RPG MAKER FOR TEENS

MICHAEL DUGGAN

Course Technology PTR

A part of Cengage Learning

COURSE TECHNOLOGY
CENGAGE Learning

Australia • Brazil • Japan • Korea • Mexico • Singapore • Spain • United Kingdom • United States

COURSE TECHNOLOGY
CENGAGE Learning

RPG Maker for Teens
Michael Duggan

Publisher and General Manager,
Course Technology PTR: Stacy L. Hiquet

Associate Director of Marketing:
Sarah Panella

Manager of Editorial Services:
Heather Talbot

Marketing Manager: Jordan Castellani

Senior Acquisitions Editor: Emi Smith

Project Editor: Jenny Davidson

Technical Reviewer: JT Hiquet

Interior Layout Tech: MPS Limited,
a Macmillan Company

Cover Designer: Mike Tanamachi

Indexer: Sharon Shock

Proofreader: Michael Beady

For product information and technology assistance, contact us at
Cengage Learning Customer & Sales Support, 1-800-354-9706

For permission to use material from this text or product,
submit all requests online at **www.cengage.com/permissions**
Further permissions questions can be emailed to
permissionrequest@cengage.com.

All trademarks are the property of their respective owners.

All images © Cengage Learning unless otherwise noted.

Library of Congress Control Number: 2011926539

ISBN-13: 978-1-4354-5966-3

ISBN-10: 1-4354-5966-0

Course Technology, a part of Cengage Learning
20 Channel Center Street
Boston, MA 02210
USA

Cengage Learning is a leading provider of customized learning solutions with office locations around the globe, including Singapore, the United Kingdom, Australia, Mexico, Brazil, and Japan. Locate your local office at: **international.cengage.com/region**

Cengage Learning products are represented in Canada by Nelson Education, Ltd.

For your lifelong learning solutions, visit **courseptr.com**

Visit our corporate website at **cengage.com**

Printed by RR Donnelley. Crawfordsville, IN. 1st Ptg. 05/2011

Printed in the United States of America
1 2 3 4 5 6 7 13 12 11

This is for Jephael, a bright and curious girl with a temperament more like an animal than a human, a natural artistic gift, and a love of all things Pokemon . . . Now you can make your own fantasy RPG worlds!

ACKNOWLEDGMENTS

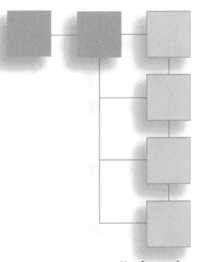

For the creation of this book there have been many supporters, especially from the RPG Maker community. Several people helped really tailor this tome into a suitable fit for our readers, including Emi Smith, Jenny Davidson, JT Hiquet, and the rest of the fine folks at Cengage Learning. I also want to thank Krystal, Levi, and Hayley for putting up with my late hours working at game play.

ABOUT THE AUTHOR

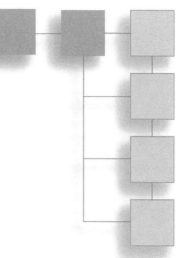

Michael Duggan is a Southern-based author and illustrator of eight textbooks on the subjects of video game design and digital media. He is also an applications developer and computer art instructor at North Arkansas College. He currently resides in the Ozark Mountains with his wife and step-children. His love for video game design comes from playing role-playing games as a kid.

Contents

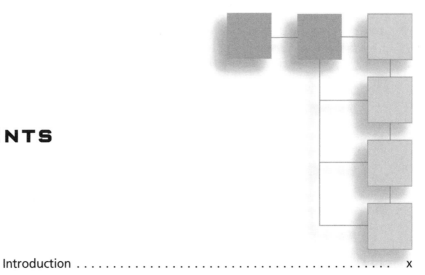

INTRODUCTION

Welcome to *RPG Maker for Teens*! This book will help you learn a complete computer game software application engineered toward creating one particular game genre: role-playing games!

Role-playing games, also known as RPGs, are those sword-and-sorcery quest games that feature turn-based combat, inventories full of unique weapons and armor, and fierce monsters prowling in dungeons.

This book shows you the techniques it takes to make your own RPG ideas come to life.

This book is written in a tutorial format, so that as you read you don't just process information but you put it to immediate use and get hands-on learning to reinforce the knowledge. Through this book, you will start by creating a game called Thug Wallow. At the same time, you will put what you've learned into practice by making your own, completely original RPG.

It's my hope that you will use the skills you learn within this book to springboard your talents into making dozens of other video games!

WHAT YOU WILL LEARN FROM THIS BOOK

In *RPG Maker for Teens,* you'll learn about the game industry, the process by which role-playing games are made, and how to make your very own RPGs using RPG Maker VX from Enterbrain. RPG Maker is a fantastic tool for someone just learning how to build games, as it requires virtually no programming!

And *RPG Maker for Teens* will break it down for you in easy-to-understand techniques.

WHO SHOULD READ THIS BOOK

Anyone who is interested in working in the game industry, who likes playing RPGs and would like to make their own, or someone who is interested in making games as a hobby and doesn't know where to start, will find the contents of this book useful. The following text goes over the specifics of creating games with RPG Maker, but it also covers the very real day-to-day responsibilities all game developers have to deal with.

Note

As this book is about designing computer games, you should have some experience with computers beforehand!

HOW THIS BOOK IS ORGANIZED

Here are some specifics about the chapter breakdown for this book.

- **Chapter 1: What Is a Fantasy RPG?**—Before delving into game development, this introductory chapter will give you a quick run-down on the RPG genre.

- **Chapter 2: Making a Fantasy RPG**—This chapter shows you the history, progression, and methods of making RPGs, as well as how to think about designing your own.

- **Chapter 3: Building Game Worlds**—This chapter delves into map-making and world construction using RPG Maker.

- **Chapter 4: Creating Characters and Writing Dialogue**—This chapter will give you everything you need to invent RPG characters, make them believable, and put words in their mouths.

- **Chapter 5: Staging Battle Encounters**—This chapter covers the intricacies of turn-by-turn combat and generating enemy characters to have to fight.

- **Chapter 6: Quest Design**—In this chapter, you'll learn to string together quests and sub-quests to give the player challenges to overcome.

- **Chapter 7: Final Touches**—This chapter shows you how to add even more custom functionality in your games.

- **Chapter 8: Where to Go from Here**—This chapter covers editing and publishing your finished games, as well as how to put your game onto disc or on the Internet for download.

- **Glossary**—At the back of the book, there is a glossary listing the most common key terms and phrases and their definitions.

What You Will Need

You will need the RPG Maker software from Enterbrain and a Windows PC capable of supporting it. The software can be found online at www. RPGMakerWeb.com. Any other programs you will use are listed in later chapters, along with details on how to access them.

Companion Website Downloads

You may download the companion website files from www.courseptr.com/downloads. Please note that you will be redirected to our Cengage Learning site.

## CHAPTER 1

WHAT IS A FANTASY RPG?

In this chapter you will learn:

- What a fantasy RPG is
- The most popular types of RPGs
- What common elements are found in RPGs
- How RPGs handle player exploration, combat, and conversation
- Why so many RPGs feature anime-style artwork

Before looking at how a fantasy role-playing game is made, it is important to know the meaning behind it. In other words, what is a fantasy role-playing game? This chapter will review the standard definition and some of the more modern cultural traditions involving this particular genre of gaming.

THE ROLE-PLAYING GAME (RPG)

A *role-playing game* (hereby referred to as *RPG*), by broad definition, is any pretend game where the players assume the roles of characters in a fictional setting. So if you've ever played Cops & Robbers or any other make-believe game with some of your friends, then you've played an RPG before.

RPGs evolved from early psychotherapy exercises. It is clinically thought to be psychologically beneficial to people to pretend they are someone else, to see things from a different perspective from time to time.

An RPG involves the participant's willingness to imagine. Visualize a therapist telling you, "Close your eyes and imagine that you are lying on your back in the middle of a summer meadow. You can hear song birds chirping in the tree boughs above your head and water trickling in a nearby creek. Clumps of clouds scuttle across the crystalline blue sky." If you can picture all that, then you are participating in an RPG. You've placed yourself in an imaginary world simply by means of your mind's inner theater.

Tip

"A role-playing game is one in which the player controls one or more characters, typically designed by the player, and guides them through a series of quests managed by the computer. Victory consists of completing these quests. Character growth in power and abilities is a key feature of the genre. Typical challenges include tactical combat, logistics, economic growth, exploration, and puzzle solving. Physical coordination challenges are rare except in RPG-action hybrids."

— Ernest Adams, founder of the International Game Developers Association (IGDA)

A Sample of Popular RPGs

Below is a brief list of some of the more popular RPGs.

- .hack
- Arc the Lad
- Baldur's Gate
- Blue Dragon
- Call of Cthulhu
- Chrono Trigger/Cross
- Dark Heresy
- Disgaea
- Dragon Age: Origins
- Dragon Quest

- Dungeons & Dragons
- Elder Scrolls
- Exalted
- Fable
- Fallout
- Final Fantasy
- Kingdom Hearts
- Mass Effect
- Neverwinter Nights
- Rifts

- Risen
- Sacred
- Scion
- Star Wars RPG
- Two Worlds
- Warhammer Fantasy
- World of Darkness
- World of Warcraft
- Xenogears

Tabletop RPGs

RPGs can be played with sheer imagination. Or the players can use rulebooks, dice, and character sheets. Games using such paraphernalia are called tabletop RPGs.

A war-gamer named Gary Gygax (Figure 1.1) invented tabletop RPGs in the 1970s. The earliest tabletop RPG was called *Dungeons & Dragons* (Figure 1.2), and it featured fantasy lands and playable characters like magic-users, warriors, and thieves. *Dungeons & Dragons* appeared briefly in the 1982 Steven Spielberg film *E.T. the Extraterrestrial* and paved the path for further tabletop RPGs that came after. So, even though there are lots of other popular tabletop RPGs available, when we examine tabletop RPGs, we'll reference the way *Dungeons & Dragons* operates.

In tabletop RPGs like *Dungeons & Dragons*, one player, titled the Dungeon Master, creates the fictional world by drawing maps on paper and placing landmarks and objects on those maps. The Dungeon Master (Figure 1.3) conveys the fictional world to the other players by describing it as vividly as he can. He also controls any character not controlled by the players, including the monsters they must eliminate and the townsfolk they might ask for clues or

Figure 1.1
Gary Gygax at a gaming convention.

Figure 1.2
Dungeons & Dragons, both then (left) and today (right).

Figure 1.3
Perhaps *not* your typical Dungeon Master.

help. The Dungeon Master makes up the challenges and obstacles the players must overcome. The players overcome them through creative cooperation and fully utilizing their imaginary characters' skills.

Besides the Dungeon Master, each of the other players creates a character to play or picks a ready-to-play character. Like the protagonists of a novel or the heroes in a movie, these player characters are central to the story the Dungeon Master evokes. The Dungeon Master's story is an adventure story and can be as simple as a dungeon crawl, rooting through catacombs looking for treasure while hacking up monsters, or as complex as a murder mystery. These adventures stage the proving ground for the heroes to perform their valiant or wicked deeds.

There's an element of rule and randomization that the rulebooks and dice serve in *Dungeons & Dragons* (Figure 1.4). For instance, if a monster is going to attack the player character, the rules say that the monster must roll one 20-sided die (1d20) versus the player character's Armor Class (AC). The die roll provides a random element, just like in gambling, so that no two moves are ever quite the same. The rule provides the framework for the action, so that the Dungeon Master can resolve the make-believe with mathematics.

Figure 1.4
Dice used in tabletop RPGs.

A tabletop RPG would be nearly identical to a fast interpretative stage play if it weren't for the rulebooks and dice. In fact, people who play tabletop RPGs can often get "into the role" just as much as a drama student in a Shakespeare play. But most tabletop RPGs do not involve stunts or moving about. Instead, players sit comfortably and say out loud what their characters are doing. They let the rules and dice interpret the actions for them.

If you think that tabletop RPGs are too old-school or nerdy, you should do a YouTube search for "Vin Diesel on *Dungeons & Dragons*," as there are several video interviews with action star Vin Diesel about playing one of his favorite games growing up. Diesel sees tabletop RPGs as a "training ground for our imagination and an opportunity to explore our own identities."

What follows is a typical script excerpt taken from a night playing *Dungeons & Dragons*.

Dungeon Master (DM): You enter the dark and foreboding crypt of Nurall. The sounds of skittering rats and dripping slime echo back at you from the pale granite walls. The space is roughly thirty feet by thirty feet, with a single torch lighting the space from a stone column rising up in the center of the crypt. Along the walls you see carved niches that appear to be filled with rotten coffins and moldering bones. There are roughly eight of these niches, four to both sides, and an iron-bound oak door set in the wall at the other end of the crypt. A circular iron grate hole rests in the lowest part of the paved floor. What do you do?

Thief: I immediately go to the right-side wall and search the niches to see if I can find any treasure in amongst the rags of the dead. Do I find any?

DM (after a quick die roll): You find ancient pocket lint and three shiny gold coins. That's it.

Warrior: Do I still have my torch? I thought I dropped it in our exit from the stairwell earlier.

DM: Your torch is lying guttering at the darkest recesses of the stairwell, where you dropped it.

Warrior: Is the torch in this room secured to the column, or can I pry it up and take it with me?

DM: You could attempt to pry it out of the sconce.

Warrior: Good, that's what I'll do.

DM: Just as you start prying it up, you hear a click noise coming behind the stones that make up the column. There's a gurgle and screech under your feet, and suddenly you see something shiny and black start to ooze out of the floor grate.

Warrior: That's not good!

Sorceress: I attempt to use Discern Intent on the ooze. Is it malign or evil in any way?

DM: Yes, it's definitely malignant.

Thief: Let's get out of here! I run to the door and check it for traps.

DM: That will take you until next turn. Meanwhile, the ooze is filling the room. It hasn't reached you, yet, but it soon will.

Warrior (to the Sorceress): Don't you have a spell or something that could plug up the grate? He said it was a circular grate hole. It can't be very big. Is it?

DM: The grate is approximately a foot in diameter.

Sorceress: Would casting Web on it do anything? The Web spell's good and sticky. Would it slow it down, at least until Thief there gets the door open?

DM: You can try.

Sorceress: Okay. I cast Web on the grate hole, then. What happens?

Pick-Your-Path Game Books

Another variation of RPG, one that developed shortly after tabletop RPGs became more mainstream, is the pick-your-path game book.

These game books, such as the *Choose Your Own Adventure* (Figure 1.5) and *Fighting Fantasy* books, are targeted toward a single player: the book's reader. Many of the books even include a character sheet the player must use to keep up with the character she pretends to be while reading the book. As the player reads

Figure 1.5
Some of the many *Choose Your Own Adventure* game books.

the book, the pages are not read in sequential order but in branching paths, meaning that as the player nears the end of each section, she is given a choice to make, and that choice can determine the progress of the story.

One of my favorite game book series was Joe Dever's *Lone Wolf*, the first eight books of which were originally illustrated by Gary Chalk. In the *Lone Wolf* series (Figure 1.6), the story centers on the fantasy world Magnamund, where forces of good and evil war for control of the planet. The player takes on the role of the protagonist, Lone Wolf, who is the last living member of a caste of warrior monks known as the Kai Lords. As Lone Wolf, the reader makes choices at regular intervals that decide the course, and eventually the outcome, of the story. If the player makes the wrong choices, Lone Wolf can die. It is therefore up to the reader to keep Lone Wolf alive and victorious in his questing.

Although out-of-print today, the *Lone Wolf* series has been distributed online through permission given by Joe Dever by a fan-based organization called Project Aon. If you would like to take a peek at the *Lone Wolf* series, just to find out more about game books, then you can do so online at www.ProjectAon.org.

Figure 1.6
The first book in Joe Dever's *Lone Wolf* series and an example of a map found within one of his game books.

A typical excerpt from a pick-your-path game book is as follows.

You dive under the fallen log just in time, as with a hue and cry you hear the goblins bound from the jungle forest to your left. You attempt to wedge yourself in tighter under the log, as goblins riding on warthogs leap the fallen log and jog further down the forested path back the way you came.

After the last warthog-riding goblin trundles off into the distance, the dust cloud from the cloven hooves fading behind them, you pull yourself out from under the fallen log, bits of spongy bark clinging to your sweaty skin. You shake off the dirt and debris and then peer back down the path, wondering to yourself where the goblins were coming from. Could they have come from that smudge-dark tower you glimpsed over the forest canopy hours ago? Or do they have a cave they normally reside in just ahead?

However, you also wonder where the goblins are heading in such a hurry. You passed a small farm not too far back, where you saw chimney smoke climbing over the canopy. Could the farmer and his family be in trouble? Is the farm the goblins' target for disaster? Or is there more afoot here?

Do you want to run back toward the farm, after the goblins, to see what is going on there? If so, turn to page 183.

Do you want to strike off through the woods in search of the dark tower you saw earlier? If so, turn to the next page.

Or would you rather follow the path and wait and see if you come across the goblin's home? If so, turn to page 212.

Computer RPGs

The electronic medium in computer RPGs removes the necessity of having a Dungeon Master. Instead of one player having to "take charge" of managing the game world and all that's in it, the computer programming does the job for you. The computer also manages the rules and randomization. Though they are still there, these game tools are nearly intangible in a computer RPG, yet many of the thematic RPG elements of tabletop RPGs are visibly prevalent in computer RPGs.

In a computer RPG, a player controls one or several adventuring party members fulfilling one or many quests. The electronic medium has progressed from simple text-based adventures, where all the story and player decisions had to be made in the form of text (such as instructions given like "Use KEY on DOOR"), like in the historically acclaimed game *Zork* (Figure 1.7), to rich immersive 3D graphics you see today.

Computer RPGs can be as simple and straightforward as pick-your-path game books, with a branching storyline and obvious decisions the player must make, or more open-ended and complex, with a huge fantasy world ripe for exploration and multiple side-quests the player can undertake any time she wants to.

Even though I refer to them as computer RPGs, contemporary electronic RPGs are found in many video game media, including consoles, handhelds, and mobile phones. They are programmed on a computer first and then ported to the appropriate output platform.

Massively Multiplayer Online RPGs

MUD (Multi-User Dungeon) became the first online multiplayer RPG in 1980. *MUD* was originally designed by Roy Trubshaw and Richard Bartle in homage to the *Dungeon* game, a variant of the text-adventure *Zork*. Later, similar online fantasy games were called MUDs, named after the original game. MUDs feature

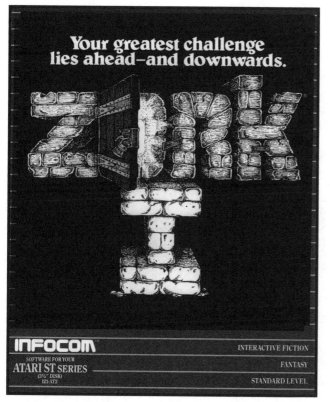

Figure 1.7
One of the earliest computer RPGs was *Zork*, where "Your greatest challenge lies ahead—and downwards."

a mostly text-based interface, similar to an online chat group, but with moderators who act like Dungeon Masters.

Many of today's massively multiplayer online role-playing games (MMORPGs), including *World of Warcraft* (shown in Figure 1.8) and *Second Life*, trace their lineage back to MUDs.

The vast majority of MMORPGs are based on traditional fantasy themes, often occurring in a game universe comparable to that of *Dungeons & Dragons*. They also have some degree of tools built around players communicating with and working together with other players, including teamwork (going on dungeon raids together) and trading (sharing resources with one another).

Figure 1.8
World of Warcraft.

The standards for MMORPGs today consist of a persistent fantasy world maintained by the game's publisher. This persistent world continues to grow and evolve even when players are not plugged in (called being "offline"). Players subscribe so they can play in this persistent world.

In 2008, Western consumers spent $1.6 billion on MMORPGs subscriptions. To keep players plugged in and paying to play, MMORPG developers and publishers have to come up with new and unique tricks to hook their audience, including innovative and rare downloadable content and expansion packs. Blizzard Entertainment's *World of Warcraft* (*WOW*) holds over 62% of all MMORPG subscribers to date and even made the Guinness World Record for the most popular MMORPG by subscribers. *WOW* exemplifies the best in MMORPGs.

Because of the amount of revenue capable in MMORPG subscriptions, video games that should not be or have never been multiplayer or online are quickly becoming so, leading to a whole new trend in game developing.

Why RPGs?

Now that you understand how an RPG is defined, you might be wondering, why only look at making RPGs?

Admittedly, you can't design a game that will delight everybody, because not everybody likes the same things. Some gamers only want to play sports games. Some only like first-person shooters, preferably military combat simulations. Others like RPGs. Since there are a great majority of gamers who like RPGs, it seems like a safe bet to make games for that audience.

RPGs are excellent games to construct for your first time, too, especially if you are new to game design and just want to get your feet wet. For a truly cross-disciplinary genre, you can look no further than an RPG. Whether you want to write game stories, make game artwork, program intricate game mechanics, or just play around with game craft, the RPG is the one genre that requires equal amounts of everything.

In *RPG Maker for Teens*, you will learn about making up stories and writing both quests and NPC dialogues. You will learn how to draw faces, maps, and backgrounds. You will learn how to code tricky game controls. And you will make a fun little game you can play through and share with your friends. With the information you learn, you can make loads of other RPGs, each time refining the rules and changing the scope of your game experience. RPGs are a great start for any wannabe game designer to cut his teeth on.

You can't know what an RPG entails without experiencing it firsthand for yourself. There's just something about going on a dungeon crawl or dashing along on a fetch quest for villagers. You'd never know the real sensation if you hadn't played an RPG before yourself. So if you haven't, you might undertake this mission: Find a fantasy RPG somewhere on the retail market and play it.

Since you're reading this book, you have shown a curiosity about RPGs, and there's a pretty big likelihood you've played them before and found them to your taste. You might even think RPGs are the coolest game genre, and I'm preaching to the choir.

Even so, let's see what separates RPGs from other video games.

Elements of Fantasy RPGs

You could say that almost every game has an element of role-play to it, because you are either being someone you're not or doing something you don't ordinarily do.

For example, in the board game Monopoly, players are big-spending million-aires trying to buy up property in order to own a monopoly on the town. And just about every video game that is a third-person shooter or platform game possesses a tiny onscreen avatar the player can control, making the player character a virtual extension of the player.

But a true fantasy RPG has much more to it than this. A true fantasy RPG must:

1. Give the player a persona, or player avatar, to control. This character can often be customized and grows over the course of the game.

2. Have a large fantastic game world for the player to explore, fight monsters, and scavenge for goodies in.

3. Have a long, winding, and branching storyline that entertains as well as serves the purpose of the game play. This storyline is told through little nuggets and quests the player undertakes.

4. Give the player items and an inventory to manage and the ability to perfect strategy in simulated combat situations. Combat can be action-oriented or turn-based.

The following are ways RPGs stand out from every other video game.

Characters: So-And-So Has Joined Your Party!

Usually, in a fantasy RPG, players control one or a small number of characters (Figure 1.9). These characters are often referred to as a *party*, not because they like to enjoy themselves but because they work together to affect a general end.

The player's party explores the game world, solves puzzles, gets involved in tactical combat, and generally achieves victory by accomplishing quests. The

Figure 1.9
Characters from the Square Enix RPG *Final Fantasy X-2*.

characters are often designed or customized by the player, making them unique to the player, and grow in power and ability over time spent in the game.

If winning the game is contingent on the survival of a single character, that character effectively becomes the player's *avatar*, or in-game representative. Even RPGs that have a party of characters will usually begin with a single character, the player's avatar, and new characters will join the party as the narrative unfurls.

The Importance of Avatars

Creator of the romance game *Dinner Date*, Jeroen D. Stout, released a paper detailing what he sees as a symbiosis between gamer and player avatar. *Symbiosis* is a concept where two or more entities form a habitual relationship where they each gain something from each other. Sharks are often followed around by tiny fish called remora, which eat the sharks' leftovers (Figure 1.10). This is one instance of symbiosis.

In Stout's paper, he states that human consciousness is not a single organism but something brought about by the collection of related thought patterns working

Figure 1.10
Remora fish and a whale shark.

together. And when a person uses a tool, such as a hammer, that tool becomes an extension of the person's self. A builder swinging his hammer is one identity; a builder who puts his hammer down and decides to sit down to watch a show on the television at home is another person. The hammer forms a symbiosis with the builder when the builder is using it, in other words.

This extension of self is played out every day in the clothes we choose to wear and the belongings we carry around with us. When a person sits down to play a video game, especially an RPG, the player character becomes an extension of that person. When the player pushes a button or mashes a key, and the avatar jumps on the screen, the player doesn't say, "My character jumped," they say "I jumped."

This sense of immersion in a video game through the use of a central figure, the player avatar, is as important to the game's creator as it is to the player, because the creator can then motivate the player by threatening the avatar. Call it emotional extortion if you will, but the core conflict behind most games depends on it.

One interesting aspect in RPGs about this "extension of self" is that the player avatar doesn't even have to be human. Lots of gamers prefer playing characters of their own specie, but the majority couldn't care less. It's the same mental

Figure 1.11
In the RPG *Chrono Trigger*, players get the chance to play Frog, a talking frog who was once a fighting champion and chivalrous guardian of Queen Leene.

reasoning we have for why kids love Disney shows and cry when the characters in those shows get hurt, even when those characters are animals. In fact, several RPGs offer gamers the choice of being human-animal hybrids (Figure 1.11), because many of their gamers are fond of that option.

Note

Did you know? The word *avatar* dates back to 1784. The word is Sanskrit and actually means "descent" or "manifestation" and refers to the incarnation of heavenly deities on Earth, especially Vishnu, a Hindu god who had ten avatars. Although its original use referenced godly beings descending to the mortal realm and taking on a physical likeness, in 1992 writer Neal Stephenson popularized the word in his cyberpunk novel *Snow Crash*. In that novel, characters could appear as avatars if they entered a virtual-reality network called the Metaverse, which corresponds to our Internet today. How your avatar looked in the Metaverse gave you social status, because a highly skilled hacker could make their avatar look really cool.

Character Class and Attributes

Besides movement controls, most of the player actions in an RPG are performed indirectly by the player characters. This means that the player selects an action to undertake and the character performs it accordingly. The success or failure of the action is determined by the character's numeric attributes. Video games have internal programming that simulates the die-rolling that generates random results in tabletop RPGs.

Some attributes in character creation are purely cosmetic, while others give the player benefits to certain actions. Attributes can also depend on a character's *class*. Class is similar to a character's occupation, and different classes have opposing strengths and weaknesses. The most common classes in fantasy RPGs (Figure 1.12) include fighters, rogues, magic-users, and clerics, with sideline classes including rangers, monks, druids, and dual-classed characters, such as fighters who also cast spells.

Fighters generally underline combat-ready attributes, such as strength and dexterity, because they need to be tough and show prowess in a fight. Magic-

Figure 1.12
In the RPG *Zenonia 2*, players can pick from four distinctive classes: Warrior, Paladin, Shooter, or Magician. The first two are melee fighters, meaning they are better prepared for fighting monsters up close and personal, while the other two stay back and shoot firearms or fire balls at the enemy from a distance.

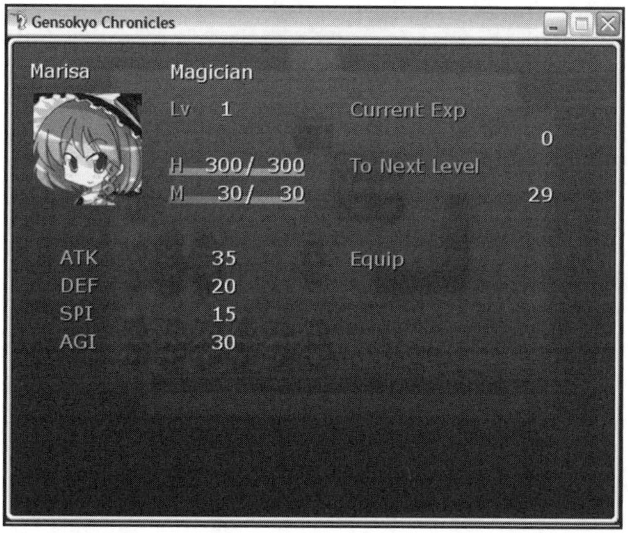

Figure 1.13
In this character screen, you see the avatar Marisa is a Level 1 Magician, meaning she can cast magic spells.

users (Figure 1.13) have to be smart, because they read spell books and comprehend complex magical algorithms, so they stress more powerful intelligence and wisdom. Rogues capitalize on quickness, stealth, and subterfuge, often in the form of attributes such as dexterity and charisma, because they have to be good at getting into places where they're not supposed to be and equally good at getting out again.

And so on. Making a great fantasy RPG character is a bit like baking a cake. Each one will be different, because each contains a different mixture of ingredients.

Gaining Experience

Although characterization is developed and grows through storytelling, RPGs demonstrate personal growth through the acquisition of experience. Almost every RPG has some version of experience point allocation. The player gains experience for beating challenges and whacking enemies in the game (Figure 1.14), and she can then spend the experience to increase her character's attributes or to purchase new abilities. This reward boosts the character's usefulness in upcoming challenges the player might face.

Let's say Gina's character Grog the Barbarian just decimated a crew of ten vile goblins. Grog receives 18 experience points for his reward. Gina can either use

Figure 1.14
Here, in this screen capture from *Dungeon Hunter 2*, the player avatar has just gained 33 experience (abbreviated Exp.) points for slaying a monster. This puts his avatar that much closer to leveling up.

part of those experience points to raise Grog's strength attribute to 14, or she can purchase a marksman skill, which will allow Grog to shoot bows and arrows. She decides she'd like Grog to have a ranged attack, so she buys the marksman skill. This decision has immediate ramifications in the way Gina will play through future combat situations.

Experience becomes a form of scorekeeping in RPGs, therefore, and amassing a certain sum of experience will cause the character's *level* to go up, an act called "leveling up." RPGs that feature character levels will start the player's character at level one and go up based on how well the player plays the game and gets involved in the storyline.

Some of the finer RPGs today use a training system for experience, such as the system developed for Lionhead Studio's *Fable* series. In a training system, the game's internal programming reacts to the actions players select most frequently and increases the player character's attributes accordingly. This means that if a player character uses a sword for a long while, the character will automatically become more proficient with the sword. If the player, instead, decides to cast a lot of magic spells, she'll become better at spell-casting.

Talk and Trade with Other Characters

Other characters managed by the computer and not the player are called non-player characters, or NPCs. This includes enemies and monsters the hero must vanquish, but it can also include characters that make up part of the backdrop and contribute to the player's journey in small though significant ways.

Speak To Me   Most RPGs handle conversations between the player and these characters via a dialog tree mechanism. The player selects an NPC in the game world to speak to. A window opens, presenting a list of possible things the avatar can say to the NPC. Most of the time, the options are limited to three or four choices, to keep it simple. The player chooses one, and depending on what option she picked, the NPC replies. Usually all of this conversation is done in text (Figure 1.15), although many newer RPGs feature audio recordings, too.

Figure 1.15
Most RPG dialogue windows showcase a close-up picture of the person talking and some text indicating what they are saying. This window overlays the action onscreen.

Asking the right questions or saying the right things elicits useful information from the NPC and sometimes gains experience points for the player. Conversation can further the game story, open up new quests, or lead to other discoveries.

Of course, not every NPC wants to stick around and chat. Some of them are little better than window-dressing, helping make the game world look more populated, and their conversations are slim to non-existent. Others don't want to talk; they want to sell you something!

Show Me Your Wares Most RPGs allow players to buy and sell goods with friendly merchant NPCs. The game world often has blacksmiths, apothecaries, farmers, and so on, who run businesses that offer to buy or sell goods and services.

The shop interface is similar to the conversation interface mentioned above, with a list or set of images of all the available items on sale (Figure 1.16). The player can choose to purchase new items or sell an item he already owns to get more money. Items purchased go directly into the hero's inventory.

Game World: A Trip to Never-land

Exploring the game world is an important aspect of an RPG. Players will travel quite extensively throughout the game world, finding objects they need, talking

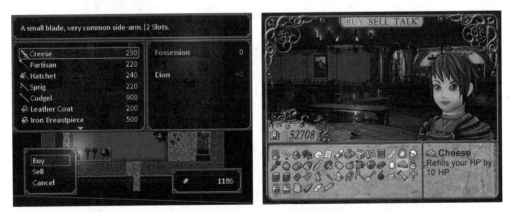

Figure 1.16
These two shop screens appear very different but operate the same. The shop on the left displays a list of tiny icons and text descriptions of the items for sale. The shop on the right displays thumbnail icons, which when clicked, will show text descriptions and prices in the right-side panel.

to non-player characters (NPCs), facing terrifying monsters, and avoiding traps. This world, therefore, has to be interesting, complex, and multifaceted. It also must be big enough to encourage exploration but small enough so the player doesn't get lost in it.

Designing a Fun Game Setting

What kind of world the player characters explore depends on the nature of the game.

Most fantasy RPGs are quasi-medieval, meaning that they use the more interesting bits and pieces from Europe's Middle Ages, Baroque, and Renaissance ages for reference but are not entirely accurate depictions of Earth's past. These games are resplendent with castles, princesses, and soldiers.

Some RPGs are *steampunk* in nature, meaning that—although the game appears faintly historic, it contains fancy technology that is purely imaginary; think of the biomechanical spider tank seen in the movie *Wild Wild West*, starring Will Smith. Technology in a steampunk universe does not have to have any real scientific basis and can even be said to be powered by magic crystal energy (Figure 1.17).

Figure 1.17
Example of steampunk technology.

A few RPGs are modern but steeped in fantasy, like the urban zombie panic games that have become popular recently.

And still others take place in a galaxy far, far away, which is almost as fantastic as the medieval ones, except the elves are replaced with aliens, and the steampunk technology is replaced with futuristic technology, like spaceships and laser swords.

Regardless of what time period or place RPGs occur in, the writers and artists almost always take artistic license with them, making the locales appear more bizarre or alien than the humdrum Earth we occupy. One reason they do this is for entertainment value. People like to be swept away. Role-playing games, after all, are a form of escape. And what better way to escape than to escape the ordinary world we all live in? In this fashion, games are comparable to theme park rides or exotic tourist destinations—and game designers are closely akin to tour guides.

A Non-Linear Game World

RPG worlds are rarely linear, as opposed to the typical linear game worlds of first-person shooters and side-scrolling platform games. A linear game world is one where the player starts at point A and struggles to get to point B, where a new area is opened up and the player must now attempt to get from point B to point C, and so on. In a non-linear game world, such as RPGs boast, the player can and often will return to previously explored areas multiple times, discovering something new each time. In the game *Planescape: Torment*, from the now-defunct company Black Isle Studios, the town of Curst is destroyed while the player is away.

Roguelike Games

Some RPGs, such as the open-source *NetHack* and Blizzard's original *Diablo*, feature a game world that is constantly changing, so that no matter how many times it is played, the dungeons are never the same. These games are called *roguelike*, because they borrow from the mechanics of the 1980 computer game *Rogue*.

NetHack (Figure 1.18) is a very small game, in fact, so it contains almost no story. But the character upgrades, quests, combat tactics, and mazelike

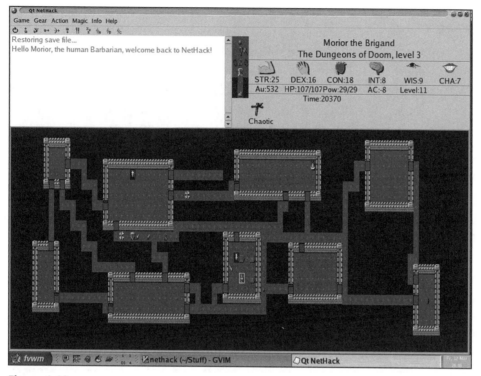

Figure 1.18
NetHack.

exploration elements of the game are remarkable for its size and keep gamers amused. When *Diablo*'s creators decided to have their dungeon maps randomly generate each time the player enters them, the game's entertainment value and overall achievement owed a lot to that choice.

Narrative: Twists and Turns in RPGs

Rather than the straightforward storylines of action games, RPGs feature robust, often twisting narratives that are just as important as the game play itself. The story unfolds as players complete challenges, explore new areas of the game world, and talk to NPCs. Story, therefore, provides the framework for the missions of the game and an explanation for why the player is doing what she's doing, why she's visiting the locales she's visiting, and why things get progressively harder and more urgent. Story entertains and enlightens.

Storytelling versus Game Play

Games, at their heart, always supply something called *game play*, which comprises challenges and interactive choices that entertain. IGDA's founder, Ernest Adams, states that one major design rule is that game play must always come first. "Game play is the primary source of entertainment in all video games. When designing a game, it is the first thing to consider."

Anybody can tell a story. You can tell a story through pictures, such as a comic book or animated movie, or through words, like a bestselling novel. But to combine story and game play is the true genius of RPGs. If you get the balance wrong, players will complain they're being "guided by the nose" and not capable of doing much—or that the game is one treacherous ordeal of "rinse and repeat" game moves and boring.

Tip

"I'm pretty damn sick and tired of all the patterns necessary to beat video games. I want a challenge, not a memory exercise. I got enough of that in history class back in school."

— Joe Santulli, *Digital Press*

Blurb It Out!   You can generally sum up a video game in a fast blurb, called a *high concept*. This is similar to the high concepts or product pitches they use for novels and motion pictures. Stephen King wrote a creepy book, later turned into a movie, called *The Shining*, and you could sum it up as, "Jack Torrance and his family go to be caretakers at a haunted resort lodge, and Jack goes crazy and tries to kill his family." That is the high concept of his story.

Similarly, you could sum up Raven Software's game *Singularity* (Figure 1.19) as follows: "You play as a U.S. agent investigating weird goings-on on the remote Russian island Katorga-12, where you discover the fabric of time and space has been altered by Cold War scientific experimentations involving an unstable element, E99. You must use the powers of temporal displacement to stop the twisted native inhabitants and rewrite history, before it's too late." See how the high concept uses both a story impression and description of game play?

Try it yourself. Think of an RPG you'd like to make. If you can't think of one, use the idea of a movie you really like and think of how it could be turned into a

Figure 1.19
Singularity.

video game. Make up a high concept for your game idea. Use both story and game play to do so.

Break It Down Into Episodes   Writers will tell you story is all about *plot*, or the sequence of events that take place over time, from beginning to conclusion.

In the story of Little Red Riding Hood, our *protagonist* (which is a fancy word for the main character or hero) Little Red Riding Hood starts out to Grandma's house before meeting a wolf. The wolf finds out where she is going and gets there before her, in an attempt to eat her. Depending on the version of story you read, Little Red Riding Hood outsmarts the wolf or gets a friendly woodsman to save her. She learns, at the end of the story, not to talk to strangers. All these events make up the plot behind Little Red Riding Hood's story.

Games usually break this down into short episodes with significant turning points in the game that come from player choices or actions. In a lot of video games, these turning points are shown in the form of *cut-scenes*. A cut-scene is a cinematic that progresses the narrative while removing the player from game play. During an episode's transition, there's usually a lot of dialogue in the form of exposition. After the cusp of the episode is through, game play is restored and the player can go back to the game.

Modern game designers are trying to make the exchange from game play to narrative episode more seamless. Instead of stopping the game to focus on a cut-scene, they let the gamer play through the episode's transition, so that—while the gamer is still getting the story information—he still feels like he's playing a game and not pausing to watch a movie.

Let's examine the story of Little Red Riding Hood (Figure 1.20). How could it be turned into an RPG?

First, the player character is the main character of the story, so we'll make the player character Little Red Riding Hood. The player starts out at home, about to embark to Grandma's house. We need one episode where Little Red Riding Hood's mom tells her to take a basket to Grandma's house and not to stop or talk to strangers along the way. Then the player can enter the Big Scary Woods.

Figure 1.20
Little Red Riding Hood versus the Big Bad Wolf.

In the Big Scary Woods, the player character can pick flowers, chase bunnies, find little keepsake treasures, and defeat snakes and spiders. She finally comes upon the Big Bad Wolf, which starts another episode, where the player can attempt to avoid succumbing to Wolf's wiles. Unfortunately, this doesn't work. When the episode's transition is through, the race is on! The player must try to get to Grandma's house before the Wolf does.

If the player has boosted Little Red Riding Hood's speed by finding the keepsake treasure Boots of Flight, then in all likelihood, the player can beat the Wolf there and fight him as he tries to get in the door. If the player doesn't make it in time, then the Wolf eats Grandma and waits to pounce on Little Red Riding Hood when she makes it there.

Either way, the game probably ends with a showdown between the Wolf and Little Red Riding Hood.

The horror game *Alan Wake* features short episodes called just that, and they are handled pretty much like TV show episodes. At the start of each episode, there's a re-cap of "what happened last time." Then the episode starts, pitting the player against a new obstacle. After the gamer comes out victorious at the end of the episode, there's a short pause between episodes with some mood music like you'd find during the end credits of a TV show.

Most games have somewhere between nine and twenty episodes in them, depending on the length of the game and complexity of the narrative.

No matter how many episodes an RPG has, it's the player's actions that determine the outcome of the game. This is significant, because a game is all about interactivity and the conclusion of it cannot seem predetermined. Otherwise, the player would find something more worthwhile to do, because what's the point in playing a game if there's only one outcome?

Study the high concept of the game you came up with in the last section. How would you arrange the sequence of events into shorter episodes, and what would be the optimal decisions the player could make in it?

Narrative Does More Than Entertain

Game designers use story for a lot more than entertainment, however. It has three other purposes, which we'll look at now.

Narrative Provides a Backdrop   Most RPGs have a *back story*, or an explanation for what came about before the player starts playing as their character in the game world. The depth of the back story varies from game to game, and often it serves only to give the player some grounding. Back stories can be much deeper and more involved, though. Players can discover reams and reams of lore and valuable information of "what happened before"—either in the game, in the form of journals, or outside the game, often in game manuals or on websites. Back stories make the game, and its component world, seem more realistic.

Narrative Makes Sense of Game Mechanics   Some games use their narrative to explain game elements that may seem nonsensical or inconvenient. For instance, the first *Might and Magic* game explained that the ever-shifting game worlds were giant terrariums hurtling through the void for some unknown purpose; this explained why the game world was roughly grid-based and had boundaries on all four sides. In the first *Fable* game, the writers explained that the reason the player could get in-game hints and tricks was through a communication device their character carried, called the Guild Seal (Figure 1.21). The Guild Seal actually became a multifaceted invention and ended up an icon for the game itself later on.

Figure 1.21
The Guild Seal.

So if something becomes ponderously ostentatious as an obscure game play element, you can always attach a story that explains why it's there.

Narrative Builds Emotional Bids   Narrative, especially in the form of NPC dialogue, can become a very strong emotional asset, too. It takes a little while for gamers to form poignant attachments to made-up characters, even their own avatar, but as the characters in the game world start talking and relating to one another, their reactions take on much larger meaning for the player. Think of the Little Sisters in the *BioShock* games or the player's allies in the *Call of Duty* games. These characters and companions add personality and warmth to the gaming experience, give emotional cues as to how the gamer should feel, and— once the gamer does start feeling something—give the designer something in the narrative the gamer has an emotional investment in.

Quests: Go Fetch!

The player must complete a series of specific quests in order to complete the RPG. This often starts with the introduction of a larger, overarching quest that has many parts to it, making it seem insurmountable at first, but over the course of the game, the player takes stabs at the quest, slowly unwrapping and evolving the storyline as the player finishes its sum parts.

Besides this focal quest, most RPGs feature side-quests. Side-quests are frequently discovered by talking to NPCs. Usually, there is no penalty if the player decides not to undertake a side-quest, but there is a reward, at least in experience.

These side-quests can appear at anytime, anywhere, and they are often formulaic. Most quests break down to the hero having to do one of the following:

- Kill an enemy or group of enemies that are lurking in a single area
- Find and return with a particular item (the *fetch quest*)
- Escort some helpless individual through dangerous terrain

A fetch quest can also involve taking an item or piece of information from one NPC to another and back again, as necessary. Fetch quests can be multipart quests, as well. Instead of finding one gilded crest piece, the hero might have to scour the maps to find 20. In this case, the fetch quest becomes a scavenger hunt, where the hero searches for multiple items over a vast area.

However, quests can get quite tedious if they appear too often and seem obvious or redundant. The player could begin to feel that playing the hero in her RPG has placed her on the fast track to being an indentured social servant, having to run gofer missions for every Tom, Dick, and Harry she comes across.

For example: "Oh, help me, help! I need to get some medicine for my sick daughter. I know I could go get it myself, but I don't really want to. I have to stay here and bake a pie. If you get the medicine for me, I'll give you a slice of my pie. Would you do that for me?"

BioWare's game *Baldur's Gate 2* won a lot of critical acclaim for its quests. Each of the quests in that game had incredible variety and always offered something new to the player. Each also had intricate political subplots and affected far-reaching consequences. The gamer was given the feeling that they had an effect on the game world, and there arose a sense of accomplishment when finally fulfilling a quest's objective.

The three main things to remember about RPG quests, in general, are:

1. They must have a well-defined objective, so the player knows what to do.

2. They must present the player significant rewards when accomplished.

3. They must further the game's narrative or add to the overall gaming experience in some way. The best thing is if completion of the quest leads to long-running consequences in the game world.

Inventory: Now Where Did I Put That?

Players of RPGs must also deal with inventory. During the course of their exploration and quest-taking, players will discover or be endowed with items such as weapons, armor, power-ups, and quest items (Figure 1.22). Each type of item is important to the overall game play.

- **Weapons**—Weapons increase how dangerous the character is to his enemies. Each weapon can deal a definite amount of damage, and ranged weapons, such as bows and firearms, can fire at a distance, harming enemies without necessitating approach.

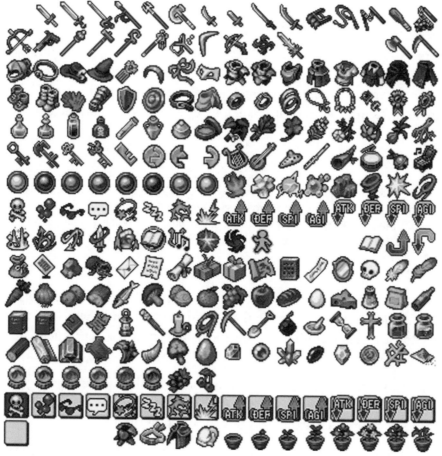

Figure 1.22
This is the standard inventory item icon set for RPG Maker.

- **Clothes and Armor**—Clothing keeps a character covered and adds cosmetic value to the character. A lot of players like to spend time using their characters as dress-up dolls, putting different outfits on them to alter their appearance. Armor actually gives the character the added benefit of defense, so enemies can't do as much damage to the character.

- **Power-Ups**—Every game features different power-ups, but the most common power-ups in RPGs are items that temporarily improve the character's health or magic, such as healing or mana potions, or items that boost a specific attribute, such as +3 to intelligence from wearing a

Cap of Knowledge. Some power-ups only take effect when used, while others give the player a permanent bonus while equipped.

■ **Quest Items**—Fetch quests require the player to find a unique item and return it to a certain place or friendly NPC. The quest item could be any of the above items, including a magic sword or nobleman's helmet. However, the item cannot be sold or traded, as it is needed to complete a fetch quest.

Note

Many RPGs use the term mana for the amount of spell-casting energy a wizard or witch has at their disposal, and mana potions can raise this energy level in order to cast more powerful spells. Mana is a native Pacific islander concept of an invisible and impersonal force residing in people, plants, animals, and (debatably) inanimate objects. It has commonly been interpreted as "the stuff of which magic is formed."

Players can travel to towns and find friendly merchant NPCs. Communicating with these NPCs allows players to trade these items for currency, which in turn permits them to buy better equipment. In most fantasy RPGs, currency, as it turns out, means gold.

Many RPGs make inventory management a logistical challenge by limiting the size of the player's total inventory, forcing the player to decide what and how much of each item the player wants to carry at any one time.

Although technically a third-person shooter, Capcom's 2005 horror game *Resident Evil 4* introduced a virtual weapons case inside which players had only a certain number of slots to fill. Players could buy a larger weapons case later on in the game, which let them fill even more slots, increasing the amount of inventory they could carry.

Combat: Turn-by-Turn

Classic fantasy RPGs, such as *Final Fantasy* and *Ultima*, separate combat from normal exploration and game play, whereas modern RPGs try to maintain a persistent experience, blending combat and exploration in one (Figure 1.23).

In a classic RPG combat sequence, the action is *turn-based*, meaning that the characters take turns. One character acts at a time, while all the other characters remain still. The order in which the characters take their turns is often

Figure 1.23
Games like *Dragon Age: Origins* blend combat and exploration into one almost seamless type of play.

dependent on their speed, quickness, or initiative. During each turn, the player decides if the character will attack, defend, use ability, or use a power-up item (Figure 1.24). The first side to reduce the other's health points to zero wins. The winner earns experience and occasionally treasure for their encounter.

Some turn-based combat sequences will permit the player the choice of running away, which is an attractive preference for those whose characters are near dead already.

The earliest fantasy RPGs featured sudden random enemy encounters that would surprise the players when they least expected it. Modern RPGs usually spawn enemies that visibly patrol areas and can be avoided if the player wishes to dodge confrontation. The former makes exploration in wilder areas tense and suspenseful, but the latter appears more realistic and less likely of generating a headache.

Many RPGs, akin to action games, include *boss encounters*. Bosses are habitually tougher than regular enemies and are strategically positioned at entrances to

Figure 1.24
In this image, the player is going up against a dragon, and he can view his four party members' health and mana, while deciding what to do this turn.

unexplored areas of the game world. Bosses act as guardians the player must trounce in order to continue the game.

Some RPG Clichés to Watch Out For

Gamers have noted that the venerable institution of fantasy RPGs is often too predictable in its constituent parts. Standards have become clichés, and many of these clichés are borderline boring for accustomed gamers. RPGs are nefarious for overused puzzle elements and character content that gets "borrowed" over and over again.

The following information can help you spot the most grating clichés and know the remedy to their use.

- **Some Call Me... Tim?**—Good guys only have first names, and bad guys only have last names or titles. If good guys have a last name, it is usually only mentioned in the player manual. REMEDY: Have carefully crafted characters. All of them should have three dimensions. Make up character details, including background, traits, quirks, and ... realistic names.

- **Who Am I?**—The amnesiac hero who must go on a personal quest to find out who he is has been used way too often. This is a device that puts the hero on the same page as the player, making for a more immersive storyline. That's why it is useful. But when one in five games use this as their device, it becomes boringly redundant. REMEDY: Have a full-fledged character who knows who he is already and let the player gradually learn his story through the game narrative.

- **Starting at Ground Zero**—The player is usually forced to start with a character at Level 1. The hero has zip for skills and no powerful weapons or powers. Some games even give the hero a toy sword and slingshot. He's expected to get tougher and find better weapons while playing the game, so that by the conclusion of the game, he is reasonably powerful. REMEDY: Start your character out where his terrific weapons or powers have been temporarily stripped from him, and he has to get them back. Or allow the players to choose whether they want to play an Easy, Average, or Hard game, and if they choose Easy they are given all kinds of powerful weapons and if they choose Hard they get to start as the 90-pound weakling.

- **No! Not My Home!**—The hero's family is killed by wicked villains. The hero's home village or planet is blown up or spectacularly destroyed by the bad guys, often before the game's beginning credits are even done rolling. This is a device that separates the hero from mainstream culture, cuts off his support base, and motivates him to take revenge on the villains. However, it is so overused it's getting tired. REMEDY: Have the story remain realistic by saying the hero is away from and occasionally writes to Mom and Dad, but they are too weak to help him when the going gets tough. Or revamp the cliché, as the creators of *Beavis and Butthead Do America* did: instead of their home being destroyed, it is Beavis and Butthead's television that is stolen, and in their ignorance, they travel the length of the United States and back to retrieve it.

- **Impossible to Kill. . . Or Not?**—Heroes are often larger-than-life, but in video games the villains always seem to be the worst shots ever, constantly missing the player character. Heroes can fall from great heights and get back up again without a scratch. They can travel through poison gas clouds and sulfurous lava fields and frozen tundra without any damage. Any medical doctor would love to study the hero, just to see how he achieves such contrary impossibilities. REMEDY: Show your hero as only human. Show the hero sweating, breathing heavy, getting tired, and having to pause for rest. Have him gasp and choke and stumble in smoky or gaseous areas. Have him shiver and act clumsy if it gets cold. Breathe life into your characters to further player immersion.

■ **Fashion Victim**—Every character in the game has only one outfit that he wears, and he wears that outfit throughout the game, even when months pass by and the outfit does not fit the climate or terrain he is traveling in. The only exception to this rule is when a sneaky character has to knock someone out, steal that person's clothes, and disguise himself to get in somewhere he's not supposed to. REMEDY: Show the hero has a pack with him, full of alternate costumes. If the hero enters a snow realm, show him donning a parka or fur-lined cloak. Entering a sweaty jungle glade? Have him put on a pair of swim trunks. Or you could introduce a wardrobe part of the way into the game, where the player character can get changed if he so chooses.

■ **Time to Save the World**—No matter if the hero really wants to relax and watch some television, his goal in every single game is no less than to "save the world." The world is menaced by a growing evil threatening to consume it. No one else seems capable of saving the world, not even a vast military force. It always comes down to one person: the player avatar. REMEDY: Instead of the world, perhaps the hero must save his grandmother. Or pay off high-interest student loans by doing night-shift work on the Late Night Dungeon Clean-Up Crew. Think outside the astronomical in nature of a primary quest.

■ **The Princess Has Been Taken Hostage!**—The princess has been kidnapped... again. What is she, danger-handicapped? Has she never taken a self-defense class in her life? Does her father not have enough gold to hire bodyguards for her? I guess the hero better go save the princess, but should he have to? In Capcom's horror game *Resident Evil 4*, the president's daughter (virtually a princess in her own right) gets captured a total of four times, and you thought Mario had it bad! REMEDY: Maybe the player character *is* the kidnapped princess, and she's tired of waiting around for someone to come save her and so she busts herself out of prison and mops up the villains on her way. Or the hero saves the princess, only to find out she is really the villain and staged the whole kidnapping plot. Or the hero is the one working for the villain and must kidnap the princess for a change. Think outside the box.

- **Carrying Swords Into a Gun Fight**—Even if the game is set in a steampunk world where giant mechanical robots pummel fire-breathing dragons, the hero's party still has the chutzpah to match bullets with flashy steel sabers, because let's face it: swords are cool! Even funnier is the fact that most of the heroes, who are shaped like skinny emo punks, carry swords the size of a Shetland pony (Figure 1.25). REMEDY: Swords are cool, and since this is fantasy, I guess you can get away with it. But try to make it seem realistic.

- **Kleptomaniac Heroes**—Anywhere the hero goes, he can open doors, walk through people's homes, subsequently trotting soil and dragon blood into their rugs, and take any of their stuff he likes. He can pick

Figure 1.25
Could this guy really heave a sword, and would it matter so much in a gun battle?

through trunks and dressers, rob them of their valuables, and think to himself, "Wow! I just found another health potion!" He never gives consideration to the people these things might belong to. Why let the players steal without consequences? REMEDY: If this is a fantasy world, perhaps make it clear that villagers set up shrines to heroes in their homes, that traveling heroes can come to and take the things on them as reward for their good deeds. Or if you want to let the player be a little kleptomaniac, set up scripted states ahead of time if he gets caught in the act, and the more times he is caught stealing the closer he comes to being handcuffed or fined.

- **But They Don't Take American Express**—It's a wonder economy even persists in a fantasy world where a merchant might get his head bitten off by a monster if he steps outside. But no matter where the hero goes, merchants are open for business and glad to see him, as he appears to be their only customer. Where do the merchants get all their goods, and how does their business not suffer from the global climate? REMEDY: Show that some merchants are busier than others, that the player has to wait in line before he can buy something from the merchant. Show armed merchant caravans along roads, or have the hero offer to transport goods for discounts at certain merchants.

- **Compulsory Dungeon No. 231**—There is this nearby dungeon. It might be a goblin cave, a hang-out for dread pirates, a banshee-ridden castle ruins, or some other kind of dungeon area. The player character has nothing better to do than go inside it and root around for treasure, all the time vanquishing goblins, pirates, banshees, or whatever. Unfortunately, this gets old fast. REMEDY: Place a specific goal for the player entering any dangerous place. No one else wants to go in there. Why should the hero? Think about it.

- **Random Ubiquitous Item No. 546**—No matter where the player goes, there are all these ever-present mysterious items. Some of them are chests, which always appear to have treasure in them when their placement makes no sense whatsoever, because anyone could've come along and looted them. Some of these items include crates, which have to be pushed, either because they're blocking the hero's access somewhere or

Figure 1.26
Why do bad guys always seem to surround themselves with conveniently placed exploding barrels? Barrels like these are found throughout the game *Bulletstorm*.

because he must use them as makeshift stairs. Some of them are barrels, which for some unknown reason the least impact will cause them to explode in a fireball that damages anyone near them (Figure 1.26). Where did these exploding barrels come from, and why do bad guys always want to use them for cover in a fire fight? REMEDY: Try thinking outside the box. Instead of treasure chests, maybe the hero finds and searches corpses of fallen explorers. Instead of crates that must be pushed, get more inventive about opening up new areas in the game. And instead of exploding barrels, use propane bottles, gas cans, or other explosive items that would be more commonly found in the game world. And if there's a fire, why wouldn't it spread, causing damage to wooden structures around it?

 Elemental Spell Casting 101—Almost every RPG has standard ice, fireball, and lightning spells, or the magic is based on elemental magic. You cast ice spells at fire imps, shoot fireballs at water spirits, and anything mechanical, such as a robot, can be blown to bits with lightning bolts. REMEDY: Start making up spells that aren't powered by colored mana or named after another game you've played. Research myths, folklore, and cultural magic systems for something more off-beat.

▪ **Bet You Can't Summarize This**—Plots for RPGs are often more convoluted than summarizing what happened on the final season of the TV show *Lost*. There's always two or three evil puppet masters at work, the hero finds he has a long-lost brother or his girlfriend is his long-lost sister, or his mother is the wicked witch who turned his father into a couch potato. Anymore, nothing is surprising in an RPG, because every wild and crazy plot twist has been used before, and the gamer is so confused he doesn't know what is going on anyway. REMEDY: Learn about proper fiction writing. Storyboard a classic struggle of good and evil with some interesting characters and an antagonist who acts like a jerk because of a glaring personality flaw. Of course, there's a lot more to it than that, but at least that's a start.

The above devices aren't the only things clichéd in RPGs. Next are the most often-found character stereotypes.

- The brooding, tortured hero who has a really cool hairdo and often spouts lines like Good Charlotte song lyrics
- The spunky optimistic kid who wears his heart on his sleeve but is obnoxiously cocky
- The spoiled rich princess who wants to run away from home and "rough" it
- The demure soft-spoken girl who's really smart and probably has a crush on the hero
- The tough-as-nails female warrior who hates men
- The old tough-skinned warrior guy who's really a softy with a heart of gold
- The hero's best friend, who is less disciplined but way cooler than the hero
- The nauseatingly cute mascot character
- The really sexy but black-hearted villain
- The villain's seductive girlfriend, who decides to risk everything to help the hero, who she's fallen for

- The villain's lackey, who usually comes in two flavors, either annoyingly difficult and mysterious or humorously incompetent

- The mad scientist who creates monsters or giant robots the hero must fight

- The hero's former ally who is now full of bitter hate

- The powerful martial artist who finds out he's on the wrong side and finally joins the hero's party

I am not saying that an RPG should *never* include a single cliché, or that there's anything inherently wrong with them. Some clichés, over time, have become staples of the genre, and gamers have come to expect them, while others—treated just right, that is—can be fun.

All I am saying is that the phrase, "Expect the unexpected," is a better one to go by when developing RPGs.

East Meets West When It Comes to RPGs

If you believe fantasy RPGs have their roots in *Dungeons & Dragons*, then the RPG was originally created in America. The first computer RPG was *also* produced in the West, and RPGs have always had a very strong Western approach, focusing on conquest and reward.

Folks in the United Kingdom have also created very popular trend-setting RPGs, including Joe Dever's *Lone Wolf* game books and the *Ultima* game series by Sir Richard Garriott (a.k.a. Lord British). Lionhead Studios, based in Guildford, Surrey, is a British computer company led by Peter Molyneux and best known for its *Fable* series. These RPGs have produced many of the standards for RPGs today.

Yet the most classic fantasy RPGs—the video games many players remember the most—were created in Japan. Titles like *Dragon Quest*, *Final Fantasy*, *Panzer Dragoon Saga*, *Xenogears*, *Rogue Galaxy*, *Kingdom Hearts*, *Chrono Trigger*, and many more, have survived virtually unscathed year after year as some of the finest in RPGs. Many of the aforementioned titles have held long-running serials and cult followers all across the globe.

RPGs received little attention in Japan until the introduction of *Ultima* in the 1980s, and then Japanese developers turned their gaze upon this new and exciting genre. In 1987, developer Square, today known as Square Enix, faced bankruptcy. Hironobu Sakaguchi, who worked for Square, created the first *Final Fantasy* game as a last-ditch effort to save the company. The title he gave to it was an example of gallows humor, because it was based on his idea this game would be the last Sakaguchi made. Instead, *Final Fantasy* launched Square into the RPG legacy it is now. *Final Fantasy* was hugely successful, with more than 97 million units sold, holding seven Guinness World Records in the *Guinness World Records Gamer's Edition 2008*.

Today, fans of RPGs continue to expect great games to roll out from the East. The Asian artwork alone has become a hallmark of RPGs.

RPGs and Anime

In Japan, a popular form of 2D animation called *anime* swept the land by the 1970s. Anime borrowed a lot from its print cousin, *manga*, which had been distinguished in the 1960s by Osamu Tezuka, whom many critics called "the God of Manga."

Anime, which is defined as "a Japanese style of animation" or "artwork done in the style of animation developed in Japan," features exaggerated physical features such as big eyes, small mouths, exotic hairdos, and exclamatory motions.

The anime genre was pioneered by such motion pictures as *Space Battleship Yamoto* and *Mobile Suit Gundam*. In the 1990s popular and successful anime such as *Pokémon*, *Sailor Moon*, and *Dragonball Z* surprised even their creators and propelled anime to the front ranks of children's entertainment in the United States. Anime continues to entertain children and young adults alike throughout the world.

Since anime was so popular at the time RPGs were being developed in Japan, the anime style was used for many classic fantasy RPGs and has become iconic for the whole game genre.

The RPG Maker software you will be using to make RPGs originated in Japan, and it relies heavily on anime-style artwork. I will show you some tricks to drawing anime characters when we get to that part, later on.

WHAT'S NEXT?

After reading this chapter, you should know the definition of an RPG and some of the most popular elements found in RPGs. You also know what's important when considering the game narrative, its characters, the quests they go on, and much more. This will help as you start making your own RPGs.

The next chapter will reveal what goes on behind-the-scenes of the making of an RPG and start you on the path to doing so yourself.

CHAPTER 2

MAKING A FANTASY RPG

In this chapter you will learn:

- How an RPG is made
- The difference between game developers and publishers
- The various roles in a game company
- The process it takes to make a game, from start to finish
- How you can start making your own games

Ever wonder how an RPG is made, or do you think that games just spring into being overnight? It takes the work and diligence of multiple people, sometimes teams of over 100, a long time to make an RPG. Often, it takes a year or more to design one game. Yet game designers keep doing it, because video games are fun, people love them, and there's money to be made making them.

In this chapter, I'll show some of the behind-the-scenes action, how RPGs are put together, and you'll start laying the groundwork for your very own RPG.

How an RPG Is Made

It takes a whole lot more than one person and a single software application to make a video game, especially an RPG. It often takes the work of a large unified team of talented individuals (some of whom are trained in art while others are more experienced at program code) and a pipeline of various different computer software.

Without further ado, let's look at how a typical RPG is really made.

Game Development and Game Publishing

The procedure of making an RPG is often two-step. One group of people, the *game development team*, actually assembles the game—while another group, the *game publisher*, puts the game on store shelves everywhere so people can buy, rent, subscribe to, and play the game.

The first group is more focused on creating an entertaining product—one that many people will want to play—while the latter group centers their attention on distribution and making money from the game.

Sometimes, as in the case of famed publisher Nintendo, the publishing company has in-house developers who make the games the publisher releases. But most often, a game development team is independent from any publisher, and they must shop around until they find a publisher who will handle their game once it's made. The contracts they sign can often lock them to a specific publisher for a time. The horror game *Alan Wake*, for example, is an Xbox 360 exclusive game. Its developers signed an exclusive agreement with Microsoft.

One motive game developers have for seeking out just the right publisher is that a publisher will often front the development team money to create a game. The developers will create a *game prototype*, which is a raw unfinished game used for business proposals, and show it off to publishers in the hopes that a publisher will give them the funds they need to finish making the game, because most game development costs a lot of dough.

While exact figures have never been made available to the public, the popular shooter game *Call of Duty: Black Ops* cost somewhere in the neighborhood of $18 and $28 million to make! You might not know it, but most video games actually rival Hollywood's top movies when it comes to production costs.

Most of the cost in making video games is in the hired talent and computer hardware/software expenses. It takes a lot of people to make a big triple-A game title these days. *Black Ops* took almost 200 paid employees to produce, including 80 voice-over actors alone. You can see a line-up of some of the employees that worked together to make the post-apocalyptic RPG *Fallout 3* in Figure 2.1.

Figure 2.1
Team photo of Bethesda Softworks developers on the *Fallout 3* game project 2009.

Note

By the way, when you hear insiders refer to *triple-A titles*, it's the same as when people say blockbuster movies, because a triple-A title is supposed to be one that costs upward of $10 million to make and is expected to sell well over a million copies. In other words, if it's a game you've seen on TV commercials before it hits store shelves at Blockbuster and GameStop, you know it's a triple-A title.

In the past, game developers could get together in small teams of fewer than a dozen people in someone's attic or garage and put together a game in just a few months. Then they would put the game on floppy discs and into Ziploc baggies and mail them to customers.

These days, most games are sold in retail outlets like GameStop or downloaded over the Internet, and game developers have scaled up to teams ranging from 75 to 300 individuals on a single project. BioWare, developer of such great RPGs as *Baldur's Gate, Dragon Age, Star Wars: Knights of the Old Republic*, and *Mass Effect*, has staff at five different offices in places like Virginia, Texas, Canada, and Ireland. And their employees may operate on more than one project at a time, because BioWare has averaged two games simultaneously every single year since 2008.

Indie Game Development

Don't be fooled by reports. Games don't *have* to take all that many people or all those riches to make.

As an example of a small, low-cost game that made it big, take the game *Braid*. It purportedly cost Jonathan Blow only $180,000 to fund this independently developed game, which went on to win critical acclaim after its release to Xbox Live Arcade in 2008. In fact, at $15 a download, *Braid* was purchased by more than 55,000 people during its first week of release (a gross profit greater than $825,000)!

Independent game developers make games "on the cheap" using free or open-source software on personal computers, and they do so without a publisher. That means that they have to rely on self-distribution channels to sell their games over the Internet for less than what commercial games go for. Indie game designers have also been called "garage game developers," after the notion that they work right out of their home garage, basement, attic, or spare bedroom. Services such as the web, the PlayStation Network, and Xbox Live Arcade make

Figure 2.2
Acclaimed indie game *Braid*.

it even easier these days for an indie developer's home-brewed game content to be distributed to wider audiences.

You can compare indie game development to the indie music scene.

You see, a rock band doesn't have to swing a licensed contract deal with a record company to play great music. They can hit gigs wherever they find them, setting up in the back of clubs and playing to the delight of their audience and not for the glory of the dollar bill. And anyone who knows the music scene knows there's some great untapped power in the indie music scene. After all, the indie musicians are playing because they have music in their souls, not because they want to sell a product.

The same is true of indie game developers. While there are some designers who get into the industry just because they want to make a profit, many of them are making games for the reason that they love games. They build the sort of games they'd want to play, and that carries over in the contents they release.

Tip

"Read, experiment, design, develop, play, and most important of all, have fun. In the end, having fun is what games are all about."

— Ben Sawyer, *The Ultimate Game Developer's Sourcebook*

Figure 2.3
Greg Costikyan.

Greg Costikyan (Figure 2.3), one of the founders of Manifesto Games, says that it is possible for a team as small as 1 to 10 developers to put together a video game for less than $1,000 and sell it online for $10 a download and make their money back in just a few short months. Several indie game developers have done it and continue to do it.

If you have a passion for designing games, and don't want to wait around for your big break into Blizzard Entertainment or whatever game company you've set your sights on, you could get a jump on your goal simply by becoming an indie game developer. This book, in fact, gives you the tools to get started.

What a Game Developer Does

"Everyone who has a computer fancies himself a game designer, just as everyone with a guitar wants to be a rock star. There is nothing wrong with that if you remember that success is a long, hard road."

— David Crane

A *game developer* is a person who, frequently with the help of others, designs video games using specialized computer software.

An ideal game developer has the following traits. Some of these come as innate inborn talents, while others are skills that can be learned and practiced over time. Don't worry if you don't have all of these traits as part of your personal make-up, because this list is broad and comprehensive to cover all types of game developers.

- **Big Imagination**—RPGs are fanciful, pretend games that exist in virtual worlds of our making. Imagination is central to coming up with game ideas and the way the artificial realities within games should look.

- **Technical Aptitude**—Technical aptitude is a general understanding of how computer programs, especially video games, work. You need to be comfortable with computers and learning new software applications in order to master game-making. If you take like a duck to new technology and have trained your cell phone to call you when you get bored, then making RPGs will be a cakewalk.

- **Analytical Eye**—Developers must have the ability to examine and break down problems in order to find resolution to them. This is very important in an iterative development process, where you are testing out new ideas and learning what works and what doesn't and why.

- **Aesthetic Eye**—Good game designers should be able to see when something looks right and when it does not. They must illuminate exactly what is pleasing to the eye, so that a game's visuals pop, while reducing ugly distractions.

- **Drawing/Painting Skills**—Because video games, by nature, rely heavily on their visual content, game artists need to know how to create really eye-catching graphics. Having training in traditional, as well as digital, art is a must nowadays.

- **Math Skills**—Game developers must have basic math skills. That includes adding, subtracting, multiplying, dividing, and working algebra problems. If you can do so without need of a calculator, even better!

- **Writing Skills**—Game developers do a lot of communicating, usually in the written word, so it is vital for every game developer to be a decent writer as well. That means that your grasp of English must be concise, accurate, unambiguous, and have little to no spelling errors. You can't

Figure 2.4
An epic fail in language localization.

get by with the "pigeon English" of cell phone and online instant messaging. Your RPG will flop if you write eligible NPC dialogue and gamers don't know what they said. Hark to the immortal lesson of Toaplan's *Zero Wing* game (Figure 2.4): "All your base are belong to us!"

There's no single homogenized description of what a game developer does, as there are several constituent parts to developing games. You could say a game developer makes games, but it is rare these days, due to the sheer bulk of labor involved, to see one person "do it all" anymore.

Therefore, game developers usually work together as a team, and each member of that team has his or her own unique role.

Game Developer Team Roles

There are many different roles within a game dev team. Many of the roles overlap, and there's quite a bit of cross-pollinating that happens within a team; for example, someone who's the director of the project might do a little user interface programming if the team is facing a deadline and have to reach their task goals sooner.

I could list every single role possible within a game dev team, but unfortunately, that would just be a waste of space. You would learn more by studying the

Figure 2.5
Just some of the team roles in game development: (A) Artist, (B) Programmer, (C) Writer, and (D) Sound Artist.

credits of one of your favorite video games, instead. The list of credits is repeated in-game, somewhere, as well as in the game manual and on the game's companion website. In the credits, you'll see roles like Lead Design, AI Programmer, Marketing Director, Scenery Designer, QA Test Lead, Web Coordinator, and much more. And not every game dev team labels their roles the same. For instance, you might see the role of game world designer named everything from Environmental Artist to World Builder.

So the list that follows (Figure 2.5) is a vague categorization based on role responsibilities and may include multiple roles in each department.

- **Artist**—The artist can be any graphic designer, 3D model artist, animator, texture artist, level artist, or other related artist that works on a game. Artists are in charge of making the video part of "video game." They create the 2D graphics, the 3D worlds and characters, and make everything look pleasing to the eye. And yes, even a boil-infested zombie in a dismal swamp must be aesthetically interesting! Artists use digital art software but must also have a strong background in traditional art, such as drawing and painting.

- **Programmer**—The programmer can be any UI (user interface) programmer, AI (artificial intelligence) programmer, game engineer, tools developer, database manager, network operator, or other related programmer. Programmers are in charge of making the game part of "video game." They make it all happen, taking the other assets and funneling them into a pipeline that works, often using a fabricated game engine. Some game engines, like the popular Unreal Engine, are purchased as premade licensed dev kits for the programmers to use. Programmers use code libraries and programming languages such as C++, C#, Python, and Lua.

- **Writer**—The writer develops the game narrative, writes the character dialogue, handles the game design documentation, and often scripts the game manual and box blurbs. Most game dev teams hire outside talent to do the writing, and often Hollywood screenplay writers are picked first—unless the director of the project chooses to do it himself. Although there isn't a huge call for game writers, there ought to be, because the job is a demanding and integral one to any game project. Writers use the native language and clever turn of a phrase to make the video game come together in a coherent whole.

- **Sound Artist**—The sound department in a game dev team has the task of giving the game its aural experience. This is as important and as big a job as designing the graphics for the game, because it has to satisfy one of our other five senses. Some sound techs record raw audio files, others edit the sound in the studio, others are in charge of coaching the hired vocal talent in their lines, to deliver spoken narration for games, and others compose or license music to be added to the game's score.

- **Lead/Producer**—Game developers have an administration side to them, too. Every department in a game dev team has at least one lead. Each lead is in charge of, and oversees, a department. So the art lead is in charge of the art department and makes sure every artist is accomplishing art task goals accordingly. On top of this micromanagement, the entire team has a single lead or director who oversees all. This is often the game designer, the brains of the operation, but not always. And this director has a supervisor, too: the producer. The producer works with the publishing department, making sure all deadlines are reached, developers are completing the game according to estimated plans, budgets aren't exceeded, and the game is advertised and ready to ship on schedule.

- **Tester**—Video game testers aid the dev team in play-testing the video game through each iterative build. Testers look for bugs, glitches, and other annoyances that need to be fixed before the game can be released. Testers may also be involved in *quality assurance*, or QA, which is a fancy term that means making sure the game ends up the fine piece of engineering the dev team wanted it to be in the first place. Testers spend long tedious hours playing the same sections of game play over and over again, filling log sheets of notes (so you have to be a clear communicator!), and reporting to supervisors. If you want to get into making video games, being a tester is often your best first step.

Besides these roles, there are also voice-over actors, who provide vocal recordings for the game characters, as well as support staff for the game dev team.

If you plan on making games yourself, you're going to have to wear a lot of different hats. But if you have some friends who want to help, find one or more of these team roles that best fits their expertise.

Game Schools

As the video game industry becomes a multibillion-dollar business and takes over the entertainment market, standards in that business have developed. One of the growing standards is that companies like to hire employees that already know what they are getting into before they start. Nowadays, it's hard to get a job at a game company if you aren't already educated in the field. Companies look for the best and brightest talent and have a pool of potential workers coming right out of college.

If you want to get a heads-up on the industry, especially if you want to go to work for a game company sometime in the future, you need to get good grades in algebra, geometry, physics, English, and art. Then, after graduating high school, seek out a college or university that offers a degree in game design or a related field.

Several places of higher learning have begun game design programs and even internships. Some of these game schools teach the software development and programming angle, while others focus on digital art techniques and 3D animation.

The following are some of the schools that offer game-related degrees.

- 3D Training Institute
- Academy of Art University
- American Sentinel University
- Collins College
- Daniel Webster College
- DeVry University
- DigiPen Institute of Technology
- Digital Media Arts College
- Emagination Game Design
- Ex'pression College for Digital Arts
- Full Sail Real World Education
- Global Institute of Technology
- International Academy of Design and Technology
- ITT Technical Institute
- Media Design School
- Pacific Audio Visual Institute
- Sanford-Brown College—St. Charles
- Seneca College's Animation Arts Centre
- The Academy of Game Entertainment Technology
- The Art Institute of Pittsburgh, Online Division
- The Florida Interactive Entertainment Academy
- The Game Institute
- The Guildhall at Southern Methodist University
- The School of Communicating Arts
- University of Advancing Technology
- Vancouver Institute for Media Arts

- Westwood College of Technology
- Westwood Online College

Getting a Job as a Developer

The responsibility of being a game developer is akin to that of being a rock star back in the 1980s. Currently, one out of ten kids wants to be involved in the game industry. That's great, because our country needs more computer geeks! I'm not kidding. Unfortunately, it's a very competitive job market.

At the time of this writing, there are more individuals seeking a game design job than there are companies hiring for positions. This means that companies have their pick and prefer the top qualified talent for the positions they have available.

The best way to get a job at a game company is to *be* that top qualified talent! You can do that by beefing up your design skills at a good game school, by entering an internship with a game company, or by working with an indie game development company in the interim.

Your work portfolio stands as a shining badge that will open doors for you, so you should start polishing it today.

That portfolio will come across even better if you have a few games you've developed of your very own. *RPG Maker for Teens* shows you how to do just that. You can craft some classic RPGs and put them in your digital portfolio to get promising recruiters eyeing you.

To look at just a few of the game companies that are doing hiring, go to http://www.gamedevmap.com (Figure 2.6).

Game Design Documents and Project Schedules

No one works in a void. That means, there is always a standard operating procedure in place, or else no one would know what to do or what steps to take to get something done. The same is true about building games.

Game developers handle each game project the same way. In order to make a game, first they have to have a plan. That's where they hash out ideas, find a great idea for a game, and narrow it down by putting it in writing. The writing they compose is called a *game design document*, which describes the game, dictates its inner mechanics, and can be as flexible or rigid as the team needs it to

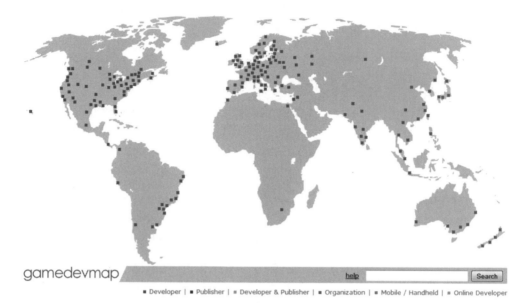

gamedevmap   help [   ] [Search]

■ Developer | ■ Publisher | ■ Developer & Publisher | ■ Organization | ■ Mobile / Handheld | ■ Online Developer

Figure 2.6
Gamedevmap.com showcases best-known game companies from all across the globe.

be. The entire design is locked down, either at this point or somewhere early into production, at which time no more features may be added to the game.

Note

The transition from game idea to game design document is a critical one. When writing the game down, many of the important decisions will be "set in stone," so to speak. Many first-time designers are reluctant to make that transition. They say they want to keep their options open, in case they change their mind about how the game will go mid-progress. They're especially afraid they might make a wrong decision or overlook something. This irresolution is dangerous. If critical details about the game are still left "up in the air" when the team starts production, the team will never be really sure what they're building, and the final product will be washed-out, bewildering, and quite likely unplayable.

Then, the team inspects the game design document to determine what different parts of the game need to be done and by whom, and they break those parts down into step-by-step tasks. They plan what software will be used and when each task should be accomplished, in order for the game to be finished by the deadline. This project schedule is overseen by the project's director and/or producer.

There is some leeway added in to each project schedule, in case there are any upsets or technological malfunctions that cause setbacks. And when it comes to intricate computer workings, there are always some of those! Almost *every* popular RPG on the market has had some technical setbacks somewhere in the course of their development.

The Development Process

Game development is broken into three sections that follow one another like clockwork. You could think of them as The Beginning, The Middle, and The End. They are as follows:

1. **Preproduction Stage**—In this stage, the original game designer, often the project director, lays out an idea for an RPG. He assembles a core team of individuals, and they look at the RPG idea from different perspectives to determine if it's viable. They tinker with it until it has approval from everybody. Then the idea is hammered into a more formal state by writing initial game design documents. A schedule of task goals is lined out, the development process is planned, and production gets underway. Often, more team members are hired on at this point to fill the needs of the production plan.

2. **Production Stage**—This stage is where the game actually gets assembled. It can take as little as four months up to three years to do. The art department works on graphics, the sound department works on sounds, the programming department programs the game, and the administration and support staff help conduct the process. Eventually, the game is tested multiple times until it reaches its final polished state and a gold master is readily available. The gold master is the best copy of the finished game and is sent to disc manufacturing or the web server to be distributed.

3. **Postproduction Stage**—After the RPG launches, it is shipped to stores everywhere or uploaded to commercial sites online by the publisher. The dev team may continue working on patch fixes and updates, or they might begin building add-ons, downloadable content, or expansion packs. Tech support also takes off, which handles gamer issues, and follow-up promotions are sponsored by the marketing people.

The way these stages are handled depends largely on the project management process. Some teams set rigorous task objectives and get as much done before reaching the cut-off dates; if a task isn't concluded by its deadline, it gets left out of the game. Other teams have a very loose organic process at first, where game elements are added or subtracted any time at will, but normally, even these teams get more precise as the final time limit approaches.

Rapid Iterative Prototyping (RIP)

Rapid iterative prototyping means that game developers will break the build process down into individual chunks. Each chunk will then be tackled, one at a time. It's a little like carving a statue out of a solid block of marble.

Let's say, for instance, that one chunk is adding Wogs to the player inventory. Who knows what a Wog is? It doesn't matter. It could be a new magical sword or a jar of fairy berry jelly. It has to be added to the player's inventory, nonetheless.

The dev team will come up with a good idea on how to add a Wog to the player's inventory. The programmers will look at ways to add Wogs to the inventory in the code, while the artists will come up with graphic designs for the Wogs and the inventory panel. If one of the developers' ideas doesn't work, then they delete what they tried and try something else instead, until they get the Wogs added to the inventory.

This often becomes a laborious process of trial-and-error. Once they get the Wogs in place, though, they can leave that part of the game mechanics alone and move on to tackle the next chunk. Eventually, the RPG will start to take shape, and by the end of the process, it will be a polished marble statue . . . er, I mean, video game.

Mark Cerny (Figure 2.7), the designer of such games as *Spyro the Dragon* and *Jak and Daxter*, often asserted that during the early stages of development, you should build, test, and then throw away no less than four different prototypes of your game, until you find the one that works best. Each new idea must be constructed and tried out thoroughly before incorporation into the actual game. Cerny's idea may sound extreme to you, involving a lot more work, and it does takes the "rapid" out of rapid iterative prototyping, but many developers see merit in the resulting quality of work.

Figure 2.7
Mark Cerny.

Scrum Development

In the last few years, a majority of game development teams have switched to a relatively new project management process called *Scrum*. Scrum is not an acronym for anything. It is a term borrowed from the contact sport rugby. Scrum development keeps teams organized and progressing toward product completion in a timely manner.

In the Scrum process (Figure 2.8), the team creates and tests updated, fully working versions of their game in short iterations called *sprints*. Sprints can occur anywhere from every week to every month. This enables the game dev team to identify and weed out potential problems early on. Plus, the directors of the team, and the team as a whole, know every aspect of the game project that's going on, which helps keep everybody in the loop and up-to-date.

On the down side, the Scrum process is pressure-intensive. If team members do not finish a task goal before the next sprint, their work might not make it into the game.

Whatever development process the dev team decides to go with in making a game, eventually they have to look at the deadline and what matters most: the game's launch date!

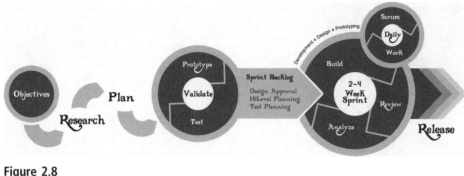

Figure 2.8
The Scrum process.

Getting the Game Out There

Before the RPG is even finished, the producer and publisher will make sure the world knows it is coming.

Most retail outlets and distribution centers have only a limited number of spots on their store shelves for video games, and they rotate their stock regularly to include the most recent and popular games that come on the market. So if an RPG is going to sell well, gamers have to be told that it is on the way months in advance. That way, when the game is released, people can buy it, the game won't flop from lack of sales, and retail outlets will want to display it because it's received a lot of hype.

The hype created by news of the game is actually orchestrated by the marketing department of a publishing company. They start by sending press releases to trade magazines such as *Game Informer* and *PC Gamer* and end with sending posters and press kits to the retail outlets themselves.

Artwork plays a huge role in an RPG's press, especially up front, and a lot of gamers will purchase games based on the quality of the box art and interior graphics. Art, therefore, makes a game more commercially feasible, even if the game turns out to be a dud from lack of innovation and poor player controls.

Being an indie game developer is harder, because publishers are more entrenched in the advertisement schemes, and indie game developers have to struggle more and spend more of their hard-earned money to put their name out there. But thanks to the Internet and web communities these days, it is not an impossible task. *RPG Maker for Teens* will show you how to advertise your game, too, once you've made it.

How to Make an RPG Yourself

Remember how I told you it is rare to find one person who can make games all by himself? Well, I lied. *You* are that person!

Soon you will make your very own RPG. You can make several RPGs, if you like, with the education you receive in this book. You can make RPGs by yourself, or you can teach your friends how to make them, and you all can work together to come up with great game ideas.

You don't need a whole lot of different software, but you will need some, in order to make an RPG. You will be using an image editor to refine your art resources, a sound editor to get your audio just right, and the RPG Maker program to put it all together.

Generating Game Ideas

Tip

"Good ideas are common—what's uncommon are people who'll work hard enough to bring them about."

— Ashleigh Brilliant

There's an app for that! No, actually, this is one area of game design that relies totally on the human element and *cannot* be done by machine.

I bet you've had plenty of game ideas. A lot of times these game ideas originate from playing other games, and you start thinking to yourself, "I wonder what would happen if they did this..." or "I could make this totally better if..." Or you might watch a movie and think, "This would make an excellent game. I bet it would be cool if..."

Write down your game ideas. Your mind is a funny thing. You might think you'll remember your idea and later find yourself scratching your head. If you write down your idea in a notebook or on your cell phone, the idea will be preserved for you later, when you actually decide to make a game. It pays to be prepared because you never know when a brainstorm might hit.

If you have difficulty thinking up a game idea, don't be forlorn. There are several ways to find inspiration.

■ **Brainstorm**—Chat with your friends. Ask them if they've ever thought of a great idea for an RPG. Or ask them what they liked or didn't like about RPGs they've played, and take notes. Tracy Fullerton, assistant professor at USC's School of Cinematic Arts, Interactive Media department, and co-director of the Electronic Arts Game Innovations Lab, says, "Some of the best brainstormers are Imagineers [the guys who work at Disney Imagineering]. They often have very large brainstorming sessions, with people from very different backgrounds, and they have physical toys to keep people loose. And somehow, tossing toys around gets the creative ideas flowing, and I find that very successful."

■ **Research**—Play a game. Better yet, play lots of different kinds of games. Don't just play RPGs, either. Try games of other genres. And don't just play video games. Try board, card, and tabletop games. This advice sounds fairly obvious, but it doesn't make it any less true. Great games beget other great games. You could make a list of what you liked or didn't like about each game, and examine ways to make your game even better. Also, you could visit your local library or scour the Internet for game ideas. Google keywords and phrases like "game ideas," and you might be pleasantly surprised how many sites you hit on the web where people have posted their own random game concepts.

■ **Frankenstein**—"It's alive!" You could use the *Frankenstein method* to come up with game ideas. This method, which is very popular in Hollywood, involves taking the best bits of disparate sources and merging them together into a single concept. For example, take *Need for Speed*, a car racing game, and *Elder Scrolls V: Skyrim*, a fantasy RPG, and put them together. Players must now race magic-outfitted berserker mobiles across vast terrains, while dodging dragons. How many racing games on the present market do you see incorporating magic fantasy elements? Why couldn't they? With the Frankenstein method, you can put several different games into a blender and see what comes out. Whatever mix you come up with, the results will probably be different!

Once that little flash of lightbulb comes on, you finally know you have a game idea. Write it down right away. Then start fleshing your idea out with more supporting details before you attempt writing a game design document.

There is no greater test for a game idea than trying to put it into articulate words on paper. Usually, ideas in and of themselves are sublingual, full of image snippets, emotions, and vague thoughts. Trying to put your idea onto paper and then reading it out loud helps you to focus and reveals weak spots that might have made it past your original mental process as you wrote the idea down. You might find there are words you used that don't work as efficiently as some others would.

After you've written down your game idea, sit on it for about a week. Come back to it later and see if it still sounds like a good idea. If so, share it with your friends. Ask them to describe your idea back to you after they hear it, based on their own comprehension, and listen to them carefully. Don't ask for their opinion or let them cut you down just yet, as this is just a game idea. Especially ignore biased, hurtful, or hasty generalizations such as, "This won't ever work because games with dragons in them suck."

The more you practice coming up with game ideas, the easier they'll come for you. You may notice yourself watching television and going, "Hey! I bet I could make a game out of this show." Best of all, with instruction you're learning here, you'll know you can.

Once you have a bunch of game ideas, you can start narrowing them down to one idea in particular you want to make now. Pull it out and write a game design document around it.

Writing Game Design Documents

Tip

"The design is not something cast in stone that has to be followed to the letter—it's more of a guideline."

— Jon Freeman

As part of their job, game developers must write a series of documents to tell others about the game design decisions. Exactly what documents they write vary from one developer to the next and one project to the next, but all game design documents share the same objective. They transmit the design to other members of the team. An edited version of the game design document can also be used to pitch the design in publisher proposals.

The process of writing a game design document (hereafter called a GDD) turns vague concepts into explicit planning. Even if no one reads it at all, a design written down is a judgment made. If there's a game feature not listed in the GDD, there's a good chance it's been overlooked. One of the developers may have to make it up on the fly, or worse, each team member will have a different opinion of what needs to be done.

A GDD is usually written in a word processor program such as Microsoft Word and distributed in paper form. It is increasingly common to find GDDs created as pages on an internal company website or wiki. A *wiki* is a website that allows for the creation and editing of a number of interlinked web pages via a browser and is often a collaborative affair, meaning that many different people can contribute to it. A wiki is a good way for a game dev team to document a game design so that all the members of the team can access it, and it can be updated easily.

A lot of times, the GDD comes multi-part, meaning that there may be one document that describes all of the game characters in full detail and another document that describes the game world with information about the kinds of things that world contains. The more features a game has, the more in-depth the GDD must be.

Typically, a GDD does two things:

- **Reveals Details**—If it isn't specified in the GDD, it isn't getting done and it won't show up in the game. The GDD tells the dev team every tedious detail going into the game, such as, "Put feature B at position X and Y and hook it up to widget C."

- **Conveys Vision**—The GDD can sometimes sound like a sales pitch. It has a load of "Let me tell you about widget C, and why it's so cool."

Some writers of GDDs get carried away with details, ending up with a dreary ponderous monstrosity that is difficult to carry around and even worse to read.

You should keep your feature lists short and to the point, missing nothing but not being over-the-top.

Fine-Tuning Your Concept

Everyone will have questions about your game, including your friends. Whether working on a GDD or not, you should refine your game idea into an eloquent vocabulary so that you can convey it to people who ask and also write it into your GDD.

To do so, answer these six questions up front to steer the direction of your thoughts.

1. **What Is This Game?**—Describe the game in one sentence or a single short paragraph. This is the answer to the most frequently asked questions you will hear, including from your mom. What are you working on? What's the name of your game? What's it about?

2. **Why Create This Game?**—Why are you creating this game? Do you love zombie games, so you're planning to make one? Do you think there is a gap in the market for another zombie game? Why make this game, then? Answering this will help you clarify what makes your game different from the rest.

3. **Where Does This Game Take Place?**—Describe the world your game takes place in. Help frame the game's setting in the reader's mind by spending a paragraph on it here. Later, you can go into it in more detail in a section devoted to describing the game world.

4. **What/Who Do I Control In This Game?**—Describe what (or rather, who) the player controls in the course of the game. Don't forget this, as this answer may make your game stand out if you have a cleverly created character.

5. **What Is the Point of This Game?**—What is the player supposed to achieve in this game world? Is he going to do something as clichéd as save the world? Is he trying to amass the largest ore mine, or find his father's secret identity? What? Generally, the answer you give here helps cement the scope of the game, because an RPG where the player has to

save the world will probably be larger and more complex than an RPG where the player must scrub several train station commodes.

6. **What's So Different About This Game?**—You must explain why your game is different from the hundreds of other commercial RPGs in the market right now. If you can't think of anything, be honest. Just say, "This is another *Diablo* clone, but it was done by me, so it's cool."

Elements of a GDD

Although no two GDDs are constructed alike, there are reasonable similarities between them all. Most have the following:

- Concept statement
- Objectives
- Target audience
- Scope of the project
- Feature set
- Work breakdown
- Asset production list
- Story and level progression

Let's take a look at each of these in turn.

Concept Statement   A *concept statement* describes what your game is all about in one sentence or a single small paragraph. Paraphrase the answer you gave in the last section here. This is the heart of the game, and whatever you write determines what you will make.

Shigeru Miyamoto (Figure 2.9), the game biz legend who invented Mario and Link and practically spearheaded Nintendo for years, advises revisiting—not *revising!*—your concept statement often, particularly when adding new features or cutting features from the game, to make sure you're still on track and keeping up with your concept statement.

Mind you, it is possible to change the core of the game partway through development, because it's happened before—although on rare occasions. When

Figure 2.9
Shigeru Miyamoto.

it does happen, and the concept statement has to be rewritten, the dev team must review all aspects of the game to make sure every feature emboldens the new concept statement.

Concept statements are often generated by starting with the words, "This game is about being a/an..." or "This game lets you..."

Here is one example of a concept statement as written by Andrew Rollings and Ernest Adams in their book *Andrew Rollings and Ernest Adams on Game Design*, published by New Riders 2003:

Diablo meets X-Files in 3D. A new threat has appeared on the streets of America: a mysterious drug, code-named Idoctrinol. No one sent to investigate it has ever come back, and it's clear that something sinister is going on. To neutralize this menace, you're given command of a super-secret team of four psychic warriors—psychically talented and superbly trained individuals drawn from the Special Forces of the U.S. Armed Services.

Objectives   Draft objectives based on what you want to see come out of your game. In essence, what do you hope to achieve by making your game?

When writing objectives, you should follow the SMART methodology as defined by James Lewis in his book *Fundamentals of Project Management*, published by the American Management Association in 2002.

Make each objective:

- **Specific**—The objective must be direct and to the point.

- **Measurable**—The objective must have a calculated outcome.

- **Attainable**—Don't say things like "This game will gross more money in its first year that *World of WarCraft*!" That objective is simply unattainable.

- **Realistic**—Your objectives should remain realistic, which here means "not crazy."

- **Time-Limited**—If you don't set a deadline for an objective, it will never end.

Target Audience

Tip

"Even though I enjoyed the challenge of programming, ultimately the motivation was the fans, the gamers themselves. I kept asking myself, 'Is that guy enjoying the game?'"

— Bob Whitehead

Define your target audience, or who you're making the game to appeal to. You cannot create something unless you know who you are creating it for. In other words, who are the players of your game supposed to be?

In many cases, it's okay to make a game for yourself and hope that other people will play it. If you have fun playing your game, chances are good others will, too. But to truly reach a broad market, consider the following.

- **Geographics**—Where does your target audience live? Are they in the United States? If so, what part? Do you want to appeal to city folk or people who live in more rural areas?

- **Demographics**—This includes statistics about your target audience. Are they male or female? Do they come from riches or do they have a moderate income? Do they still live with their parents?

- **Psychographics**—Values, attitudes, and beliefs of your players are important in what they will play. What kind of ethics do your players adhere to, do you think? Would they consider stealing or killing wrong? Do they have an immature mentality?

It is just as important to consider who will be reading your GDD, too. Don't write your GDD to be aimed at gamers, because they will never see it. Usually, a GDD is read by the dev team, producers, and publishers. So don't be vague or offer cryptic references in your documents. Everyone who reads it must be able to comprehend the information they read.

Instead of saying, "Players can fire laser cannons at dirigibles," state in clearer terms, "Players can operate laser cannons that have infinite ammo by standing next to one and pressing the spacebar on their keyboards. Each laser cannon takes 12 seconds between shots to recharge. Cannon fire has a range of 300 feet and can do 150 points of damage to dirigibles." See how more concise and accurate this sounds? Plus, the game's programmers won't have to make up the numbers when they're setting up the combat system, because all the information they need is right there.

Scope of the Project   Each game project is unique. Remember that your game can only be as successful as the preparation that's put into it. Determine the scope of your game before moving on, and never make assumptions about the project. If you leave any gray areas, you might get lost in them later on—so be careful!

To determine the overall scope of your game, you must be able to look at the big picture. You should establish the following items, most of which are resolved for you when using RPG Maker.

- **Platform**—Is this game being developed primarily for the computer or another platform? You have to have special porting software to port games to console or handheld platforms; the software is not cheap. As you will be making your game in RPG Maker, you should know it only works on Windows PC platforms.

- **Genre**—What is the game's genre (for example, is it a first-person shooter, RPG, strategy game, or something else)? You will be making an RPG, so that's easy here.

- **Player Mode**—Is the game a single-player, multiplayer co-op, or multiplayer versus game? RPG Maker is used to make single-player games.

- **Player Point of View (POV)**—Which camera perspective will be forced through most of the game (for example, first-person, third-person, isometric, or other)? RPG Maker makes top-down perspective games, similar to the classic *Zelda: Link to the Past* and *Final Fantasy* games.

- **Time Interval**—Will the game be real-time, turn-based, or time-limited? RPG Maker features two modes: real-time for exploration and turn-based for combat.

- **Technology**—What technology will be required to make the game? As you are going to use RPG Maker, we'll go with that.

- **Interface**—How will users navigate through all the information in the game? What type of interfaces will be required? How do you want those interfaces laid out? Remember, an RPG usually has a menu screen, a character creation screen, an inventory panel, a buy/sell merchant screen, and a combat menu screen.

- **Content**—What content should be included in your game?

- **Style**—What sort of aesthetic style do you want applied to your game? What will the look and color scheme be like? What mood do you want to effect?

- **Audio**—How will audio be used in the game (for example, music, sound effects, dialogue, and so on)?

Feature Set   List all the essential selling points about your game right here, including all the features you've decided to put into your game. If they are purely technical features, then you can put them into a separate tech specs section later on.

The feature set is critical to understanding the overall direction of a game before creating it. The feature set should also depict how the player plays the game and the highlights of the game play experience. Feature sets consist of 5 to 15 things that make up your game, each one making your core concept stronger. Remember, if a game feature doesn't strengthen your concept directly, the feature should be revised or excluded.

To see feature sets for other games, check out the back of any game box you happen to have. Though these lists will usually be written in marketing speak, the desire of the designers is clear.

Here is a feature set you might see for a typical RPG:

- Play as one of five different character classes: Warrior, Berserker, Bard, Druid, or Thief.

- Pick one of four character races to play: Human, Elf, Dwarf, or Halfling.

- Choose one of six different magic schools to use: Fire, Water, Earth, Sky, Night, or Time.

- Use a combination of melee weapons (e.g., daggers, swords, maces, mauls, and so on) and ranged weapons (e.g., bows, crossbows, flintlocks, rifles, and so on).

- Explore eight different maps, including Jungle, Mountain Range, Coastal Region, Cave Tunnels, Deep Forest, Savannah, Sky Realm, and Capital City.

- Experience turn-based combat versus 120 different monsters and boss enemies.

Work Breakdown   A *work breakdown* simply breaks down your game project into tasks and sub-tasks, assigns team members to those tasks, and estimates the hours it will take to get those done.

Task Determination

Tip

"Ideas are cheap. A dime a dozen, as they say. It's the implementation that's important! The trick isn't *just* to have a computer game idea, but to actually create it!"

— Scott Adams

Tasks can be either specific or general to the project.

- *Specific tasks* are the steps needed to complete a feature of the finished project. A feature may be a player character. To create this character, you or your team need to write a character description, draw concept artwork, design a character model, and animate the character in motion. Each of these would be a specific task.

- *General tasks* include the broad steps applied to almost every feature within your product to create the best player interface, style, story, and game play—including quality assurance.

Estimating a Timeline   Once you've generated all your tasks, you can begin estimating the time it would take to complete each one.

There are interdependencies that can stand in the way of progress. You can't begin play-testing until all your assets are put into place, and you can't finish assets until the concept artwork has been reviewed. You can't finalize the enemy artificial intelligence until the first prototype is finished. Steps like these are points in a project where nothing else can be accomplished until that step has been completed. These points are considered specific tasks, but they can also become bottlenecks if you don't figure them into your timeline wisely.

Estimating Costs   The next step is to identify how much everything will cost. You don't have to really worry about this, unless you decide to purchase a license of the RPG Maker software to continue using the application after the 30-day trial is over. But for most game companies, budgets are very important to track, and estimating how much money you might spend will save you money in the future.

Cost factors in the following elements:

- **Employees**—Costs associated with your team, including paying their salaries, benefits, bonuses, and reimbursements.

- **Talents and Licenses**—This consists of expenses for outsourced staff or companies, such as composers, writers, visual effects artists, programmers, and voice-over actors.

- **Equipment**—Servers, workstations, networking equipment, scanner beds, digital cameras, printers, and software packages you need to complete the project cost money.

- **Overhead**—This takes account of maintaining your office and work environment, such as rent, utilities, and office supplies.

Asset Production List   Assets here mean any viable element that will go into your game—especially visual art and audio. Asset production is done through a collaboration of designers working on characters, milieus, recordings, and more.

Typically, you want to have many of the major assets halfway completed before starting to script the game so that programmers will have something to test with.

List all the major assets that must be created for the finished game, including the following.

- **Setting**—You should break down the game world into smaller component pieces, such as towns and landmarks, and describe what's important about each one. Draw maps on paper to show what each area should look like from a bird's-eye view.

- **Characters**—Then, explain each and every character that will appear in the RPG, including the player characters, NPCs, monsters, and enemies. Provide statistics and full descriptions of each. The more onscreen time a character gets, the more details you should mention here.

- **Items**—Write a short overview of each of the items players might find in the game, including weapons, inventory items, quest items, keys, and so on. You can draw pictures of the items and give them unique looks based on the game's aesthetic style.

Story and Level Progression   This portion of a GDD records the large-scale story of your RPG and the way the game progresses from one area to the next. You're not trying to record *everything* that happens in the game, but rather a general outline of the player's experience from beginning to end, much like the walkthroughs that people write for games posthumously.

If the game's story diverges based upon the player's actions, this is the place to put it in writing and point out what decisions cause the game to take one course rather than another.

Reading an espionage fiction story, you might encounter something like this:

Daphne looked at the high-rise and realized the only way to get inside to steal the important documents she needed would be the roof of the next-door building. That night she cut a hole through glass in a fifteenth-story window and slipped through, dressed in black Lycra. She proceeded down the corridor and hid behind suits of armor as security guards patrolled by...

This sounds interesting, but it doesn't sound like a game. A game has interactive choices to it. Consider this (Figure 2.10):

Figure 2.10
Stealth games like *Splinter Cell*, shown here, broke new genre ground with a single game mechanic.

You play as Daphne. Your mission is to get into a high-rise corporate office and steal important documents. If you use your binoculars, you see a rooftop of a building next-door parallel to the fifteenth floor of the high-rise, allowing access through one of the windows. You show up that night after getting the gear you need. You have the choice of slipping through a window using stealth or blasting the window out with your shotgun and dashing in as fast you can, blazing a trail of destruction in your wake. Or--if you did not use the binoculars to start with--you might approach the front door, where you learn there is a tour starting for new employees. Get a fake badge or steal someone else's and you could invite yourself in. Pretend to be a new employee for a while, and then make an excuse to go to the bathroom, at which time you change into your black Lycra jumpsuit and slide through air ducts to take your own (sneaky) tour of the high-rise...

The second writing excerpt has more excitement to it. It's fresh and has playability built into it. Not only are there choices for the player to make, but there are enough choices that the player might want to play the game a second or third time, just to see what happens each time. You're inviting the player to collaborate in telling the story, giving her room for exploration, decision-making, and co-storytelling. You are not limiting the direction the story has to go in, which adds to the player's creativity and sense of wonder. This attribute makes game media a much more intimate experience for the audience than any other known media.

Remember, when giving the player choices, each one must be:

1. **Tangible**—The choice has substance and is not thrown in willy-nilly. Don't ask the player, "Left or right door?"—when both lead to the same room.

2. **Entertaining**—If you ask a player, "Take the fun scenic view or the dull boring one?" he will pick the more exciting one every time, guaranteed.

3. **Long-lasting**—The results of the player's choice should change the course of his path and have dramatic repercussions later on in the game.

4. **Informed**—The player should be given enough information in order to make the choice. Don't ask him, "Red or blue?"—when he doesn't know what you're referring to. If he makes a wrong choice, he will blame it on you for not giving him enough clues to go by.

Just how much choice should you give the player?

In a tabletop RPG, the narrative is completely open-ended, and the players can choose to do whatever comes to mind, because a Dungeon Master curbs the narrative to fit their decisions.

In a video game, you—the designer—do not have such luxury. You have to be able to predict all of the player's likely choices. You have to create, support, and test each possible choice. And, when choices are stacked on other choices, you are creating an interconnected web of content, of which your player will witness but a single path. Each middling or halfhearted choice you present reduces the odds your player will see your best stuff.

You don't want to rail the player into a locked track, either. You have to learn to balance the choices you give him versus the tale you're entertaining him with.

Remember the use of episodes we looked at in the last chapter? You can break down your game narrative into separate episodes and describe the open and close of each of those episodes here. In the example given above, the episode with Daphne would start with the player across from the high-rise, binoculars in hand, and would end whenever the player exits the high-rise with the important documents stolen (or not).

Planning the Development Process

If you plan to make an RPG all by yourself, which is commendable and very doable for your first time, you must understand that you will be responsible for every task. You will have to come up with your game scheme, write your documentation, draw your art assets, record your audio, construct your game world, program your code, and all the rest.

However, if you have the option and choose to do so, you could recruit some friends and start your very own game dev team. Find someone to be an artist, someone else to be a writer, someone else to be a programmer, and so on. If you do so, you would drift from being a project director to doing lots of interdisciplinary tasks, in the process of running the whole team.

If you work by yourself, then you are the only person you have to worry about. Building RPGs solo requires discipline and dedication. It's often too easy to give up after getting started, unless you have serious motivation. You can plan on the project taking you longer and requiring more labor and determination working alone than if you had the help of team members. Justly, it is more rewarding when you design an RPG all by yourself.

Finding the Right Resources

You will need the following components before you can begin making an RPG:

- A desktop or laptop computer with Windows Operating System 7, Vista, XP, 2000, or ME installed on it; this computer must have at least 128MBs RAM, an 800 MHz or better processor, 100MBs free disc space, a video adaptor with 1024 × 768 or better screen resolution, and a DirectSound-compatible sound card. These system requirements are practically "old hat" nowadays, so just about any computer *should* suffice.

- An image-editing program installed on your computer. If you have an image-editing program of preference, then by all means, use it. If not, you will find a list of available free resources below.

- A sound recording/editing program installed on your computer. Micro-soft Windows OS comes with a basic sound recorder you could use. If you have an audio program you'd prefer using, go right ahead. If not, see the free resources listed below.

- The RPG Maker program installed on your computer. See below for instructions on how to get it.

- Art supplies. You will need (at minimum) several drawing pencils, pens, markers, and paper. A ruler, compass, or guide can also help. More art utensils will be mentioned in the directions on drawing.

List of Free Resources

Herein you will find open-source or freeware programs you can download and install on your computer at your leisure. These are graphic or audio-editing programs that can make your game-making easier. You can investigate the applications on your own and see what you think. Use what is comfortable, because the software you're most comfortable with will make you more productive.

The following applications are just a small sample of the software that's out there. If you have the time and Internet research skills, you could get on a web search engine and look for keywords such as free, application, software, freeware, 2D/digital art, image editing, photo editing, and sound editor.

Photoshop Express   Photoshop, a program developed by Adobe, is the most-used image-editing application for Windows. It has lots of capabilities, including photo touch-up and paint tools and layer stacks for creating professional 2D pictures. I use Photoshop for most of the digital image work that I do.

Photoshop, unfortunately, is expensive. At the time of this writing, Photoshop CS5 costs $699 for an individual license. You can also get it as a part of the Creative Suite package, which includes Dreamweaver (Adobe's web-editing app), Flash (Adobe's 2D animation app), and many others. But it's hard to throw down that much money unless you know what you're getting into.

Thankfully, die-hard Photoshop fans can check out Adobe's special online application, Photoshop Express. Released in 2008, Photoshop Express is a far cry from the full version (it has no layer ability, for instance), but it'll get the job done in a pinch. You can also register for a free account to get 2GB of space for your photo upload needs.

To find out more about Photoshop Express, go online to http://www.photoshop.com.

Paint My daughter prefers to use Microsoft Paint. It comes free as part of the Microsoft OS, so you will find it on any computer that has Windows (look under Start > All Programs > Accessories). She likes it for the close-up pixel-by-pixel painting she can do with it, because she prefers drawing 2D sprites. Paint is not a terrific program when it comes to adding effects or touching up photos, but it is a versatile drawing app.

You can find a complete tutorial on using Paint online at http://windows .microsoft.com/en-US/windows-vista/Using-Paint.

GIMP The GNU Image Manipulation Program, or GIMP, is cross-platform, with a large community of support. It's come a long way from its early days of difficult interfaces and gnarly configuration setup. Now you can customize your editing interface and get nearly all the advanced photo-editing techniques of Photoshop in one simple and absolutely free application. Plus, GIMP is part of the GNU Project with development and improvements ongoing.

To find out more about GIMP, or to download it, go to http://www.gimp.org.

Paint Dot Net Paint Dot Net, which is jointly developed by Washington State University with support from Microsoft, is a free Paint look-alike that lets you create, edit, and manipulate 2D images on your computer. Similar to Paint or Photoshop in many ways, Paint Dot Net (Figure 2.11) supports multiple layers of depth, has a simple and uncluttered interface, unlimited undo functions, several commercial-quality special effects, and a wide variety of paint tools. There's also an active and growing community of digital artists who use and collaborate with Paint Dot Net that can help support you if you decide to use it.

To learn more about Paint Dot Net, or to download it, go to http://www .getpaint.net.

Picnik With Picnik, a web-based application connected to the photo service Flickr, all editing is done within your web browser. No download or registration is required. Simply upload an image from your computer or one you have found on the Internet, and start manipulating the image in clever and quick ways using Picnik's intuitive tools. In addition to using your Flickr account, you can edit your photos from your Picasa Web Albums, Facebook, Yahoo! Mail, or Photobucket, too. The premium version of Picnik is available for $24.95 for an annual

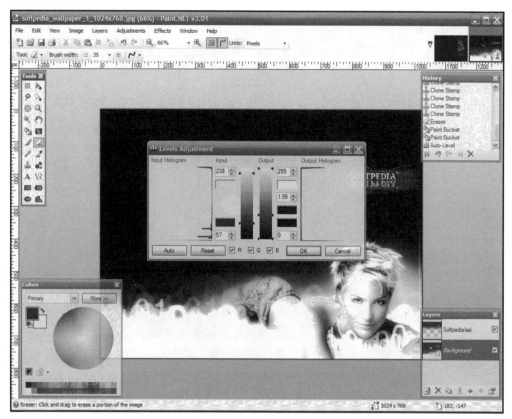

Figure 2.11
Paint Dot Net.

subscription. But for most users, it's a fast and easy replacement tool for Photoshop.

To try Picnik (Figure 2.12) and see if it's what you want to use, go to http://www .picnik.com.

Phoenix The founders of Worth1000.com, a community of image manipulation talents of over 500,000 digital artists and growing, started a New York–based indie company called Aviary. Aviary is a word that means, basically, a bird cage, and each of the software applications Aviary has developed since their beginning is named after a different—often mythical—bird. Their premier image-editing program, Phoenix, is no different.

Phoenix, in mythology, is a bird that is reborn from its own ashes, and so, too, are many of the application user's digital images. Like Picnik, Phoenix is entirely

Figure 2.12
Picnik.

web-based, which means you don't have to download any software in order to use it, and it is entirely free. Phoenix combines the robust photo retouching and paint tools of Photoshop with the ease and simplicity of an online website. Many digital artists who are not used to or cannot afford Photoshop, are switching to Phoenix.

If you'd like to see what Phoenix is all about, go to http://www.aviary.com (Figure 2.13).

Pixlr   With Pixlr Editor you can retouch digital images with basic and advanced tools, or create new images with the paint tools. It's fast, fluid, and easy—all within your web browser. If you're out of time or in a rush, Pixlr Express has quick and easy editing options for you. And for a faster editing experience, install Pixlr Grabber into your Firefox or Chrome browser, or onto your Windows desktop.

To experiment with Pixlr Editor, go to http://www.pixlr.com.

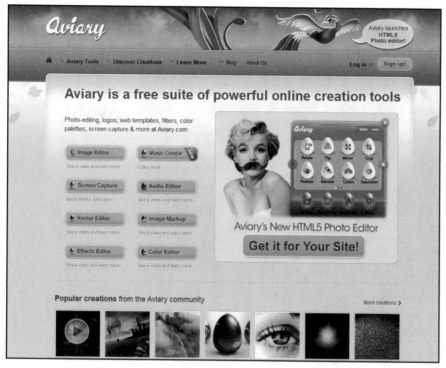

Figure 2.13
Aviary.com.

Myna and Roc   Besides Phoenix, Aviary also has two sound-editing programs that shouldn't be missed. The first one, Myna (named after the noisy myna bird), is an audio editor, while Roc (named after a legendary thunder bird) is a music creation program. Both are fairly easy and intuitive to use and operate through your web browser, so you don't have to worry about installing any software and can work on your digital audio anywhere you find Internet access.

To try out Myna or Roc, go to http://www.aviary.com.

Audacity   Audacity, created by Dominic Mazzoni, is kind of like the GIMP of the sound-editing world. With this small cross-platform application (under 3MBs), you can record, slice, and mix audio. There are a lot of robust options that don't clutter up the interface, because they are hidden in menu bar drop-down lists, and the way most of the editing is done is through simple playback controls and click-and-drag highlighting, all of which is very intuitive. Although Audacity supports WAV, OGG, and AIFF sound file formats, you have to

Figure 2.14
RPG Maker VX (RPG Tsukūru).

download and install a LAME encoder (a third-party plug-in) to be able to export out MP3s. The best thing about Audacity is that it is free.

To learn more about Audacity or to download it, go to http://audacity .sourceforge.net.

Installing RPG Maker

In 1988, the Japanese group ASCII first released a program called RPG Tsukūru (Figure 2.14). Tsukūru is supposed to be a pun, mixing the Japanese word tsukuru, which means "to make" or "create," with tsūru, which translates to English as "tool." RPG Tsukūru, often romanticized as RPG Tkool, was a program created for the development of fantasy RPGs.

The software series continued, its title evolving into the English name RPG Maker, and its developer, ASCII, was later succeeded by Enterbrain, Inc. RPG Maker underwent several incarnations, including RPG Maker 2000, RPG Maker 2003, RPG Maker XP, and (the latest) RPG Maker VX. Most versions include a tile-set-based map editor, a simple scripting language for scripting events, and a battle editor. All versions include initial premade tile-sets, characters, and events, which can be used in creating new games from scratch quickly and efficiently. PC users can also create and add in any new tile-sets or characters they like.

Starting with the RPG Maker XP version, the program uses Ruby, a dynamic, general-purpose, object-oriented programming language that combines many of the syntax elements of Perl with Smalltalk features. RPG Maker runs at 1024 × 768–pixel resolution, although the games made with it run at 640 × 480, and RPG Maker VX has a framerate of 60 frames per second (fps), which greatly enhances the animation quality, especially over the choppy 20 fps of earlier versions of the software.

Because of its ease-of-use and intuitive interface, RPG Maker is the simplest tool to use when making RPGs. Plus, it has been used in schools to help students learn mathematics and programming while having fun creating video games. As of 2005, RPG Maker's games as a whole have sold about 2 million copies worldwide.

You will use RPG Maker VX to make your very own RPG with the help of this book. In order to do so, go to Enterbrain's website at http://www.rpgmakerweb .com and download the 30-day trial version of the software. If you'd prefer to own RPG Maker VX, it will cost you or your parents around $60. Then follow the instructions to install it on your machine.

WHAT'S NEXT?

Now you should be ready to get started. You still have to learn the software and adopt certain skills with drawing and writing and synthesizing a game, but that's what the rest of this book is for. The rather dry academic beginner stuff is out of the way. All you have to do is turn to the next chapter and begin building your first RPG world.

Tip

"It is the greatest of all mistakes to do nothing because you can do only a little. Do what you can."

— Sydney Smith

CHAPTER 3

BUILDING GAME WORLDS

In this chapter you will learn:

- Why you should use a game world
- How a game world sets up action, fences players in, and more
- How to make maps on paper and add details to your make-believe world
- Creative ways to make your game world unique
- How to build worlds in RPG Maker

A *game world* is a complete background setting for a game. Creating an original, believable, interesting world is a genuine challenge. World-building is complex and time-consuming, although it can be very fun.

To design a historical game world will require hours of research. Worlds based on fiction (novels and TV series, for instance) require research, too, to make sure every detail conforms to the source, and to fill in logically where the original story gives no information.

In this chapter, we will look at what it takes to build a game world and how to design one using RPG Maker.

Purpose of a Game World

A game world gives the player an allusion for where his character is and where he should go. An RPG has to have a background for reference, a playing field for the player to explore, find resources, and beat combatants in. The game world reflects the game's setting, and as such, the setting can be just as important as the characters that are in it.

A game world serves an even larger purpose. Here are the top reasons why you use a game world:

- To set the stage for the game action.
- To create game flow.
- To set the mood.
- To fence the player in.

A Game World Sets the Stage

"Where are we? What are we doing here?" These are two very important questions players ask as soon as a video game loads, no matter what the game's genre. Creating a whole game world, not leaving anything out, and making that world as apparent to the player from the beginning will curb the player's curiosity and put him right into the action (Figure 3.1).

However, the game world is merely a backdrop, and with just a few simple brushstrokes and imagination, the setting can be set in place, with little to no fuss.

Impressiveness and decoration are the only ways that real-life construction influences game construction. Places in virtual space do not suffer with usability concerns. Windows and doors can look just like windows and doors, but the game artist doesn't have to worry about sizing them correctly so the game's inhabitants can use them; they just have to *look* right.

Game environments are little more than cardboard props to support the game action. Even in pseudo-realistic games, the buildings don't have any weight, they don't really exist, and many of them exist as "false fronts" that have no real depth to them beyond what the player can see.

Designing a game world, therefore, is more about game play than it is about a perfect simulation of the real world. Compare game settings to movie sets in that

Figure 3.1
In Bethesda's *Elder Scrolls IV: Oblivion*, the varied backgrounds serve as a stage for the character interplay.

they both support the narrative by putting details into graphic context for the viewer or gamer. They do this by mimicking real-world objects and buildings, but they do so only as necessary to the story.

A Game World Creates Proper Flow

The most important function of a game world is to support the game play. The pacing of the game's action can be short and fast-paced or long and sweet and is often dictated by the size and complexity of the game's levels and their content.

You can liken game flow to *feng shui*, the Oriental art of object placement and engineering based on the premise that invisible but tangible streams of *chi* energy moves all around us and gathers in tight corners. You want to promote flow just like *chi* flow, and guide the player's attention throughout the game world, by placing objects in just the right spots.

You can imagine that *chi* moves a lot like water, so it travels from areas of heavy concentration to areas of lesser concentration, filling voids as it goes. You certainly don't want it to stop and pool in one area, or else it will stagnate. The same is just as true about game flow.

Proper pacing in a game is even more important than how the game looks. Pacing is imperative, a real sink-or-swim mark for a game creator. A balance between player resources and game objectives is one of the keys to pacing your game. You should alternate between forcing the player to struggle to stay alive and reflectively exploring and solving puzzles. This will increase the playability of your game.

A Game World Sets the Mood

People respond on an emotional level in reaction to familiar settings. A creepy candle-lit castle in Carpathia has a vastly different emotional atmosphere, say, than a bright cheerful glen with chirping birds and flowers.

Take a look at the different regions in the *Silent Hill* horror games (Figure 3.2). The fog world, with its muted daylight and fuzzy—albeit normal-looking— surfaces, is more laid-back, allowing the player to explore with less worry and hesitation, than the nightmare world, where all that can be seen in the dark labyrinthine milieu is rust and blood splatters—and the darkness hides fiendish monsters that pounce on you. You just know when you hear the sirens and start to enter the nightmare world that you are in for trouble!

World-building, when used appropriately, sets up the game atmosphere and provides the backdrop that reflects the mood and emotional string-pulling you, the game designer, want to accomplish.

A Game World Fences the Player In

World-building also serves to hide the fact that the player character is actually inside one big invisible box he cannot escape. The box must have visual constraints as to how far, and where, a game character can explore. Without a proper frame of reference, the player would not be able to get around in the virtual world you will be creating.

Keeping the gamer from wandering off the game field you've constructed or going places you don't want him to go is called *"fencing the player in."* Nobody likes being told where they can and cannot go, so your fences will be frustrating for the player as a general rule of thumb.

Figure 3.2
As you can see in these two examples from *Silent Hill: Homecoming,* the fog world (top) and nightmare world (bottom) have two distinct moods.

Your player needs to understand that your fences are part of the game world and not merely thrown in to aggravate him. Essentially, if you put these boundaries into graphical context, they are less frustrating. For example, you could use uncrossable bodies of water, treacherous escarpments, thick brush, steep walls, and other visual structures to show the player his boundaries.

CREATING A PAPER PROTOTYPE MAP

So what defines a game world? What are the components of a game's setting?

Take a moment to consider everything you would have to do in order to record planet Earth as a game world. There are major continents to fill, each with its own range of climate, landform, culture, resources, history, and religion. An uncounted variety of plant and animal life forms populate the Earth's surface, and several new species are still being discovered. All in all, the Earth is an incredibly rich and diverse place. In fact, there's never been a game world nearly as complex as our real one.

Some things you might want to consider when world-building are:

- Maps and landforms
- Weather and climate conditions
- Cultures and customs
- Technology and communications
- Transportation
- Medicine
- Weapons and combat
- Work
- Political climate and conflicts
- Religion
- Monsters and animals

Frankly, you will need to get a notebook and make copious notes on each of these items and any other ideas or observations you can think of when developing a game world.

Getting Inspiration

Tip

"The books one reads in childhood, and perhaps most of all the bad and good bad books, create in one's mind a sort of false map of the world, a series of fabulous countries into which one can retreat at odd moments throughout the rest of life, and which in some cases can survive a visit to the real countries which they are supposed to represent."

— George Orwell

Creating a rich RPG world is a daunting task. The following are the top ways you can find inspiration for your game worlds.

- **Watch a movie**—You'll find cool settings and environments in most movies, and not just fantasy epics.

- **Read a book**—Read a good fiction book and pay attention to the description given for the setting.

- **Borrow from tabletop RPGs**—Almost every tabletop RPG has a world map and descriptions for game settings within it.

- **Travel the world**—Remember your own trips, if you ever go anywhere, and what it felt like to visit strange locales.

- **Pick up a travel guide**—Travel guides, especially the Frommer's kind, can give you lots of rich details and maps for any place you can think of to visit.

- **Ask your friends what kind of game world they'd like to play in**—This might just help you choose some features for your newborn world.

- **Watch the Travel Network**—You can check out exotic locations without ever leaving home, through some educational TV programs.

Maps and Landforms

Take some time when sketching your world map. Back in the day, I would rush home from school, pull out my latest notebook, and continue drawing on a map that would take me all week to finish. You want your world map to be indicative of the place you will build later in RPG Maker, so put some exertion into it.

Even though it may take some effort, drawing a map is very easy to do. All you need to know is what symbols to use. That's where a map legend comes into play. Each map maker uses a different kind of legend, one that works for him. You must first design a map legend, like the one in Figure 3.3, and build your map using those symbols.

Drawing Your Map

Tip
_____

"Map out your future—but do it in pencil. The road ahead is as long as you make it. Make it worth the trip."

— Jon Bon Jovi
_____

Figure 3.3
An example of a map legend.

You will need to take the game setting you invented when writing your game design document in the last chapter and make a map for it. The examples I show here are going to be used for the game project Thug Wallow we'll be designing in RPG Maker, just to get your feet wet, but I encourage you to make up your own game world.

Land and Sea   First, you need to determine how much of your game world will be covered in water. Obviously, if you want a mostly desert world, you'll deliberately select a very low H_2O percentage, while a seafaring adventure would have some sizable water bodies. Once you've determined how much of your world consists of seas, lakes, and oceans, your next step is to sketch out the continents, inland seas, and major islands. The distribution of land and water over the surface of your game world depends on what you've decided.

The next step is to sketch the actual shapes of the continents and major islands on your paper map (Figure 3.4). The regional distribution of land and water may suggest a pattern to you, but, overall, sketching out the coastlines of each imaginary land mass is a very creative process.

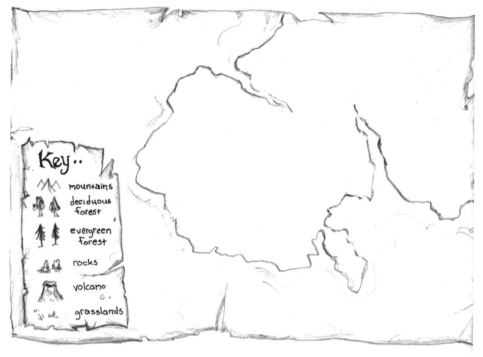

Figure 3.4
An example of continents.

Hill and Dale   The solid portion of Earth's crust is not one humungous unit. Instead, it is divided into a number of plates that continents and oceans rest on. Mountains are created where these plates collide, the stress long ago having pushed up the land mass. Valleys are results of the reverse of this collision process, where plates move apart, causing deep rifts. So draw some mountain chains and valleys where you imagine these plate collisions have taken place (Figure 3.5).

Escarpments mark sudden changes in elevation, and may mark the edge of a plateau or a crease in the face of the continent. Escarpments can represent long, unbroken grades, or sheer cliffs cutting across the face of the land. They work wonderfully for fencing the player in.

River and Lake   When it comes to bodies of water, lakes can be located anywhere, even in the heart of mountains, while rivers are born in and around major lakes and mountains or uplands, where rainfall, snowmelts, and deep

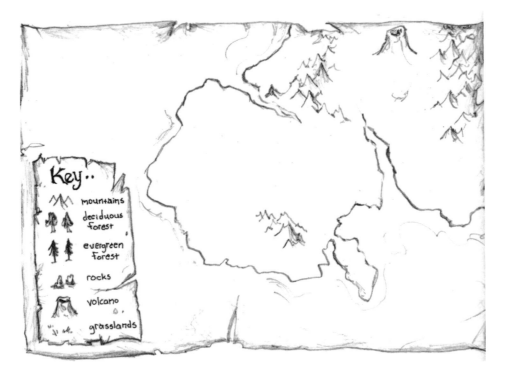

Figure 3.5
An example of highs and lows in land elevation.

springs feed streams. Since water flows downhill, streams gradually combine into greater and greater rivers as they join together on their way to the sea. Along areas where the land shifts in elevation rapidly, waterfalls and rapids will be most abundant.

The placement of lakes, rivers, and other bodies of water may influence the location and shape of your other map features by suggesting more realistic boundaries between terrain areas. For instance, many townships are found along river ways because it's faster and easier for them to do trade along water routes.

Sketch your bodies and tributaries of water where you'd imagine them (Figure 3.6).

List of Typical Landforms   The following are some of the most common fantasy RPG landforms.

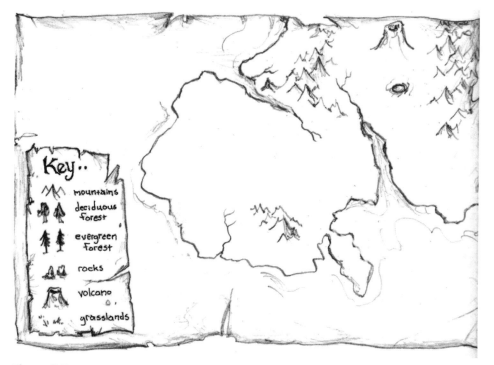

Figure 3.6
An example of rivers and lakes.

- **Aerial**—Mountain-top kingdom, airship, flying cloud castle, or cliff-side city.

- **Archipelago**—No large continents exist, only numerous small islands (Ursula K. Leguin's *Earthsea* series is a prime example).

- **Arctic**—A glacial or snowy place where cultures rely on animal husbandry, nomadic hunting, whaling/sealing, or fishing.

- **Desert**—The world is unusually arid, with vast reaches of waterless waste. Water could even be a valuable commodity.

- **Extraterrestrial/Other**—Occasionally, a strange realm that exists outside of our known time and space is ideal for meeting odd beings.

- **Forest**—Virgin woodland makes homes for sylvan creatures and agricultural societies.

- **Grasslands**—This covers a variety of terrain types, from tropical grasslands to dry northern steppes to African savannah to prairie.

- **Jungle**—Fetid, tropical forest covers much of the land.

- **Moors**—Moors are elevated regions with poor drainage, covered with extensive heath and scattered bogs. Misty valleys and foothills make for excellent moors.

- **Mountain**—Humped mountain ranges and arid hilltops make for treacherous trails and closed-in homesteads.

- **Oceanic**—Almost no land masses exist, only vast aquatic life. This would be ideal for a game involving mermaids.

- **Subterranean**—The focus of the game world is underground, in caves and tunnels deep beneath the earth.

- **Swamp**—Large portions of the setting are watery lowlands and marshes, filled with snapping crocodiles and stinging gnats.

- **Unstable**—For some reason, often of sorceries, large portions of the setting are mutable, changing, or formless. Lands could belong to powerful deities, who change their look on a whim, or break apart and reform by shifts in magic polarity. Take a look at the animated film *Dragon Hunters* for a great example of this (Figure 3.7).

- **Volcanic**—The land is marked by volcanic activity, including earthquakes, lava flows, and ash falls.

List of Important Sites

The following are the most common sites found in game worlds.

- **Castles/Towers**—These may be found in or near many villages, towns, and cities, and serve as the home of the local lord or knight, fortification against invaders, and barracks or headquarters of militia and constabulary.

- **Cities/townships**—The burg is a principle adventure site, urban in its sprawl and reflecting the personality of its people.

Figure 3.7
The setting in the 3D movie *Dragon Hunters* is constantly shifting.

- **Dungeons**—Classic underground delving adventure sites are monster-ridden dungeons. Although an actual dungeon is a medieval prison or torture chamber, dungeons in fantasy RPGs are seen as long, twisting underground mazes filled with diabolical traps and hideous monstrosities.

- **Ruins**—An ancient culture left behind ruins with fantastic wealth, magic, and hidden dangers inside. Locating unknown ruins could be the goal of an archaeologist or treasure-hunter.

- **Shrines**—Lonely sites scattered across the land are often the hubs of unusual eminence. Shrines could exist as shrouded temples to forgotten deities or focus nodes for mystic power.

- **Trade Routes**—The most traveled roads, pathways, bridges, and ferries in the kingdom are the merchant trade routes, which could still be harrowing, due to brigands.

- **Wilderness**—Exploring vast reaches of pristine wilderness, blazing trails along old trade routes or getting hopelessly lost, is the mark of many adventurers.

You can see the sites I added to the game map for Thug Wallow in Figure 3.8.

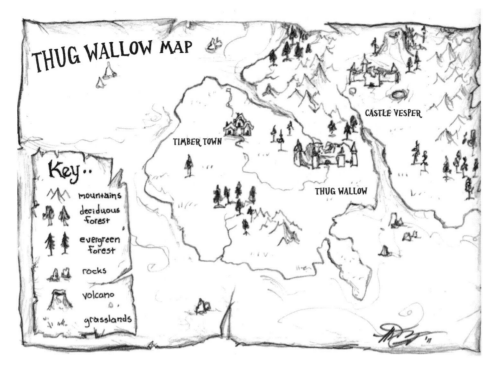

Figure 3.8
The finished map sketch for Thug Wallow.

Weather and Climate Conditions

Tip

"Weather is a great metaphor for life—sometimes it's good, sometimes it's bad, and there's nothing much you can do about it but carry an umbrella."

— Terri Guillemets

Our planet has specific weather patterns and climates based on the balance of chemicals in our atmosphere and the radiation given off by the Sun. Taking this into consideration, your game world should seem just as real and have its own weather patterns and climate conditions, even if you rarely exhibit them during the course of your adventures.

You can use Table 3.1 to create random weather and climate conditions for your world.

Table 3.1 Weather and Climate Conditions

Temperature	Condition	Precipitation
Sweltering	Sunny	Arid
Hot	Clear	Humid
Warm	Hazy	Foggy
Mild	Cloudy	Stormy
Chilly	Overcast	Drizzle
Cold	Thunderheads	Downpour
Frigid	Windy	Showers
	Breezy	Snow

Cultures and Customs

Culture is the method by which a society operates. Holly Lisle, in her *Create a Culture Clinic*, states that every culture has the same components:

- Its members share some form of common ground.

- They all adhere to specific goals.

- They set aside their differences in order to work together.

- Each member sacrifices some of his time, effort, or resources.

- They all work for the good of the group to sustain it.

- Everyone works to survive, propagate, and grow beyond their lifetimes.

If you feel like your game setting's culture is lacking, or that it appears thin, you might rethink some of the details. Consider what the day-to-day life is like for the citizens of your culture. Chiefly, study their home life. Where do they sleep and eat? How do they talk to one another? Where do they go when they're sick? What taboos exist? All these details will help flesh out a thin or droopy fictional culture.

When establishing a culture, here are some more quick ideas to mull over:

- **Architecture**—Lack of timber in one area might lead to buildings being carved from stone, while a community in a heavily forested area might prefer making log or wooden structures. Also, most communities have one or more prominent sites within them that stick out to visitors, such as armories, post offices, palaces, apothecaries, wizard towers, or libraries.

- **Fortifications**—For defense against intrusion, most communities surround themselves with a wall, palisade, or dome.

- **Layout**—Many communities are organized by the class of resident, so a city might have an area just for nobles and another for commoners.

- **Population**—A community may be largely deserted or only consist of a few close families, or it could be booming and choked with people.

- **Wealth or Poverty**—Prosperous communities feature buildings in good standing repair, stronger fortifications, and busier commerce districts. Impoverished towns lack the funds to maintain appearances and may be filled with beggars.

List of Popular Historic/Fictional Cultures

You might also want to explore the use of one of the following cultures, at least for inspiration.

- **Barbarian**—The glory days of Vikings and Celts could prove useful for you in building a barbarian culture. Think of the Cimmerians of Robert E. Howard's *Conan* stories.

- **Colonial**—The early days of American colonization, with its muskets, cannons, wood fortresses, and civil unrest could provide you with lots of cultural flavor.

- **Egyptian**—Your world could have a decidedly ancient Egyptian flavor to it, with pyramids and sand dwellers.

- **Feudal**—The primary culture could be based on the feudal society of medieval Europe, as many fantasy games have used.

- **Frontier**—America's Wild West, with its gun-toting cowboys, saloon girls, and native peacekeepers, was rife with adventure because of the lawlessness of the early settlers.

- **Greco-Roman**—Toga-wearing philosophers and trained soldiers could mark a mythological tale patterned after the ancient Greeks or Roman Empire.

- **Modern**—There's nothing holding you back from creating a thoroughly modern RPG, either. You could place your setting in your own backyard or in whatever rural town or metropolitan city you prefer.

- **Oriental**—The principle culture is Oriental in flavor. Medieval Japan, China, or India are all good examples of societies that could be recreated. So is ancient forgotten Persia.

- **Renaissance**—A world filled with swashbucklers and rakes, the Renaissance provides for nuances of technology and advancement in art, literature, and politics.

- **Seafaring**—The culture is reliant on fishing and sailing for trade and survival (Figure 3.9). Piracy may be abundant, or the wharf villagers could be mysterious icthynonic cultists like those found in H. P. Lovecraft's Cthulhu mythos.

- **Steampunk**—Frequently combined with another background, steampunk provides its world's citizens with steam-powered gadgets and uncanny imaginary inventions that often border on science fiction.

Figure 3.9
Just at a glance, you can tell that this province is probably seafaring.

- **Tribal**—Imagine the African or Native American tribal hut-dwellers and nomads, or you could invent a Lost World place, with dinosaurs and Pleistocene mammals such as cave bears and saber-tooth tigers.

- **Victorian**—Equal parts creepy and romantic, the gaslit grottos of Queen Victoria's time, with its Jack the Ripper and Sherlock Holmes, has inspired many tales.

Mapping Your Cultures

Where is each culture you've created located on your world map? How many separate states exist in each one? What resources do each of them control, and how do they survive and prosper? In this step, you will create the rough boundaries of each kingdom or area, building a political map of the region. For now, all you want to do is get an idea of the distribution of cultures across the map.

As you sketch out the political boundaries of your map, keep an eye open for particularly interesting areas that you think deserve special development. Is there a great old empire surrounded by fierce monster-dominated lands? Or balkanized areas of several rival cultures, all crowded together?

Technology and Communications

Tip

"Any sufficiently advanced technology is indistinguishable from magic."

— Arthur C. Clarke

Technology is a sign of scientific advancement in a society, from the invention of the wheel and discovery of fire to modern medicines and computers to laser battles in star-flung quarters of outer space. Most fantasy RPGs take place during the glorified European Middle Ages, but you can place your RPG anywhere and in any technological age.

Plus, different regions on your world map could have very different technology. One society could have progressed into a steampunk futuristic civilization, using robots to do the chores they don't want to or even developing war-scarred mecha machines—while a society further away from them could still be living a pastoral feudal society of simple farmers who think anything more advanced than a plow must be magic.

Think about what level of technology to give to the cultures on your world map. What sort of day-to-day devices do they use? How do they get to work; is it by horse or buggy or motor vehicle or rocket ship? How do they heat their food? Cool and heat their homes during extreme weather? Entertain themselves?

Although agricultural, construction, engineering, and transportation technology are all very important items to think about when considering technology as a whole, military technology will have the widest reach of effect in your RPG. The main thing players will want to know an answer to is "Do we get guns? What about rocket launchers? Or are we back in the sticks-and-stones age?"

Language

The language of a region or kingdom is almost as important a marker as its boundaries. What, and how many, languages are spoken in your game world?

As a rough guideline, most fantasy races (elves, dwarves, and so on) should have their own racial language, plus every separate culture ought to have its own. For trade and commerce, perhaps a common language should be spoken, so everyone can get along, or else people might have to depend on skilled translators. Even when a common tongue is shared, different groups within a single community may have their own distinct cant. For example, a rough dock worker would speak very differently from a pious castle nobleman.

Tip

"Language is the armory of the human mind, and at once contains the trophies of its past and the weapons of its future conquests."

— Samuel Taylor Coleridge

Written Language

Possession of written language is a key characteristic of a progressive culture. But your culture's written language could look very different from ours. Consider the Viking runes and the Egyptian hieroglyphics. If you want, you can invent your own special code language of symbols for use as your pretend

Figure 3.10
An example of a make-believe code language.

society's written heritage (Figure 3.10). If you do, you will have to teach your gamers how to interpret the code writing.

Transportation

How your world's inhabitants get around is linked directly to their technology level. If your game world is set in the Dark Ages, the inhabitants won't be making any sudden jaunts in automobiles or airplanes any time soon. They would be more likely to use horse and cart or long wooden paddle boats.

In classic RPGs like the ones you create with RPG Maker, the characters get around by walking. Most of the world should reflect this by having clearly marked walking trails.

Medicine

Medicine is another area that is defined by technology and society's advancements. Doctors and scientists work together to come up with new surgical methods and pills for patients to take.

In medieval times, most doctors were actually religious scholars. Surgery back then was crude, consisting of sawing off limbs that showed defects or to

Figure 3.11
Some health potions.

prevent the spread of infection. Medicine (or the apothecary science, as it was considered then) was little better than herbalism, mixing different plants into tinctures that could give some benefits. Most fantasy RPGs borrow from this history, using health potion bottles as the cure-all for any sort of character distress (Figure 3.11). Some games even require players to collect different plants to mix their own medicines.

Examples of modern medicine used in RPGs are first-aid kits, which, presumably, contain antiseptic, gauze, painkillers, and more. Or players might visit medical stations, staffed by human or robotic doctors, where their ills may be cured.

Weapons and Combat

Mankind's history has been replete in battle and armaments since the dawn of time. Depending on the technology level of the culture, the combatants may use clubs, bows, spears, swords, and other melee or ranged weapons. Or people may have discovered gunpowder, at which point the weapons become high-impact, including muskets, rifles, cannons, pistols, and other firearms. Futuristic weapons could include lasers, phasers, ion cannons, or some other form of weaponry based on theoretical science.

The three main things that gamers want to know, when it comes to weapons, are as follows:

- Is the weapon a melee weapon, requiring me to get close-up to the enemy, or is it a ranged weapon, meaning I can fire it from a distance?

- Does the weapon require ammunition, and how often will I have to reload the weapon?

- How much damage does the weapon do?

Tip

"I believe everybody in the world should have guns. Citizens should have bazookas and rocket launchers, too. I believe that all citizens should have their weapons of choice. However, I also believe that only *I* should have the ammunition. Because frankly, I wouldn't trust the rest of the goobers with anything more dangerous than string."

— Scott Adams

Work

The professions people do for a living, the sort of work that they do, is often dictated by the kind of culture they grow up in and what they find that either (a) they need to do to support society or (b) what they like doing and have a knack for.

1. What sort of work is most fitted for the culture you've created?

2. What sort of work runs most counter-productive to the culture you've created?

Commonly, mountainous or cave-dwelling cultures do a lot of mining. Woodland cultures do a lot of lumber and gaming (not video gaming, but hunting animals for food). Seaside cultures do a lot of fishing and trawling. Land-bound cities have a lot of factories and office jobs.

Trade and Currency

Everyone needs something, so some kind of trade must exist between nations and tribes for the exchange of goods. Mountain men will want paper, which is made of wood, and may want to eat sushi, so they will have to trade with traders

Figure 3.12
Gold coin is the most common fantasy game currency.

from other lands to get these things. This need for goods that indigenous peoples do not possess leads to trade routes, commerce, and currency. *Currency* is the use of script notes or coins to pay for things you cannot or will not barter for.

In most fantasy RPGs, currency consists of gold coin (Figure 3.12). In America, money is measured by the dollar. Your game world could use colored gems, funny Monopoly money, or anything else you can think of.

Employment

Here's a list of typical places/types of employment you might include in your town or province:

- Apothecary
- Armorer
- Assassin/Bounty Hunter
- Baker

- Barber
- Blacksmith
- Bookbinder
- Brewer
- Butcher
- Cheese Shop
- Clockmaker
- Cobbler
- Cooper
- Dyer
- Engineer/Architect
- Fence
- Furrier
- Glassblower
- Grocer
- Hostel
- Inn
- Jeweler
- Leatherworker
- Locksmith
- Mason
- Miller
- Minstrel
- Navigator/Cartographer
- Potter
- Scribe/Clerk
- Shipwright

- Stable
- Tailor
- Tavern
- Woodworker

Political Climate and Conflicts

Realms in fantasy RPGs typically fall into three broad types of categories:

- **Kingdoms or Nations**—Kingdoms are realms as fantasy readers tend to imagine them, consisting of a collection of cities and populated rural townships and farmlands in between them, all governed by a central body.

- **City-States**—City-states are political units based around a major capital city and a lightly settled hinterland. Generally, city-states emerge in areas where terrain discourages a dispersal of the population.

- **Tribes or Tribal Federations**—Cultures that do not build large cities or townships can be described as tribal. The individual tribes may be organized into one large tribal federation, or they may exist as independent clans and villages.

Who Rules?

Tip

"I believe there is something out there watching us. Unfortunately, it's the government."

— Woody Allen

In each realm, you have to decide who runs things. How do the characters relate to the ruling class? In a fantasy RPG, there are hundreds of possible government systems for nations and tribes. You can examine the samples below and pick one that is appropriate.

- **Autocracy**—One hereditary ruler wields unlimited power.

- **Bureaucracy**—Various departments and bureaus together compose the government, each responsible for some aspect of rule.

- **Confederacy**—Each individual place governs itself, but each contributes to a league or federation that has a purpose for promoting the common good.

- **Democracy**—Democracy is government by the people and for the people, either through their own words or by elected representatives.

- **Dictatorship**—One supreme ruler holds absolute authority, but it is not inherited.

- **Feudalism**—The typical government of Europe during the Medieval times, a feudal society consists of layers of lords and vassals, with peasants at the very bottom.

- **Geriatocracy**—Often favored in primal tribes, this is government reserved to the very old, such as a Village Elder.

- **Magocracy**—Government is led by a learned body of wizards.

- **Matriarchy**—Government is led by women only, especially the eldest or most important females.

- **Militocracy**—Military leaders rule the nation under declared martial law. Only elite soldiers may rise to power.

- **Pedocracy**—Government is by erudite sages or scholars.

- **Plutocracy**—Government is by the wealthy or rich landholders.

- **Republic**—Government is by representatives of an established electorate who rule in behalf of the electors. The American government system is a democratic republic by definition.

- **Syndicracy**—Government is by leaders or representatives from multiple syndicates or guilds. For example, a crooked township might be run by the local Thieves' Guild.

- **Theocracy**—Government is by society's religious leaders. Imagine the Papal Church taking control of all of Rome, and that's what you'd get.

Mired in Political Conflict

In your government, everything could be perfect, but this makes for a very dull environment. To add some spice, there are several ways you can inject conflict and tension into your make-believe government. The sorts of conflicts that become a political issue include the following:

- **Cataclysm**—Natural disasters such as earthquake, flood, hurricane, or volcanic rupture could change the way a society exists.

- **Feud/Rivalry**—Important noble families, wealthy merchant houses, or other powerful individuals of note could engage in a serious confrontation or several smaller clandestine battles.

- **Intrigue/Scandal**—Some sort of far-flung conspiracy or shocking behavior could rattle the leaders of a community.

- **Invasion**—The kingdom could be invaded at some point, or even conquered.

- **Migration**—A flock of refugees, the fall out of a passing war or victims of disaster, could pass through the area or even attempt to settle, perhaps against the wishes of the kingdom.

- **Plague**—Disease could sweep the realm, decimating the population and changing the way people live their lives.

- **Raiders**—The community could be continually beset and pillaged by foreign raiders or an organized band of outlaws.

- **Rebellion**—The government could, indeed, be unjust, inspiring several groups to band together to revolt.

- **War**—War might be fought during this time period. Most war is fought over landholdings. A civil war, failed revolution, or grab for power is an internal war. A crusade is a religious war, where one set of believers clash against another.

Religion

Tip

"There is only one religion, though there are a hundred versions of it."

— George Bernard Shaw

Making up a religion can be almost fun. Before creating your own religion for your game world, however, be advised. Tell your parents and anyone else that asks that you do not *really* believe in this religion. It is just something you invented. You don't want any confusion causing you problems further on.

In and of itself, religion does many things for a game world. It can:

- Relieve people from mediocrity.
- Guide its followers and give them direction in life through a codified moral philosophy.
- Provide rituals, ceremonies, and holy days (holidays).
- Give hope and joy in moments of tremendous suffering.
- Produce miracles and a sense of awe.
- Institute a hierarchy of people in power, besides nobility.

A religious belief is also the rich sponsor of education and personal enrichment (Figure 3.13). During Earth's past, many religions were seen as the only source of tutelage. If parents wanted their kids to learn anything, they'd send them to a monastery or cloister.

Religions can also lead to religious wars, religious persecution, religious reformation, and open rebellion. Just consider the Spanish Inquisition, a

Figure 3.13
A scholarly religious man figure from RPG Maker makes an imposing character.

group of believers that transformed into earnest zealots seeking out and putting to death anyone they considered a *heretic* (a non-believer).

In fantasy RPGs, there are often multiple religions, each worshipping a different—entirely made-up—deity. A *pantheon* is a group of gods and goddesses recognized and worshipped in a certain area. Your characters may even believe that their magic stems from these deities as a gift. You may even want these gods and goddesses to take interest or a more direct role in the lives of their followers. Usually in a pantheon, each divine being governs a sphere of interest, such as fertility, mischief, thunder, or the arts, and they always have a sigil or crest that represents them.

Other believers may persist that magic energy itself is worthy of worship, as the Jedi Knights do the Force in George Lucas' *Star Wars* saga or the Taoists do the Tao (a form of *chi* that flows through and interconnects all living creatures).

Tip

"Businesses may come and go, but religion will last forever, for in no other endeavor does the consumer blame himself for product failure."

— Harvard Lamphoon, *Doon*

Here are some questions you need to ask yourself when creating a make-believe religion.

1. What do your religion's members believe defines the Truth?

2. How do believers benefit by following this religion? Or do they suffer by following it?

3. Is the religion taught as part of public education? Or is it confined within its members' community?

4. Is the religion tolerant of others? Does it attack other religions or non-believers?

5. What is the moral code that dictates its members' actions and behaviors? How is this code reinforced? Are insubordinates shamed or punished in some other way?

6. What are the followers' restricted to do or not do? Do they all practice a vow of silence or celibacy?

7. What are the most notable ceremonies? What about their holy days or celebrations? Are they focused around the seasons or around commemorating mythical moments in history?

8. Does the religion proselytize, or seek out new converts? How so?

9. Are members allowed to quit?

Monsters and Animals

Scientists have identified over 1.7 million of the world's species of animals, plants, and algae, as of 2010. There are more than 60,000 spiny animals called vertebrates, and more than a million animals without spines, called invertebrates. All of these creatures have unique habitats, eating habits, and mating rituals.

Fantasy fiction is populated not only with human and human-like races (like dwarves and elves), but with fabulous beasts and creatures straight from legend. You can peer at the fringe of mythology and folklore and extrapolate hundreds of bizarre animals that have never truly existed. Any of these could appear in your RPG world.

For each creature you want roaming your game world, think about its appearance, its size, where it would likely be found, and what sort of defense mechanism it has. Not all creatures have to be ferocious man-eaters, but most have some form of self-protection. Besides natural beasts, you could also invent man-made or magic-made monsters or mutations, which could be even weirder than the natural denizens of the game world.

List of Mythical Creatures

The following is just a sample of the kinds of creatures commonly found in fantasy RPGs (Figure 3.14) and in our own folk tales and mythology. A great resource to review the descriptions of these creatures is the weighty tome *Bulfinch's Mythology* or the website www.MythCreatures.co.uk.

Below is a list of sample mythical creatures:

- Banshee
- Basilisk

Figure 3.14
A bunch of mythological monsters found in RPG Maker.

- Bogeyman
- Brownie
- Centaur
- Chinese Fox
- Cockatrice
- Cyclops
- Demon
- Dinosaur
- Dire Wolf
- Doppelganger

- Dragon
- Dryad
- Fairy
- Genie
- Ghost
- Ghoul
- Giant
- Giant Ant
- Giant Spider
- Gnome
- Goblin
- Gorgon
- Gremlin
- Griffin
- Harpy
- Haunt
- Hellhound
- Hippogriff
- Hobgoblin
- Lamia
- Leprechaun
- Manticore
- Mermaid
- Minotaur
- Mummy
- Necromancer
- Nightmare

- Nymph
- Ogre
- Orc
- Pegasus
- Phoenix
- Pixie
- Rat Man
- Roc
- Sasquatch
- Satyr/Faun
- Skeleton
- Sphinx
- Thunderbird
- Titan
- Tree Man
- Troglodyte
- Troll
- Unicorn
- Vampire
- Werewolf
- Wraith
- Zombie

WORLD-BUILDING IN RPG MAKER

Take what you've created on paper, and you can put it into RPG Maker as your game world. The information you've collected will help you frame each scene of your game and make your world more compelling and coherent to your player.

For the purposes of your learning, you will make an RPG based on a premise created for you. I have set up a story, maps, and characters for this RPG, called Thug Wallow, and you can follow along, step-by-step, in making it. After each section of Thug Wallow instruction, however, you are obliged to use what you've learned to make your own game, one based off the game design document you've made up and the maps you've drawn for it.

Different Types of Maps

If you look carefully at classic fantasy RPGs, you will see that there are roughly three different types of maps used.

- **General Maps**—Some maps, like the ones you see throughout *Zelda: Link to the Past*, are for general exploration and adventuring. These can include maps of forests, towns, dungeons, and so on. Players can face monsters, find items to pick up, and encounter NPCs and road signs in these maps. RPG Maker has a random dungeon creator just to create dungeon maps for you, but they are still considered a general kind of map.

- **World Maps**—These maps are zoomed out, the land as it would be viewed from far-away, like an expanded map of the continent. In these maps, players can do major traveling from one area to another without stopping to sightsee. Only the most dominant travel locations are marked, and random encounters are rare to nonexistent. World maps like these don't have to demonstrate or represent the entire globe. Often, like in the case of *Chrono Trigger*, a world map will show one section of the current game world, like the town of Leene, the Millenial Fair, the Woods, and Queen Leene's Castle all on one world map (Figure 3.15). When the player interacts with any one of these travel locations, he is taken to a general map of that area, which he can then explore in earnest.

- **Room Maps**—When exploring a general map, players might choose to enter a building, whether it's a witch's hovel, innkeeper's establishment, or person's home. As opposed to a large area to explore in, these places are small enclosed areas often with only a single doorway to enter and exit from. Usually, walls separate the player from the exterior view of the building. It's a bit like seeing the inside of a place with the roof removed.

Figure 3.15
World map from *Chrono Trigger*.

Note that an interior space can appear larger than its exterior indicates, because there are no physical size constraints in a digital art world.

What Are Tile-Based Maps?

Maps may *look* like a single picture, but in reality, they're made up of many pieces fitted together like a jigsaw puzzle. These pieces are called *tiles*. Building maps in RPG Maker involves painting squares with these tiles. Each tile contains information such as whether characters are allowed to pass through or around it.

The tiles you place on your map are selected from the tile palette on the upper-left side of the editor window in RPG Maker. You can select multiple tiles at once by clicking and dragging your mouse cursor within the tile palette. Selected tiles can then be "painted" in the map view on the right side of the editor window. To do so is like using a painting program.

You set the tile placement method through the drop-down menu list under Draw in the main menu. There are four different draw tools:

- **Pencil**—This is the default draw tool. It places a tile wherever you click the mouse in the main window.

- **Rectangle**—You define a rectangle by clicking and dragging out a diagonal section with your mouse. When you let up on your mouse button, the rectangle you've defined will be filled with the selected tile.

- **Ellipse**—You define a circle by clicking and dragging out a diagonal section with your mouse. When you let up on your mouse button, the circle you've defined will be filled with the selected tile. This makes for smoother borders.

- **Fill**—Wherever you click in the main window, all identical squares adjacent to the tile you click will be filled with the selected tile.

You can also right-click anywhere in the map view to automatically select and draw with the tile placed at that point. This function is known as the *eyedropper*. Making use of the eyedropper allows you to skip selecting tiles within the tile palette.

Note that the tile palette has multiple tabs, each with a different kind of tile set.

- **Tab A**—Most of the indoor and outdoor ground cover is found under Tab A.

- **Tab B**—World map decorations and basic tiles are found under Tab B.

- **Tab C**—Interior decorations are found under Tab C.

- **Tab D**—Tab D hosts dungeon-type decorations.

- **Tab E**—Tab E is blank. You can import a custom tile palette into Tab E for you to use.

Creating a New Game Project

Before creating a map, you will have to set up a new project in RPG Maker. Each project encapsulates the entire game you are making, from the graphics and audio files you'll use, to the game world and actions available. Project titles will describe the game, so you should use the game title for the project title.

Figure 3.16
Name your new project "Thug Wallow."

If you don't already have RPG Maker open, open it now. Once you have RPG Maker open, go to File > New Project from the main menu to open the New Project dialog box (Figure 3.16). The Folder Name will be "Thug Wallow," and the Game Title will be "Thug Wallow." The location is created for you by default, and depending on your machine setup, should work just fine. Click OK to close the New Project dialog box when you are done setting up your new project.

You should now see the main editor screen of RPG Maker, and you'll see one prefabricated tile-based map, MAP001, which is created by the program by default. Because MAP001 is at the top of the map list hierarchy, it will be the first map the game opens to when the player chooses New Game from the Start menu.

Building Maps for Your Game Project

Making maps in RPG Maker is fairly easy, through the use of painting tiles. Each map requires a uniform method. If you practice this method to building maps, you will find that they are easy and fun to make. Here is the method:

1. Paint your ground cover, terrain, roads, and buildings. These tiles are found under Tab A in the tile palette.

2. Add a little flair. Paint decorative elements from Tab B, C, and/or D on top of your map. This must be done in stages.

3. Add more decorations as needed. This includes animated graphics to make your map "come alive."

4. Done with the basic map? Then it's time to add events such as interactive items and NPCs.

You will start with a world map and then work your way down, creating Timber Town, Thug Wallow, and the environs therein. Finally, you'll put together a dungeon for your player to explore.

Your First World Map

Let's make MAP001 into our world map. Right-click on the MAP001 name in the bottom leftmost panel and select Map Properties from the options list. In the Map Properties dialog box that comes up, you can configure all of your selected map's parameters, including its name, dimensions, type encounters, and parallax background image. Most of this you won't need to know just yet, but change the map's main parameters as follows:

- Name: World Map
- Width: 35
- Height: 21

Click OK to close the Map Properties dialog box and save your changes.

Try the Eyedropper tool now. Right-click on one of the squares in the map editor containing water. The water tile, found in the tile palette Tab A, is selected. Use the Fill tool to click anywhere in the map editor. This will fill your entire map with water, if it's not already. You will find all the ground cover tiles you need to draw base land masses in tile palette Tab A. Using non-regular shapes, draw the world map in the map editor window that you see in Figure 3.17. The easiest way to do this is to start with the Ellipse tool and then move to the Pencil tool.

Note
_____

Remember that if you mess up, it's very easy to undo your work. You can tap the pink Undo button, go to Edit > Undo on the main menu, or use the key command Ctrl + Z to undo your last action.
_____

Add more terrain details to help fence the player in. Using three separate tiles from tile palette Tab A (the mountain and tree on grass tiles, plus the lighter-colored grass tile beside them), draw the ground pattern like you see in Figure 3.18. Try for a rough, natural impression, because you'll find it's always difficult to make tile-based maps that do not look man-made. Also, make sure the upper-right corner of your world map is inaccessible by the player, cut off by mountain ranges and trees.

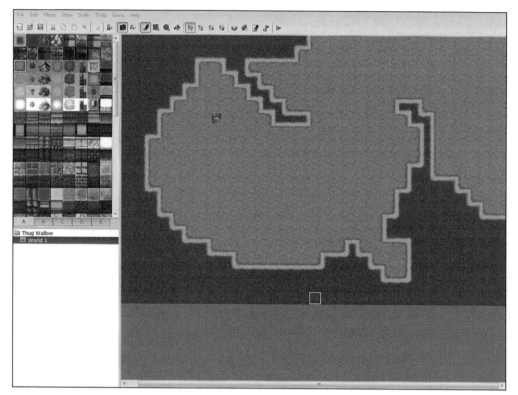

Figure 3.17
Create the main continent of your world map by drawing grassland on water.

At this point, stop to add more details to the sea. You can draw some rocks in the water and some darker areas of water, to indicate deep rifts.

Then switch to tile palette Tab B. This tab is filled with items that can be used to dress up your terrain. Scroll down the tile palette until you see the buildings. Draw Castle Vesper first. Click-and-drag to select the red-roofed castle tiles and paint them in the upper-right corner of your world map, where your player won't be able to travel because of the mountains and trees you've painted in the way. Use the crumbling gray castle ruins tiles to paint around the castle, making it look bigger, older, and more menacing.

After painting Castle Vesper, draw Thug Wallow. It will dominate the center portion of your map. You can use the plain-looking village tiles for the center of Thug Wallow, the red-towered castle town tiles for the front sides, the crumbling

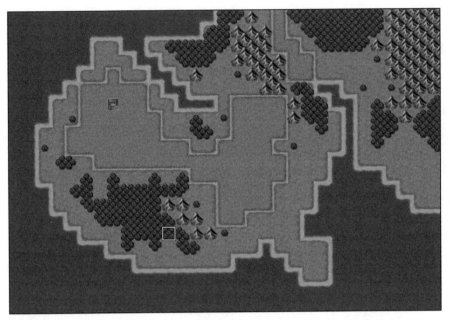

Figure 3.18
Add terrain elements like grass, trees, and mountains.

ruins for the back sides, and more. Experiment until you have a large, decent-looking port town. Thug Wallow is where most of the game's play will take place, so be sure that it looks interesting enough from a distance.

Last, but not least, draw Timber Town. It's a small farm village, so just use some quaint village tiles to create an L-shaped town with a single noticeable entrance way. It rests on the other side of the bay from Thug Wallow. Compare your finished work with Figure 3.19.

Changing Tile Passage Settings

By the way, you might wonder, when choosing tiles to "paint" in the map editor, if the tile will allow the player character to walk on top of or behind the picture. There's an easy way to check. Go to Mode > Passage Settings on the main menu (hotkey F3) or click on the Passage Settings button, which looks like an orange guy walking. This toggles your Passage Settings on.

The symbols will not appear in the map editor, but will appear in the tile palette on the left. The symbols give you (the designer) a heads-up on passage settings. If a tile has an O symbol over it, it means the player character can walk on or in

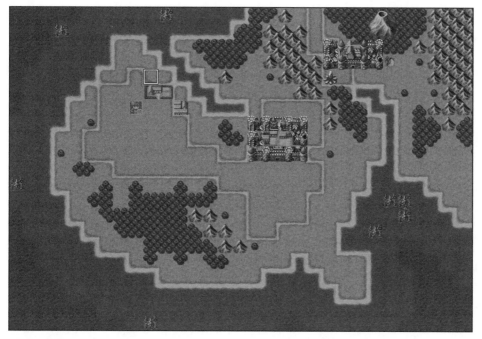

Figure 3.19
The completed World Map.

front of the tile. If a tile has an X symbol over it, it means the tile blocks the player completely, and he will have to go around the tile when he comes to it. If a tile has a star symbol over it, it means the player character can go behind the tile, in the case of treetops and overhangs.

You can click on the symbols in the tile palette to change them, which you probably don't want to do until you get more comfortable with them. Click on the tree-on-grass tile you used in the world map until its O symbol changes into an X symbol. You don't have to repaint the tree tiles on your map, because the new settings take over automatically. Now players won't be able to walk on top of the forests you created in the world map. This helps you fence the player in.

Press F3 to toggle the Passage Settings off again when you're through with them.

Your First Town

Timber Town is the player's first stop and where the quest begins. It is a small farming community plagued by evil. The key site is an inn.

We must design each new map before we can add pathways for the player to get from one map to another. Right-click on the Thug Wallow folder icon in the lower-left list and choose New Map (hotkey Insert) from the options list. In the New Map dialog box that comes up, give your map the following details:

- Name: Timber Town
- Width: 30
- Height: 24

Click OK to exit the dialog box and return to the map editor, where you'll see your new, blank map. The black-and-blue checkerboard squares indicate transparency, or no-fill. With the main grass terrain tile selected from tile palette Tab A, use the Fill tool and click somewhere in the middle of your map to fill the map with grass. Select the thicker, lighter-colored grass tile and, using the Pencil tool, create a one-to-two-square wide border all the way around, leaving a gap for the entrance at the bottom of your map. In this border, use the fence tile to create a brown wooden fence or palisade to go all the way around the map, closing the village in (Figure 3.20).

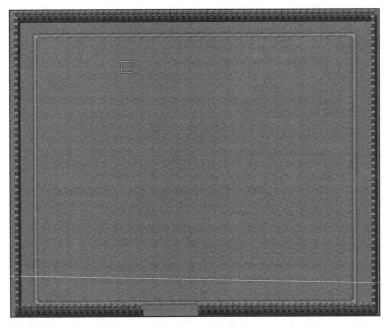

Figure 3.20
This is what your base map for Timber Town should look like.

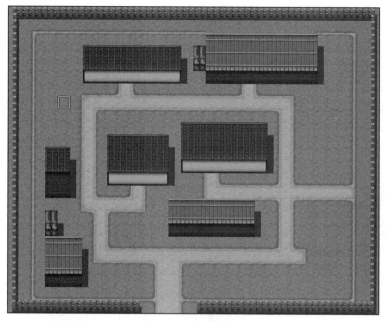

Figure 3.21
You should add pathways and buildings to your Timber Town map.

Use the sand tile in tile palette Tab A to sketch walkways through the town. The paths only need to be one square wide. You can add one square to the front door of each building, or where you believe you'll put the doors, so that it looks like the people there have a front step.

After you are done with the walkways, select house wall and/or roof tiles before painting in the buildings with the Rectangle tool. You should use a selection of multiple different building tiles to create a varied affect, because each house shouldn't appear as if it were made with a cookie cutter (Figure 3.21).

Now you can use tiles in tile palette Tabs B and/or C to "dress up" your Timber Town. You can choose some trees, plants, stumps, rocks, flowers, rain barrels, and much more. You can use Figure 3.22 as a guide, if you like, or get creative with it. I also added windows, climbing vines, flowers, signage, and more to the buildings, to make them look more authentic.

Lastly, you need to place a wooden signpost at the front entrance to the town. You will add an event to it later that will tell the player where they are.

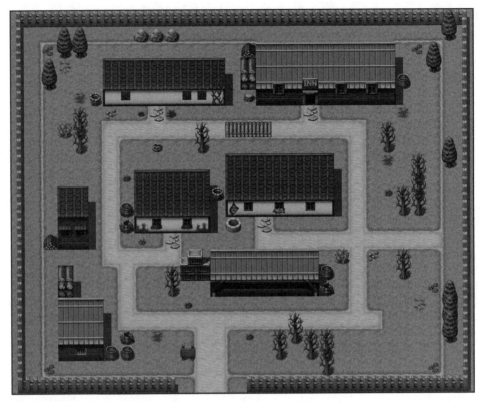

Figure 3.22
Finish decorating your Timber Town with tiles from Tabs B and/or C.

Connecting the Two Maps

It has come time to connect World Map to Timber Town. First, click on World Map in the lower-left list. World Map will appear in your map editor. Press F6 or click on the Events button (Ev) to switch to Events edit mode.

Besides maps, events are one of the core features driving RPG Maker. An *event* is any entity with an attached behavior and/or graphic representation or animation. For example, non-player characters (NPCs) are considered events, because they have an animated picture representing them and they communicate text to the player when the player interacts with them. You don't *have* to attach a behavior to an event, especially if you just want to add an animation such as a flickering torch in a dungeon. You don't *have* to attach a graphic to an event, either, especially if you want an invisible trap to trigger a behavior.

In the first map you create, you have an event that is unique, called the *player start position*. You will see it is already created for you, by default, and shows an image of the player character. Move your play avatar to wherever you want the player to be positioned when they first start the game. Do not move the avatar on top of mountains or trees, because you the player will become stuck if you do so.

The next event you need to know is the transfer. *Transfer events* allow you to set up portals between maps the player character can use to move from one destination to another. You should right-click on a square somewhere in front of Timber Town, where you want your entrance to Timber Town to be. Select Quick Event Creation > Transfer from the options menu to open the New Transfer Event dialog box.

Click the [...] button beside Destination to browse for a destination. This is where the player will travel to when he crosses your event trigger. Select Timber Town from the left-hand list and pick a square somewhere on that map next to the wood sign you created close to the town's entrance. You do NOT want to pick a square right at the entrance, because we'll be adding another transfer event there in a moment that takes the player back out to the world map, and you do not want the poor gamer warping back and forth on accident. Click OK when you've chosen your destination.

Under Direction, you can choose which direction you want the player character to be facing after he's traveled to this new destination. If you pick "Retain," the character will automatically face whatever direction he was facing when he triggered the event. This is fine for events where you have control of where the avatar's facing when he triggers them, or when you don't care where the avatar is facing when he triggers them. In this case, select "Up" from the drop-down list, so the avatar is facing up, into town, right after traveling there (Figure 3.23).

Click OK to close the New Transfer Event dialog box.

After the event has been created, it can be edited. Right-click on the event you just created and select Edit Event (hotkey Enter) from the options list. On the left, under the Graphic heading, double-click on the blank tile to open the Graphic picker window. Scroll down the list until you find !Flame. Pick one of the sparkle star images and click OK to close the Graphic picker window. Put a check next to Walk Animation, Stepping Animation, and Direction Fix beneath the Options (Figure 3.24). Click OK to close the Edit Event window.

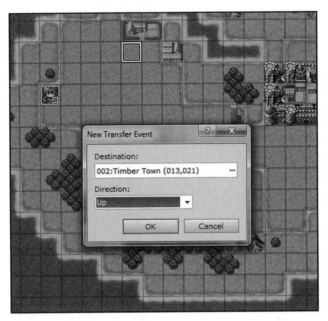

Figure 3.23
Create a quick transfer event.

Now it's time to save your project and try it out. Go to Game > Playtest in the main menu (hotkey F12) or click the Playtest button, which looks like a green play arrow. You will be prompted to save your game project, which you should do. After you have done so, the game will open, and you can play through it just as your gamers will when you're done. Select New Game, which is selected by default, and press Enter to open a new game. Use the arrow keys on your keyboard to move your character. Approach the sparkling icon next to Timber Town, and watch as you're transported into the town. It's as simple as that! Click the exit button (X) to close the game window when you're through testing.

The reason that I suggest using a sparkle icon or any symbol at all for this event is to limit player frustration. Sure, the sparkles are not very realistic, but none of the gates or doors provided will look very realistic, either, and we do not want to leave this event blank, in case the player should ignore it.

Your First Room Map

Now you can create the interior of Toad Inn, the tavern in Timber Town. Right-click on the Timber Town map in the lower-left and select New Map from the

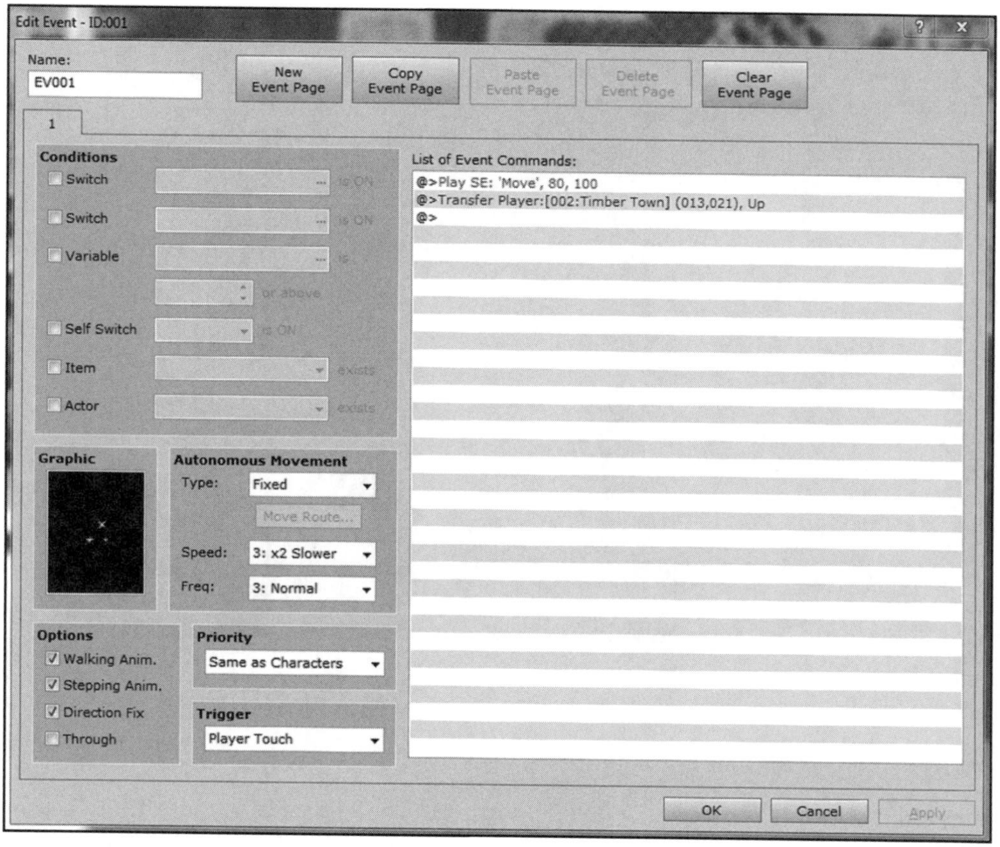

Figure 3.24
Edit your transfer event so that it sparkles.

options. Name your new map Toad Inn, and set it to Width 20 and Height 13. Press F5 or click the Map button to return to map editing mode, if you're not there already.

In tile palette Tab A select a floor tile to paint your floor with and create a wall border to hem in the room, leaving a square-wide opening for the entrance/exit. Keep in mind that with room maps, you don't have to fill the whole map area. Transparent areas will be rendered with black color or with a custom background.

There are countertops tiles in Tab A that you can make into tables and counters in the upper-right portion of that tile palette. These will allow you to paint tiles from Tabs B, C, or D on top of them, without deleting them. You see, although there are table tiles in Tab C and D, if you try to paint another tile on top of

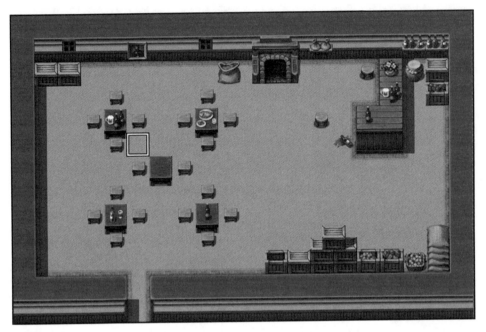

Figure 3.25
What your finished room map should look like.

them, such as plates of food or drink cups, you will erase the table tiles. Using the countertops tiles from Tab A fixes this problem.

Once you have the building's underlying structure designed, you can add furniture, props, and other decorations. You can use tiles from Tab B and/or C to decorate your room map, making it look like the interior of a tavern. There should be tables, stools, food and drinks, crates, and baskets. You can even place windows along the uppermost wall and a fireplace, to make it seem cozier (Figure 3.25).

Connect the inn to the town, and vice versa. Switch to event editing mode by pressing F6 or clicking the Events button. Go back to your World Map and right-click on your transfer event that carries the player into Timber Town. Select Copy (hotkey Ctrl + C). Go to the Toad Inn map and right-click on the very last square going out the door. Select Paste (hotkey Ctrl + V). You've just copied and pasted the transfer event from the world map to the inn.

Now we have to edit the inn's copy. With the transfer event in the inn still selected, press Enter to open the Edit Event dialog box. Look on the right side of the dialog box and you'll see a large text field area called List of Event Commands. In the List of Event Commands, you should see a line that reads like:

`@>Transfer Player:[002:Timber Town] (019,007), Down`

Click on that command line to select it. Then press Delete to clear it. Double-click in the blank line where the command line once was to open the Event Commands dialog box. Event Commands is where several premade code scripts are stored. It allows you to execute a lot of different code scripts without having to type a bunch of program lines in by hand, which is still an option if you'd prefer.

In Tab 2, under Movement, you need to click on Transfer Player. Click the [...] button beside Direct Designation to browse to your destination. You don't want to deposit the player right at the doorstep of the inn, so go to Timber Town and select a square just a little ways down from the inn. Use the drop-down list to set your Direction to Down, so that the player, on exiting the inn, will be facing down and away from the inn. Click OK to close the command dialog. Your new command line will appear in the List of Event Commands. Click OK to exit the Edit Event dialog box.

Go to your Timber Town map and right-click on the front door of the inn. Select Quick Event Creation > Door from the options. *Door events* are the same as transfer events, except they are associated with animated door images. Double-click on the Graphic and choose the tile set showing a normal-looking closed wood door with brass knob and click OK to save your changes. For the Destination, choose a square two or three squares in past the Toad Inn entranceway (not right on top of the exit transfer event you just created). Click OK to accept your changes when you're done.

Save your project and test it out. You should now be able to walk from the World Map to Timber Town, and there you should be able to enter the Toad Inn and exit it again. Exit the playtest when you are through.

Interactive Decorations

Return to your Timber Town map. Here, you need to set up *interactive decorations*. These are items that communicate messages to the player without seeming like actual NPCs.

Right-click on the wooden sign you drew in a tile near the entrance to Timber Town. Select New Event from the options list. Name your new event "TT Sign." In the New Event dialog box, double-click in the first blank line of the large text field on the right under List of Event Commands to open the Event Commands dialog box. Go to Tab 1 and click on Show Text. In the Show Text dialog box, type "Welcome to Timber Town!" Note that you can click the Preview button to see what your text window will look like, before exiting the Show Text dialog. Click OK when you're done.

This event is different from others in two important ways. First, it does not activate when the player touches it. Instead, the player has to walk up to the event and press the Enter key to activate it. That's what the Trigger option Action Button states. Second, this event is on top of a tile (the wooden sign) that the player cannot walk on top of to actually trigger. We have to change that. The Priority option needs to be set to Same as Characters. You can find that in the Priority drop-down list. Click OK to exit the Edit Event dialog box when you're satisfied.

Let's make a locked door. You should right-click on a square where a door to a building should exist (not the inn, but one of the other buildings in the town). Select New Event. Name this event "Locked Door."

Double-click the Graphic representation. Scroll down and click on the !Door 1 group. Select the first door graphic in a set that you like. A trick here is to pick a *different* door graphic than you will use for *actual* door events. This helps the player see at a glance that, "Oh, this door will probably be locked just like the last one I tried that looked like that," so it saves him time, trial, and effort.

Double-click in the first blank line of the large text field on the right under List of Event Commands to open the Event Commands dialog box, go to Tab 2, and click on Play SE under Music and Sounds. Scroll down until you see Knock. Select the Knock sound effect in the list (Figure 3.26). Once the sound effect sounds the way you want it, click OK.

Double-click on the next line of the List of Event Commands. Go to Tab 1 in the Event Commands dialog box and click on Show Text. In the text field of the Show Text dialog box, type "It appears no one is home." Click OK to save your changes. Before leaving the Edit Event dialog box, make sure the Priority is set to Same as Characters and the Trigger is set to Player Touch. Click OK to exit.

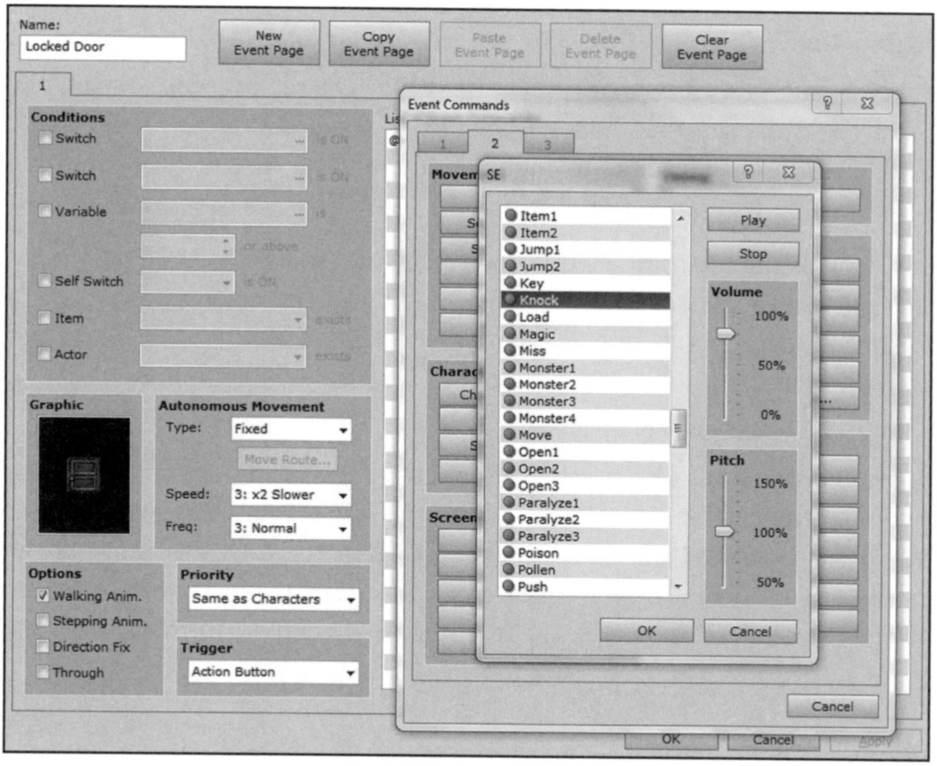

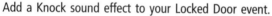

Figure 3.26
Add a Knock sound effect to your Locked Door event.

Copy and paste multiple copies of your Locked Door event throughout Timber Town, placing the events where you need doors to buildings but don't want to go through the trouble of creating room maps for the interiors of homes. This satisfies curious players, who will no doubt investigate every area of your map in the hopes of finding nifty hiding places for treasure.

You could also set up events like these for other decorative elements in your maps. Players who touch or try to interact with a well could get a message saying, "It appears to be a wishing well," and if they try interacting with open chests or barrels, you could tell them, "You find nothing valuable here." The more little details you can add to your game, the more dynamic and fun it will end up being.

Save your project and test out your new interactive decorations.

Customizing Text

You can customize the text that shows up when interacting with objects or NPCs. You could display the character's name that's speaking or have specific words written in another color, to highlight them. This is done by inputting markup tags in the text as you're writing it.

Let's try this with the welcome sign you created for Timber Town. You should right-click on the TT Sign event and select Edit Event from the options list. In the List of Event Commands, right-click on the top line, where it says "Text" and select Edit to open the Show Text dialog box. Edit the text as follows:

```
Welcome to \c[3]Timber Town\c[0] !
```

Typing \c[3] sets a new color (green), and after the text, you turn the rest of the writing back to the default white color by typing \c[0]. Click OK twice to exit. Save your project and test out your Timber Town sign. Now, the name of the town should show up in a bright green color. You can use this neat trick any time you're writing a text message, to add emphasis to certain words or phrases.

Here are some other ways you can alter the look or behavior of text messages:

- \.—Pauses the text readout for 0.25 seconds.
- \|—Pauses the text readout for 1 second.
- \c[x]—Changes the color of the text following it, where X is the number of the color you want to use; default is set to white (0).
- \G—Opens an additional text box displaying how much money the player has.
- \N[X]—Shows the actor name of the party member speaking, where X refers to the number of that actor.

Animated Graphics

Just like the sparkle animation graphic you set up for the transfer event to and from Timber Town and Toad Inn, you can add *animated graphics*.

You should right-click on a map square and select New Event. In the Edit Event dialog box, click on the Graphic representation. Select a group and then click on the first graphic in a set you want displayed on your map. Just to test this out, you might pick the !Flame group and click on the first lantern or candle flames you see in a set. Click OK. Make sure that Walk Animation and Stepping Animation have a checkbox checked. Click OK again to close out of Edit Event. Save your map and playtest it to see that your new animated decoration works. The lantern should glow slightly, and the candle flame should flicker. It's as simple as that!

The more animated graphics you place in your level, the more "alive" your game's setting will appear.

Inn Events

An *inn event* will let the player's party members restore their health and mana points in exchange for money. This is usually done inside a map structure representing a place to sleep, such as an inn or hotel.

Go to your Toad Inn map, and with Events edit mode still active, right-click next to the back counter of your inn and select Quick Event Creation > Inn to open the New Inn Event dialog box. Here, you can choose a graphic representation for your innkeeper and set the price to rest one night. You can set these options as you like (Figure 3.27) and then click OK to save your changes.

Save your project and test out your new inn event (Figure 3.28). Now your player can come to Toad Inn whenever he or she needs to rest up and heal after a battle.

Tip

For advanced users, you can edit the text in your inn event to show the player how much gold he or she currently has. To do so, open the event for editing and look for the Show Text line in the List of Event Commands. Right-click that line to edit it, and type "\G" somewhere in or at the end of your text message. \G is a command that tells the program to reveal, in the upper-right corner of the game screen, a small box showing how much gold the player has.

Treasure Chests

A fantasy RPG wouldn't be as exciting to explore if it weren't for the hidden rewards—especially those iconic treasure chests, which are often stuck in hard-to-reach places in the game world. Making a treasure chest is easy as 1-2-3 in RPG Maker, using the *treasure chest event*. Let's put two treasure chests into the game world we've made so far, just to test it out.

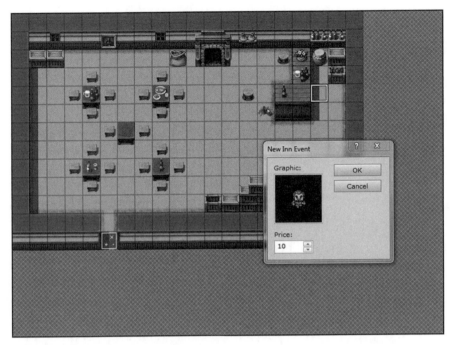

Figure 3.27
Alter your settings in the New Inn Event dialog box.

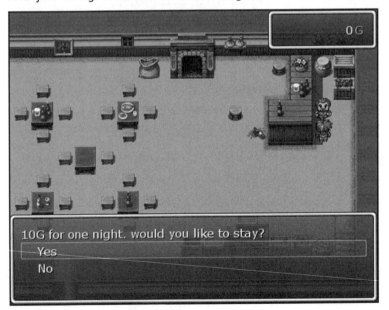

Figure 3.28
What an inn event will look like in the game.

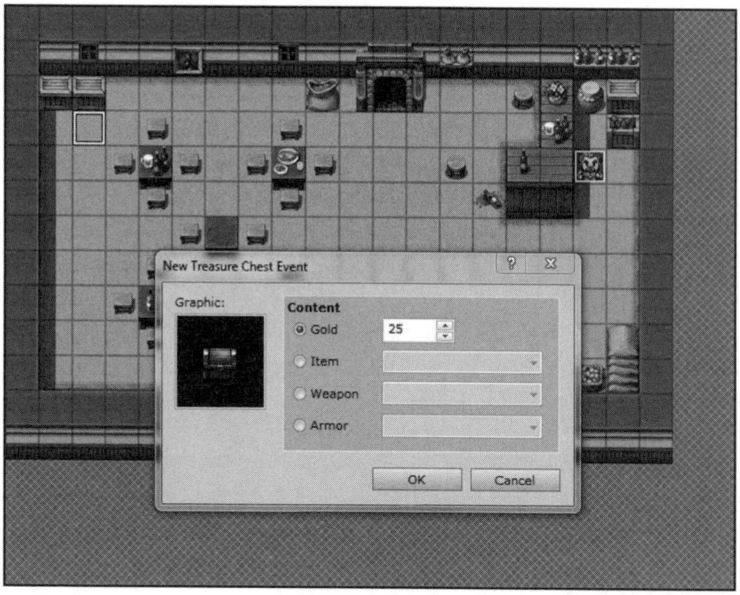

Figure 3.29
You can adjust your settings in the New Treasure Chest Event dialog box.

In Toad Inn, you need to right-click on a spot that's not in the middle of the room but not hard to get to, either. We want the player to see this treasure chest, because he'll need some currency to start the game with. After right-clicking on your chosen area, select Quick Event Creation > Treasure Chest from the options list.

In the New Treasure Chest Event dialog box (Figure 3.29), you can double-click the graphic to change the way your chest will look. You can also set what will be in the treasure chest. You can put gold, weapons, items, or armor in chests. To control game flow, vary what you place in treasure chests. You don't want to give the player too much of one thing, or he'll be overburdened and hurting for the one thing he can't find—or the game will seem too easy to beat.

Set your Gold to 25 for the player to start with and then click OK to save your changes.

Go to your Timber Town map and find someplace that's not invisible but maybe a little harder for the player to reach. In other words, find a place the player would have to be actively exploring the map to really find. Add a second treasure chest event there. Set its Gold to 50. This gives the player 25 Gold for sure and 75 Gold total, if he really looks around Timber Town to find all the goodies.

Save and test your game. See how easy that was to set up? Now you can do the same with chests containing weapons, items, or armor.

The Town of Thug Wallow

Thug Wallow is not a nice place. It's supposed to be a place of danger and a messy maze of streets. Before we create the functional aspects of this ominous town, we have to generate the maps. You should do so just as you did for Timber Town. You will start by laying down the ground cover. Then you will add buildings and props. And lastly, you will touch up the map with some decorative pieces. However, you want Thug Wallow to be much bigger, so it will exist as an interconnected set of four different street maps.

Study Figures 3.30 through 3.33 as guidelines in building your Thug Wallow street maps. Name your maps the same as the names given in the captions. Map sizes are given in parentheses.

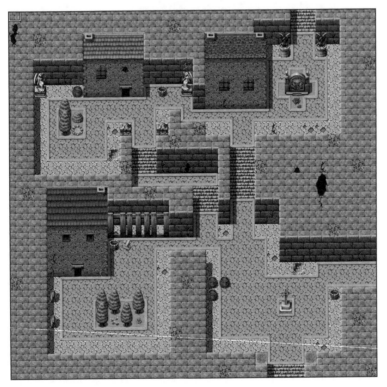

Figure 3.30
Candle Street (Width 30, Height 30).

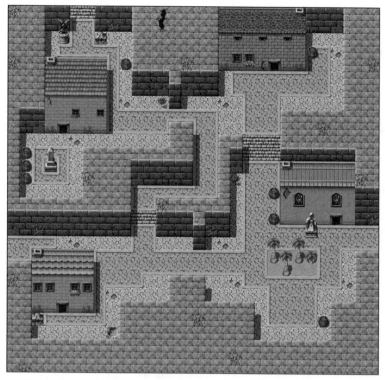

Figure 3.31
Market Street (Width 30, Height 30).

Thug Wallow will also have some important room maps, besides the general maps you just built. These are for stores, warehouses, and other interiors players will be able to navigate as they explore Thug Wallow and the narrative. You can make as many as you want, but these four are the ones you need for game continuity. Go ahead and build these room maps now, following Figures 3.34 through 3.37 as you do so. Remember to name them the same as you see in the captions. Again, map sizes are given in parentheses.

Dungeons

Unbelievably, designing dungeon maps is actually much faster and easier to do in RPG Maker than designing just about any other kind of map. Whenever you have a large-scale mazelike map to create, and it does not matter to you how it is laid out, then you can auto-generate it randomly using RPG Maker's built-in dungeon creator.

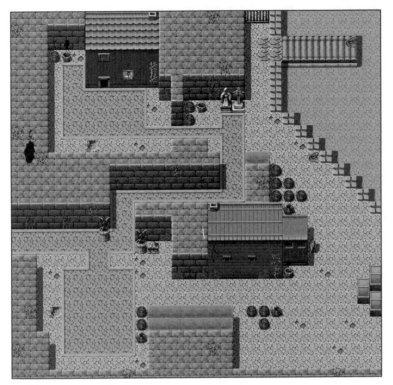

Figure 3.32
Anchor Street (Width 30, Height 30).

Create a new map with the following values:

- Name: CVesper 1
- Width: 45
- Height: 65

After you have created it, right-click on your new map's name in the bottom-left panel and select Generate Dungeon from the options list. For Wall, select the gray tile 6 over and 1 down. For Floor, select the first tile you see. Click OK when you are ready to create. A random dungeon layout will be generated for you, featuring twisting hallways and rooms. Yours will look different every time you use the dungeon creator. If you don't like the way your dungeon looks, you can do it again—as many times as you like—until you are satisfied. The way my random dungeon looks is shown in Figure 3.38.

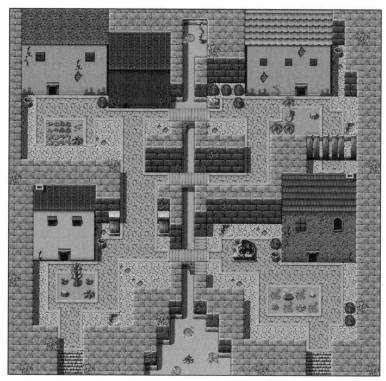

Figure 3.33
Clog Street (Width 30, Height 30).

Note

If you want to design an outdoorsy dungeon or a cavernous lair, you probably don't want your map appearing so boxy. After you manufacture the dungeon with RPG Maker's built-in dungeon creator, you can use the Circle tool and the same tiles you implemented for generating the dungeon to paint over the top of your map. You can make smoother, rounder-looking spaces and tunnels that way, using the dungeon auto-generated for you as more of a guideline.

Scroll down to the bottom half of your map. Find a central room or area to be your entryway. Take the same tile you used for the floor and paint a one-or-two-square-wide alcove leading down, out of the map. Scroll to the top of the map and create an exit going upstairs in the same manner. You will need to scroll down to the bottom of Tab A and select one of the stairs tiles to paint stairs into your alcove, so the player knows he'll be going up.

Figure 3.34
Black Lobster (Width 20, Height 15).

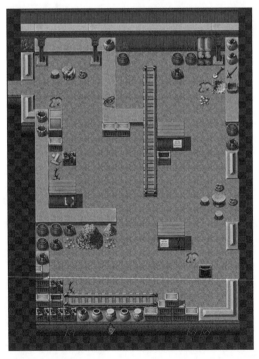

Figure 3.35
Warehouse (Width 18, Height 24).

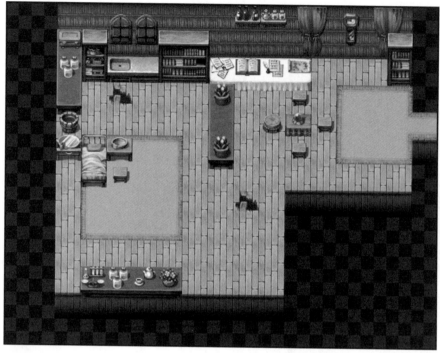

Figure 3.36
Parlor (Width 17, Height 13).

Now put in as many decorations from Tab C and D as you'd like to dress up your dungeon. You will want to add statuary, tables, rubble, debris, cracks, rugs, beds, steel cage doors, suits of armor, framed pictures, and much more. You can see what I did with my dungeon in Figure 3.39.

The very end of the dungeon is the last map you will create. This final map will be where the quest goal rests for your game. Name your new map CVesper 2, and set it to Width 20, Height 17. Design it as you would a room map, along the same lines as the Parlor map you made before, but containing tiles befitting a castle. Add decorations, and be sure to put in a crystal column and a throne. Compare your CVesper 2 map with the one in Figure 3.40.

Don't Forget to Add Animated Graphics and Interactive Decorations!

Spend a little time now adding animated graphics (such as flickering candles, glowing lanterns, and curling smoke) and interactive decorations (such as locked

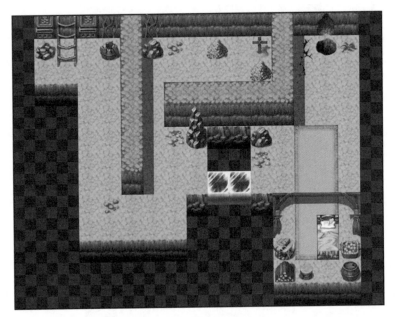

Figure 3.37
Hut (Width 17, Height 13).

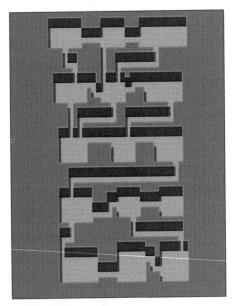

Figure 3.38
An example of what your random dungeon might look like.

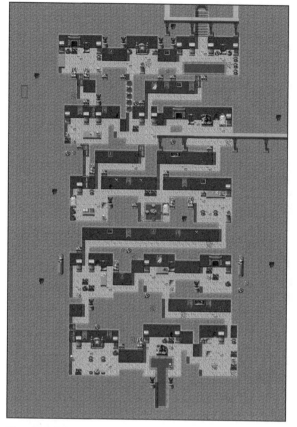

Figure 3.39
You can add visual interest to your dungeon map by adding decorative elements like these.

doors, sign posts to read, and other objects that react to the player) to your Thug Wallow and Castle Vesper maps, if you have not already done so.

You can go to Timber Town and copy one of the locked door events you made there and paste it on the static doorways of the buildings you have made throughout Thug Wallow. Just be sure the locked door graphic is different from the graphic you plan to use on your door events. This helps the player to understand by sight what doors are locked and unlocked, so he doesn't waste a lot of time checking every single one.

The more you spruce up your maps and make them yours, the prouder you'll be with the final results and the more gamers will delight in them.

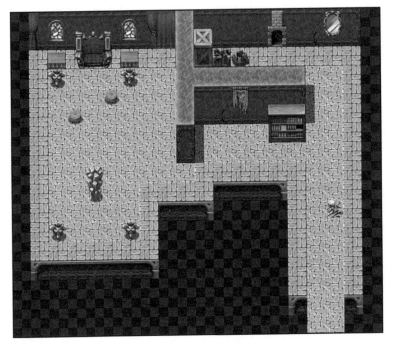

Figure 3.40
Create a throne room for the game's quest goal.

Connecting Your Maps

Before you can fully test your maps, your player character must have a way of getting from one to another, so that you (the designer) can playtest them properly.

To do so, add transfer or door events to every map. Use a fluid scheme so that the connections are two-way. Your gamer should be able to go from one map to another and back again, just like you did with the Timber Town and Toad Inn. Remember to place the entry and exit points so they don't overlap and the player doesn't inadvertently travel back and forth when he doesn't wish to.

There are some tricks to make your transfer and door events more consistent and less frustrating for your player. First, make all your transfer events so they show the animated sparkle graphic. This helps the player see where he should go. Second, give your door events a different door graphic than the locked doors you add to the other buildings. Last but not least, for entrances or exits that are more than one-map-square-wide, you should copy-and-paste duplicate transfer events to fill up the space.

1. **World Map**—Here, you should already have a transfer event to Timber Town. Add a transfer event in front of Thug Wallow that takes the player to the bottommost passageway to Candle Street. Add a second transfer event in front of Castle Vesper that takes the player to the passageway of CVesper 1. Note that this event should be blocked off to the player by mountains or trees. You don't want the player getting to it until he has accomplished his tasks in Thug Wallow.

2. **Candle Street**—Place a redundant transfer event at the bottommost passageway that takes the player to the World Map (just outside and facing down and away from Thug Wallow). Place a transfer event on the rightmost passageway that takes the player to the leftmost passageway on Market Street. Place another transfer event at the topmost passageway that takes the player to the bottom-left passageway on Clog Street.

3. **Clog Street**—Place a redundant transfer event at the bottom-left passageway that takes the player to Candle Street's topmost passageway. Place another transfer event on the bottom-right passageway that leads the gamer to Market Street's topmost passageway. Add a door event on one of your buildings that leads the player to the entryway of Warehouse.

4. **Market Street**—Add a redundant transfer event at the topmost passageway that takes the player back to Clog Street's bottom-right passageway. Add another redundant transfer event at the leftmost passageway that takes the player back to Candle Street's rightmost passageway. Add a door event on one of your buildings that leads the player to the entryway of Parlor. Put a transfer event at the rightmost passageway that takes the gamer to Anchor Street's leftmost passageway.

5. **Anchor Street**—Place a redundant transfer event at the leftmost passageway that takes the player to the rightmost passageway on Market Street. Add a door event on the front of the tavern that takes the player to the entryway of Black Lobster.

6. **Parlor**—Add a transfer event at the edge of the entryway that takes the player just outside the building on Market Street.

7. **Black Lobster**—Add a transfer event at the edge of the entryway that takes the player just outside the tavern on Anchor Street.

8. **Warehouse**—Put a transfer event at the edge of the entryway that takes the player just outside the building on Clog Street. Where you put the hole in the ground with the rope ladder, place a transfer event in front of it that leads the player to the bottom of the rope ladder in the Hut map.

9. **Hut**—Put a transfer event at the top of the rope ladder that takes the player inside the Warehouse map, beside the hole with the rope ladder.

10. **CVesper 1**—Place a transfer event at the topmost passageway that takes the player to the entryway of CVesper 2.

What's Next?

A lot of groundwork (in an almost literal sense) was covered in this chapter. You learned all about creating make-believe game worlds and coming up with details about the societies existing in them. You drew paper prototype maps for your own game. In RPG Maker, you created the game maps for Thug Wallow. Next you will add characters to make the setting more interesting. And you'll add character dialogue, which is important to further the narrative.

For now, take some time on your personal game project. Use the GDD you wrote and the sketches you made at the beginning of this chapter to develop RPG Maker maps to go into your own project. When you come to a good stopping place, continue on to the next chapter.

CHAPTER 4

CREATING CHARACTERS AND WRITING DIALOGUE

In this chapter you will learn:

- How writers make up believable characters
- What makes people (and characters) tick
- How to write dialogue that sells
- How to customize the player's party members
- How to put NPCs into your game and make them do things

Your game's really coming along. You've documented the design and planned what will go into it. You've established the game's setting by creating maps the player can travel around. You've even inserted some objects, such as inn events and treasure chest events, which the player will be elated to locate. Now the next stepping stone in the path of learning game design approaches. It's time to attach characters to your game.

Characters don't have to be human. In video games, as in cartoon media, they don't even have to make sense all the time. But they *do* have to be believable, and for the purposes of your game narrative, many of them *should* be lovable. So how do you make RPG characters? This chapter will tell you all about it.

INVENTING RPG CHARACTERS

There are roughly three types of characters in an RPG (Figure 4.1):

- **Player characters**—Player characters are controlled by the player. This starts with the first or primary player character, also known as the avatar. The avatar struts across the game maps and represents all the characters in the player's party. These characters are also referred to here on out as *actors*.

- **Non-player characters (NPCs)**—Any character not controlled by the gamer but by the game is referred to as an NPC. In most cases, the term NPC is reserved for characters that are neutral in nature. They may aid the player by giving him items or information or sending him on a quest, but they do not get involved in player battles.

- **Enemies**—Also signified as monsters, these characters are the game opponents. They attack the player characters and defend against the player's attacks. Enemies often lurk in dungeons and wild places. They can also guard undiscovered treasures or bar the player's path. They must be overcome to win the game.

What follows are the instructions for coming up with player and non-player characters. Enemies will be dealt with in a later chapter.

Figure 4.1
Example characters from the RPG *Torchlight*: (A) Player, (B) NPC, and (C) Enemy.

Getting Inspiration

Potential characters are all around you. You see them walking to school. You see them shopping in the mall. You see them hanging out or talking to your friends. If you close your eyes, you can see them in your memory. Memorize what stands out about them, what makes them appealing (or appalling).

Believable characters come from and share a lot in common with real people, so use what you learn by studying others to invent your make-believe characters.

Many writers will actually sit quietly in a public venue and "tune in" on strangers they find interesting. These writers will make as many notes as they can about the person they're studying, in order to maybe understand them and also to use them later as a character in a story. You could do that, too.

However, a word of caution here: Don't put your friends or family members into your story. That can lead to trouble, especially depending on what you do to their characters. But you can use their essence—what makes them such an outstanding person to begin with—instead.

Creating Memorable Characters

Tip

"Character is what we do when we think no one is looking."

—H. Jackson Brown, Jr.

Creating a memorable character that audiences will care about is definitely rewarding, from a commercial standpoint and an artistic and technical one.

To create memorable characters, you have to keep in mind the following rules.

- **Characters do things**—People don't do something for no reason. Every action someone takes is because of motivation, or a direct psychological urge to do something. To show your character's actions in context of his personality, you'll have to know a little something about him. Why does he do what he does? A gallant knight wouldn't ride off and leave a damsel to be molested by monsters, because a gallant knight has applied himself to a long-held moral code, which includes saving damsels in distress

Figure 4.2
Gallant knights are motivated by duty, because they're sworn to protect the innocent.

(Figure 4.2). Once you understand a character's personality and motivation, you can make his actions seem more believable.

■ **Characters think things**—Everyone has personal opinions and beliefs, so why shouldn't your characters? These opinions or beliefs may be shared by a group of other characters, or they could be unique to that one individual. The thoughts they think could even be wrong. For instance, ponder what feudal peasants would think if a young sharp-tongued outcast girl tells them, "Bad things are going to happen!" and then the milk cow dies. The peasants will probably think that she's a witch and *made* the cow expire.

■ **Characters feel things**—Thoughts are rational, because they usually follow patterns of logic and reasoning, but real people aren't always rational, are they? Especially in tense situations, they are not. In addition to thinking with their heads, people feel with their hearts, their stomachs, or wherever you believe their deepest emotions arise. People get afraid, they get angry, they fall in love, and they feel overwhelming joy.

■ **Characters want things**—Believable characters, just like real people, want things. These may be simple things that come from universal desires, like being loved, accepted, popular, or wealthy. Or they could be more specific things, stemming from events that have occurred in the character's lifetime.

Giving a Character Personality

One of the most important elements of a character's particular appeal is personality.

There used to be this funny college-education commercial on an Oklahoma City TV channel where I'm from. In the commercial, would-be recruiters asked a young lady what skills she had, and she answered (over and over again), "I have a brilliant personality!" in an upbeat voice. The recruiters, needless to say, were not impressed. They would just shake their heads, because what they wanted were hard, concrete skills, not "a brilliant personality." However, what that TV commercial also hit on is that every real human being has a personality.

Personality is the basis of who we are as individuals. Skills are what we do.

Personality is important, not only because it influences the game audience's reactions, but also because it can shape the character's looks, behavior, actions, and dialogue. All of the most successful game characters have well-defined personalities. Some may even appear as exaggerated or larger-than-life caricatures of ordinary personalities.

Look at the Nickelodeon cartoon character SpongeBob SquarePants. He's a nerdier-than-life fry cook who is *so* perky he is almost unbelievable. But then again, his environment of Bikini Bottom and the circumstances he finds himself in are equally unbelievable, so he fits.

Pop Psych: Creating Nested Personalities   Noted psychologist Sigmund Freud says people are complex constructions of multiple personalities and that we all have different sides we show to other people or to no one but ourselves.

Here is how his theory of nested personalities breaks down (Figure 4.3):

- **Ego**—The character's core identity, which must be protected at all costs. A character's main motivation in life is to nurture and protect his innermost self. If anything threatens his being, he rallies against it.

- **Superego**—The character's parental inner voice or higher self. Imagine this as the angel sitting on one shoulder, telling the character what not

Figure 4.3
The ego, superego, id, and demeanor.

to do. This is also who the character strives to become, over time, and who he looks up to.

- **Id**—The character's childlike and impulsive inner voice and general whimsy. You can imagine this as the devil sitting on the character's other shoulder, telling the character that it's okay to have fun and cut loose once in a while. Both the superego and id are important for the character, because without one or the other life would be very dull or the character would slip into a rut.

- **World Mask/Demeanor**—Actually, this tidbit of nested personalities comes from another psychologist named Carl Jung. He suggests that people hide their true selves behind layers of expectations. The world mask or demeanor is how the character appears to the rest of the world, which can change depending on the setting and circumstance just like donning an outfit.

Selecting Character Personality Archetypes

Tip

"Lara Croft is attractive because of, not despite of, her glossy blankness—that hyper-perfect shiny, computer look. She is an abstraction, an animated conglomeration of sexual and attitudinal signs ... whose very blankness encourages the viewer's psychological projection. Beyond the bare facts of her biography, her perfect vacuity means we can make Lara Croft into whoever we want her to be."

—Steven Poole, "Lara's Story"

Figure 4.4
Can you tell their archetype?

There are some personalities that are so well-known that they have become conventional character types.

An *archetype* is an original model of a person, ideal example, or a prototype after which others are copied, patterned, or emulated. Personality archetypes can help make fictional characters seem more three-dimensional and thus more realistic. These archetypes are instantly identifiable, because they appeal to your audience's subconscious and are symbolic in nature.

Decent archetypes can help you by providing a jump-off point to develop new characters. What follows are the most often used archetypes in fiction, from the 1940s to today (Figure 4.4).

- **Best Friend** (male)—Decent regular Mister Nice Guy (think Tom Hanks).

- **Boss** (female)—A take-charge kind of woman.

- **Chief** (male)—The quintessential alpha male, someone who is used to barking orders.

- **Free Spirit** (female)—Playful, fun-loving hippy/artist type.

- **Librarian** (female)—Prim and proper but repressed spirit, brainy but insightful.

- **Lost Soul** (male)—Tortured brooding loner type.

- **Nurturer** (female)—Capable and comforting caregiver or mothering type.

- **Professor** (male)—Logical but introverted bookworm or genius.

- **Rebel** (male)—The bad boy image, who is also a bit of an idealist.

- **Smooth Operator** (male)—A fun irresistible charmer.

- **Spunky Kid** (female)—The mousy girl-next-door with moxie.

- **Survivor** (female)—A mysterious and manipulative cynic.

- **Swashbuckler** (male)—Physically daring and daredevil explorer type.

- **Waif** (female)—The typical damsel in distress who is more concerned with her looks than protecting herself.

- **Warrior** (female)—Thoroughly modern heroine, tough-as-nails fighter.

- **Warrior** (male)—The weary white knight or reluctant protector of the weak.

That may seem like a fairly comprehensive list of archetypes. Yet modern archetypes can come even closer to simulating real human attitudes.

Table 4.1 list some more modern personality archetypes. The name of each is separated by parentheses. To combine two archetypes, take the word in

Table 4.1 Personality Archetypes

Expression 1	Expression 2
(Artsy) Creator	Artistic and imaginative eccentric
(Babe) of the Woods	Young, naïve, and innocent
(Caged) Animal	Frustrated, wild, and impulsive
(Charismatic) Mediator	Natural-born leader and speaker
(Chic) Elegant	Stylish and graceful
(Cloaked) Enigma	Mysterious and secretive
(Controlling) Critic	Cynical and judgmental
(Detached) Thinker	A serious scientific mindset
(Dreaming) Sleepwalker	Mystic, all-knowing, and psychic
(Dueling) Action Hero	Noble, gallant, and romantic
(Fanatic) Phoenix	Visionary and prophetic believer
(Grunt) Worker	Diligent and hardworking
(Lone) Warrior	Reckless, hotheaded, and mercenary
(Mischief) Fool	Joking, witty, and playful
(Miscreant) Alienist	Antisocial, psychotic, and scary
(Mooch) Slacker	Easygoing, idle, and lazy
(Plotting) Kraken	Paradoxical, deep, and selfish
(Sensual) Hedonist	Indulgent and pleasure-seeking
(Sniveling) Sycophant	Flattering hanger-on

parentheses from one archetype and combine it to the second archetype's expression. For example, a combination of (Artsy) Creator and (Dueling) Action Hero becomes an Artsy Action Hero.

Choosing the Perfect Name

Another element of character appeal, and one that should carry forth your chosen personality, is the character's name. Your character's name is really important, as it reflects who the character is and gives the audience a way to identify them. It can also be spoken so often as to become symbolic of the character. Thus, the choice of name is important.

If you name a character Grunt Masterson, you automatically assume just by his name that he is tough or surly. Whereas someone named Guybrush Threepwood (the hero of the LucasArts adventure game series *Monkey Island*) sounds like a complete goofball. Names should fit the character. They should also fit the story setting where your game takes place.

Avoid making too many characters' names similar to one another or homonyms. You run the risk of confusing your audience or causing undo frustration for the player, who often has to remember some character based solely on name alone. For instance, you should probably never have a character named Sandy and another named Cindy, because they run together when you hear them spoken out loud.

If you need help picking out a really good name, your best bet is to use a baby name guide. This may sound weird, but that's exactly what a lot of fiction writers have used. Baby name guides will even tell you the name's meaning and origin.

Sometimes, when you have a specific character in mind, it's easier to find a descriptive word tag for the character and then cross-reference a baby name guide to find a name with a meaning matching the word tag. For example, the Irish name Braon stands for "tear drop," so it would match a sad, depressed, or brooding character perfectly. And the Hebrew name Gideon stands for "mighty warrior," so it's perfect for a fighter character. Try coupling name meanings with your character's personality.

Don't have time to raid your local bookstore or library for a baby name guide? You could also look online at places like Babynology.com (Figure 4.5) or Cool-Baby-Names.com.

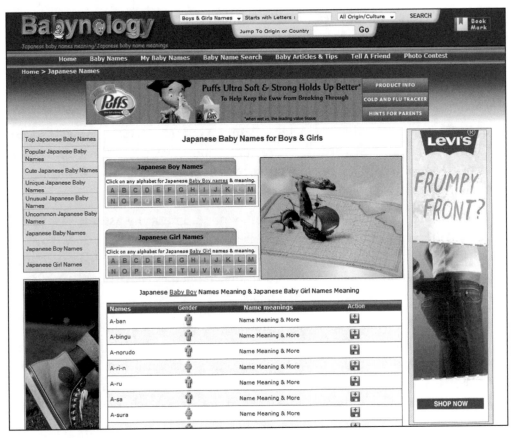

Figure 4.5
Japanese boy and girl name lists at Babynology.com.

Writing a Character Profile

Tip

"As you design the avatar for your game, think about how you want the player to relate to him. Do you want an entirely nonspecific avatar, really no more than a control mechanism for the player; a partially specified avatar, which the player sees and knows little about, but who doesn't have an inner life; or a fully specified avatar, separate from the player, an individual with a personality of his own? The more detail you supply, the more independent your avatar will be."

—Ernest Adams, *Fundamentals of Game Design*

Get yourself a piece of notebook paper, and get ready to fill in some blanks.

Using the old-school approach to character generation, much like the paraphernalia used in tabletop RPGs such as *Dungeons & Dragons*, you make up details about your character, almost as if you were interviewing that character about his most intimate particulars or creating a Facebook profile about him.

Main Info   Details you want to know about your character include, but are not limited to:

- **Name**—What's the character called?

- **Age**—How old is the character?

- **Place and Date of Birth**—Where and when was he born?

- **Gender**—Is the character male or female?

- **Size**—How tall is the character and how heavy is he?

- **Eye and Hair Color**—Blue, green, or brown eyes? Blonde, redhead, or brown hair?

- **Education**—Where did he go to school, or is he still attending?

- **Residence**—Where does he live, and who else lives there?

- **Family/Friends**—Who are his friends/family?

- **Interests**—What does he like to do, especially during his time off?

- **Likes/Dislikes**—What are his favorite and least favorite things?

- **Background**—What was life like for him before the game narrative starts?

- **Typical Costume**—How is he normally dressed?

Classes   In most RPGs, *class* is a term that refers to a player character's calling or what he does for a living. Therefore, a character's class does not refer to how well-mannered or rich the character is, but how he occupies himself in the fantasy game world. Each RPG has different classes, and each player-controlled character belongs to one of these classes.

RPG Maker begins with the default classes listed below, which you can edit, add to, or take away from.

- **Paladin**—Besides being a strong character similar to a knight, a paladin has the noble blessing of a religious deity and can perform miracles similar to a priest.

- **Warrior**—The character is an obvious soldier, tough and trained in physical combat.

- **Priest**—A priest can pray for blessings and miracles from his deity. The boons granted priests are holy versions of magic spells, the most powerful of which is healing others by lay-of-hands.

- **Magician**—A witch, wizard, sorcerer, or other character skilled in the forbidden arts of spell-casting can perform all sorts of magic tricks on enemies.

- **Knight**—Similar to the warrior, except that the warrior is often a mercenary, whereas the knight has trained within castle environs to protect the kingdom and thus is better armed.

- **Dark Knight**—The dark knight is the evil opposite of the paladin. Instead of being blessed with a holy power, this fighter has the powers of darkness on his side.

- **Grappler**—To grapple means to wrestle or fight without the use of weapons. In RPG Maker, a grappler is essentially a martial artist or monk fighter who has sworn to fighting hand-to-hand.

- **Thief**—A rogue in every way, a thief is quick and nimble, able to pickpocket people, and is handier playing dirty than clean.

Stats   Next, you need to rate the following character stats on a scale from poor to average to legendary. These can be used to modify actor parameters in RPG Maker later.

Stats (Rate: poor | average | legendary)

Max HP—HP stands for hit points and is an indication of how robust and healthy the character is and how many hits he can take before needing first aid.

Max MP—MP stands for mana points and is an indication of how much magic energy the character can possess (in order to cast spells).

Attack—Attack reflects how hard the character strikes an enemy in combat.

Defense—Defense shows you how well the character can defend itself in battle.

Spirit—A priest, witch, wizard, or other spell-caster should have a high spirit, as it is the stat used to muster the energy needed for effective magic use.

Agility—With a high agility, a character is nimble enough to rapidly recover, get in a few fast strikes, and avoid enemy attacks by dancing out of the way.

Skills   Next, list the top-five most frequently used skills the character possesses.

If you don't have a clue what skills are, or what skills may be included, take a look at the following list. These are the default skills that come with RPG Maker and are used by many fantasy RPGs. Some of the skills listed here are more potent than others, so don't make your starting characters too powerful by giving them those. By the way, these skills are not only available to actors but to their enemies, too.

You can edit the skill list later on in the RPG Maker Database, which I will show you how to do (Figure 4.6).

Here are the default skills in RPG Maker:

- Dual Attack (damage 1 enemy many times)
- Double Attack (damage 2 enemies)
- Triple Attack (damage 3 enemies)

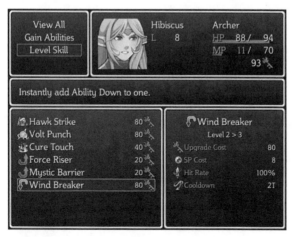

Figure 4.6
An example of custom skills being used in-game.

- Poison Attack (changes Poison status)
- Darkness Attack (changes Darkness status)
- Confusion Attack (changes Confusion status)
- Sleep Attack (changes Sleep status)
- Paralysis Attack (changes Paralysis status)
- Flame Breath (deals fire damage)
- Ice Breath (deals ice damage)
- Electric (deals lightning damage)
- Tidal Wave (deals water damage)
- Gravel (deals earth damage)
- Sickle Weasel (deals wind damage)
- Poison Breath (poisons all enemies)
- Deadly Poison (poisons all enemies)
- Sand Dust (blinds all enemies)
- Dazzling Light (blinds all enemies)
- Uncanny Fog (silences all enemies)
- Silence Song (silences all enemies)
- Supersonic (confuses all enemies)
- Temptation Song (confuses all enemies)
- Sweet Breath (puts all enemies to sleep)
- Sleep Pollen (puts all enemies to sleep)
- Paralysis Breath (paralyzes all enemies)
- Paralysis Glare (paralyzes all enemies)
- Leg Sweep (stuns your enemy)
- Body Attack (stuns your enemy)
- Warcry (stuns all enemies)
- Vampirism (absorbs HP from 1 enemy)

- Meditation/Weak (restores a little of 1 actor's HP)
- Meditation/Strong (restores 1 actor's entire HP)
- Heal (restores 1 actor's HP)
- Heal II (restores 1 actor's HP)
- Heal III (restores 1 actor's HP)
- Recover (restores entire party's HP)
- Recover II (restores entire party's HP)
- Self Recovery (restores user's HP)
- Cure (cures poison/paralysis)
- Cure II (cures poison/paralysis)
- Raise (revives fallen actor)
- Raise II (revives fallen actor and restores his HP)
- Poison (poisons all enemies)
- Blind (blinds all enemies)
- Silence (silences all enemies)
- Confusion (confuses all enemies)
- Sleep (puts all enemies to sleep)
- Paralysis (paralyzes all enemies)
- Weapon Bless (raises ally's Attack)
- Armor Bless (raises ally's Defense)
- Spirit Bless (raises ally's Spirit)
- Quick Move (raises ally's Agility)
- Weapon Curse (lowers enemy's Attack)
- Armor Curse (lowers enemy's Defense)
- Spirit Curse (lowers enemy's Spirit)
- Slow Move (lowers enemy's Agility)
- Life Drain (absorb HP from 1 enemy)

- Mana Drain (absorb MP from 1 enemy)
- Fire (deals fire damage to 1 enemy)
- Fire II (deals fire damage to 1 enemy)
- Flame (deals fire damage to all enemies)
- Flame II (deals fire damage to all enemies)
- Ice (deals ice damage to 1 enemy)
- Ice II (deals ice damage to 1 enemy)
- Blizzard (deals ice damage to all enemies)
- Blizzard II (deals ice damage to all enemies)
- Thunder (deals lightning damage to 1 enemy)
- Thunder II (deals lightning damage to 1 enemy)
- Spark (deals lightning damage to all enemies)
- Spark II (deals lightning damage to all enemies)
- Water (deals water damage to 1 enemy)
- Wave (deals water damage to all enemies)
- Stone (deals earth damage to 1 enemy)
- Quake (deals earth damage to all enemies)
- Wind (deals wind damage to 1 enemy)
- Tornado (deals wind damage to all enemies)
- Saint (deals holy damage to 1 enemy)
- Starlight (deals holy damage to all enemies)
- Shade (deals dark damage to 1 enemy)
- Darkness (deals dark damage to all enemies)
- Burst (deals non-elemental damage to 1 enemy)
- Newclear (deals non-elemental damage to all enemies)

Idiosyncrasies

Tip

"If you want your characters to be fully fleshed-out human beings, you will not make them perfect."

—Holly Lisle

Identify at least three, preferably more, idiosyncrasies in your character's makeup. An idiosyncrasy is defined as a personal peculiarity of mind, habit, or behavior—a quirk, in other words. These quirks can be totally useless skills or absurd qualities that stand out. Everyone has them, and they're what make us such great individuals.

Look at Scooby-Doo and his human companion, Shaggy. Both can eat super-hot jalapenos and odd food combinations all day long without putting on any weight. They are also dreadfully afraid of ghosts and monsters. However, they can be bribed to venture into forbidding territory in exchange for a Scooby Snack. These lovable quirks about them are what make them so cool.

Here are some suggestions if you're stuck thinking up idiosyncrasies:

- Afraid of doctors, medicine, or shots
- Always getting into trouble
- Always a klutz
- Bends into yoga pretzel positions with ease
- Can change outfits in a second
- Can do higher math in his head
- Can find his way even in the dark or blindfolded
- Can pick up stuff with his toes
- Can sleep with his eyes open
- Carries an odd smell
- Color blind and the way he dresses reveals it
- Compulsively clean and tidy
- Cracks knuckles really loud

- Easily angered and prone to tantrum throwing
- Extremely lucky, but only in the weirdest ways
- Gossips continuously
- Hair grows exceedingly fast
- Happy and bubbly all the time
- Has a nightmare frequently
- Haunted by bad memories or a ghost
- Immodest to the point of being vulgar
- Lazy and mooches off others
- Likes and eats weird food concoctions
- Makes perfect paper origami
- One eye is a different color than the other
- Picks nose in public
- Picks up stray kittens
- Really excellent thumb wrestler
- Speaks only in whispers
- Speaks to himself
- Suffers from mistaken identity all the time
- Thin blooded (gets cold easily)

NPC Dialogue: "I'm Sorry… You Said What?"

You should also do what you can to show that your NPCs are *not* mindless programmed robots. Players hate it when NPCs are so stupid they do not try to protect themselves or so monotonous when they talk that they are a bore to listen to. If you bother to put NPCs into your game, at least make them *seem* like real people.

Start by Selecting NPC Traits

You can make a complete character profile sheet for each and every NPC you plan to put in your game. Or you could do what lots of other game writers do and give each NPC at least three main character traits. These traits can be any adjective you can think of.

To make your NPC appear better-rounded, try to bestow traits that aren't similar in nature or expected. Instead of saying that a prince is heroic, dashing, and noble (all gag-me Prince Charming qualities), you could say that your prince is brooding, good-looking, and unwise. Now you have a character that will probably mope about a lot, have girls fawning over him, but won't ever notice because he's clueless.

You don't tell the player what these NPC traits are; instead, you show him through the NPC's actions and speech. For instance, consider the following interchange:

THOMAS walks up and tells you, "I am here to help." Immediately you are beset by goblin raiders, and THOMAS helps you out.

This excerpt is okay but flat. The speech is flat, too. It seems completely devoid of character. THOMAS, for all you know, could be a cardboard dummy. However, if you assume before writing your game that THOMAS is a swaggering, swashbuckling vegetarian (Figure 4.7), then you would write the same dialogue this way:

Figure 4.7
Thomas swings to the rescue!

```
You are trapped in an alley with no escape, surrounded by goblin raiders. Suddenly
you hear, "Ho! Take this, you silly meat-gobblers!" and THOMAS swings in to the
scene, kicking three goblins down. He pulls out a rapier and says, "Hey, mate. I
didn't figure you needed a hand, but I couldn't resist. Have at them!" And THOMAS
helps you out.
```

Admittedly, this revision is a little longer than the first one, but it is a small compromise to make your game better. A good writer knows that game dialogue must be kept short and to-the-point, because the space in each text box is limited, but he overcomes this by adding character nuance where he can, so that the dialogue does not sound stale.

Giving everyone the player associates or identifies with some character traits is vital. Each of your characters should sound distinct, since his voice springs from his personality.

Spice Up Even the Shortest Exchange

Give your NPCs interesting dialogue to speak instead of flat drivel, no matter how brief the exchange is supposed to be.

Take the following example:

```
AGENT (to the player): Go see the Boss. He has a mission for you.
```

This is awful. It's flat and carries no emotion or inflection to it at all. It is boring, even though it does get the player's mission across. If you were the player, you'd now know that you have to see some other character to get some information from him, someone named "the Boss." But if you were the game's writer (which you are!), consider jazzing up the dialogue a little:

```
AGENT (to the player): Boss told me he wants to see ya. He said somethin' about ya
taking a mission for him—one of those few come back from!
```

Now this bit of dialogue (Figure 4.8) still tells the player what he or she must do next, but it also sets up the story with some foreshadowing (meaning, a little taste of what is coming later). Plus, it cleverly reveals the NPC's background with all the "ya's" and shows that the NPC has sincere feelings.

Create Realistic Relationships

Show that the player's character and these NPCs cohabitate—that they can love, have fights, or share complex and realistic relationships. You could even have

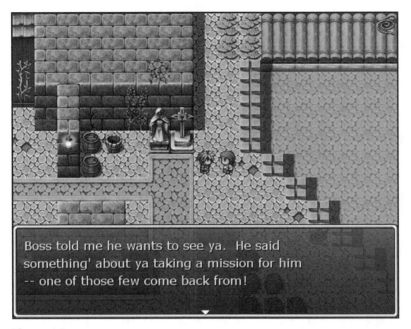

Boss told me he wants to see ya. He said
something' about ya taking a mission for him
-- one of those few come back from!

Figure 4.8
You meet with an unsavory agent.

some NPCs admire, fear, or respect the actors based on the player's choices in the game.

Lionhead Studios did this with their game series *Fable* (Figure 4.9): the gamer's choices change the world around him, modify the way the player character looks, and alter the NPC's perceptions of him (if the player has been mean to a few people in one village, neighbors in the next village might react with hostility or scream and run away in fear; yet if the player shows love and generosity to the NPCs, he will be treated with adoration).

Not every NPC lives alone, in a void. Give him other NPCs he can chat with, family and friends he can see on a daily basis and have to take care of, and more believable connections to the rest of the game world.

This can be a tricky accomplishment to achieve in an undersized 2D sprite game, but it's not unattainable.

Figure 4.9
Being bad is not so easy in *Fable III*, shown here.

Putting Characters in Thug Wallow

For this exercise, you will want to start RPG Maker and open your Thug Wallow project that you worked on in Chapter 3, if you do not have it already open. If you did not complete the Thug Wallow project or have chosen not to, you can go to Data Files > Chapter 4 > Game Project > Thug Wallow on the companion website (www.courseptr.com/downloads).

You will start by customizing your player's avatar and list of party members. Then, I will show you how to place NPCs into your game maps and make them talk.

Customizing Your Party

First, who is in your party now? Test your current game to see.

When in the game, you can press Escape, X, or number pad 0 to open the player select menu (Figure 4.10). This will show you four characters, including Ralph, Ulrika, Bennett, and Ylva (four prefabricated actors). Your primary avatar is the first actor in that list, Ralph. If you were to be attacked by a troop of enemies in the game, these four characters would be used to fight. In this screen, you can view their stats, equip/unequip weapons and armor, and use items within their possession.

Figure 4.10
The player select menu.

Exit your playtest when you're through playing.

You can set who is in your initial party in the Systems tab of the RPG Maker Database.

The RPG Maker Database

Go to Tools > Database on the main menu (hotkey F9) or click the Database icon button in the toolbar (it looks like a stack of papers). This will open the Database dialog box (Figure 4.11).

The Database is the dialog in RPG Maker where the main information about the game is kept. It is split into multiple tabs, each of which is explained below. All the tabs, excluding System and Terms, feature a list on the leftmost side, where the item in the Database you want to edit is selected.

- **Actors**—This tab contains descriptions of all the actors (player party members) in your game.

- **Classes**—This tab is where you define the various classes of actors.

- **Skills**—This tab is where you define the skills your actors and opponents can use.

- **Items**—This tab is where you define the items that your actors can pick up and use.

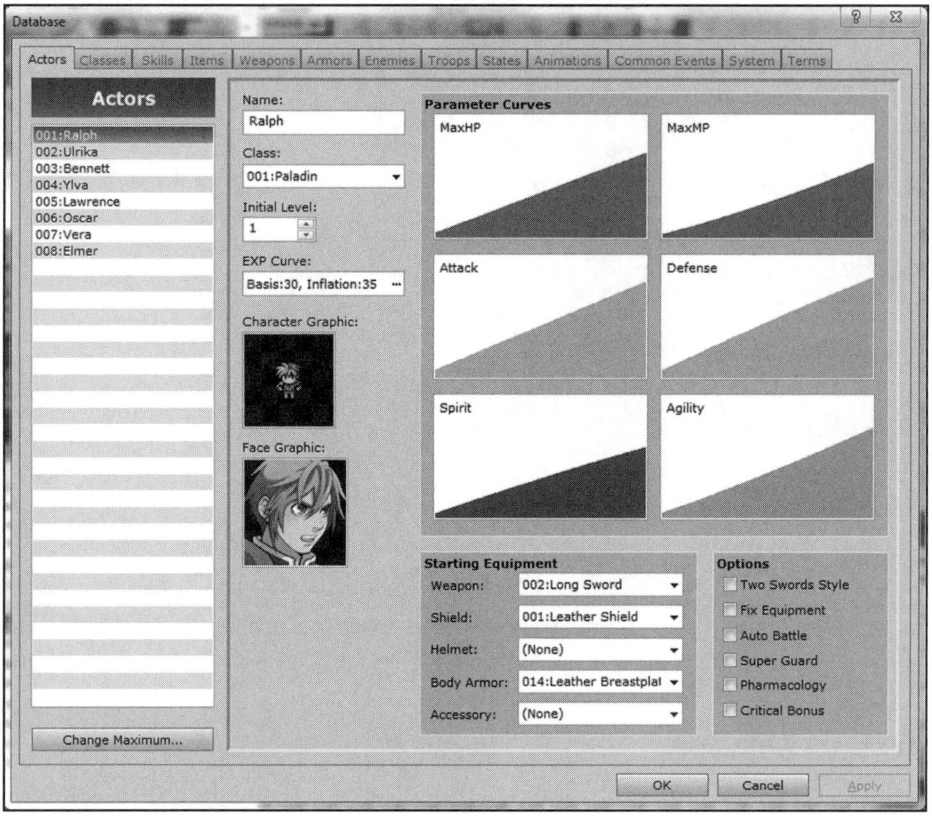

Figure 4.11
The RPG Maker Database.

- **Weapons**—This tab is where you can create weapons for your actors.

- **Armor**—This is where you can create armor for your actors.

- **Enemies**—This tab is where you can generate enemies for your actors to slay.

- **Troops**—This tab allows you to set up individual battles.

- **States**—This tab lets you craft your own state effects that can be used on a character.

- **Animations**—This tab lets you revise the animated look of an attack or other state.

- **Common Events**—This tab allows you to append code that runs in the background of your game.

- **System**—This tab is where you can modify the main settings for your game.

- **Terms**—This tab allows you to adjust all the phrases used for definite values in-game, including what character stats and player commands are called.

Creating New Classes

Click on the Classes tab to go there. Classes are the jobs available to actors. Each class has different skills and equippable weapons and armor types. You are going to have five different classes in your game.

Instead of deleting the existing classes, simply change the maximum number allowed. Click the Change Maximum button in the lower-left corner. Raise the number to 13 and click OK. You should now see five new class slots on the left, from 009 to 013.

Naming Classes   Click on each of your new classes one by one and give them the following names:

- Mummy
- Stein
- Vampire
- Were
- Witch

Positioning Classes   Set the position of each class. The position is where they stand in battle. Below are the typical positions you can select from the drop-down list for each class.

- **Front**—The character is tough and imposing. This is usually the best placement for warriors, thugs, and knights, because anyone on the front lines will be attacked more often.

- **Middle**—The character is better at ranged attacks but not completely frail. This is usually for archers, thieves, and the like.

- **Rear**—The character is best at using magic, especially for support. Susceptible to attack, they are kept in the rear so they don't get hurt. This is usually for priests, magicians, and the like.

Stein and were should be in the front. Vampire and mummy can be in the middle, and witch can take up the rear.

Restricting Classes The middle part of the window, where it says Equippable Weapons and Equippable Armors, is for restricting what each class can equip. For instance, in most fantasy RPGs, magicians cannot equip heavy weaponry or wear heavy armor. They are restricted to wearing robes and magic apparel and wielding rods or staves. This offsets their great ability to do magic. The same goes for thieves. They are often restricted to light armor and simple weapons, because they have the added bonus of their speed and wiliness.

Editing Weapons You will want to edit your weapon and armor names first, before editing their restrictions.

Click on the Weapons tab and rename the weapons below as follows.

- **001: Club > Bat**—Change the description to "A simple wood baseball bat."

- **004: Long Bow > Bow**

- **012: Battle Axe > Axe**—Change the description to "Not used for chopping wood."

- **019: Mithril Claw > Silver Claw**—Change the description to "Claws made of a magically enchanted silver."

- **022: Golden Staff > Staff of Ages**

- **024: Great Crossbow > Repeater Bow**

- **025: Wizard Rod > Voodoo Rod**—Change the description to "A voodoo doctor's rod, covered in gris-gris."

- **026: Dragon Whip > Cat-o-Nine Tails**—Change the description to "A vicious whip with many ends, each covered in sharp points."

Making New Weapons Click Change Maximum and raise the limit to 31 weapons. In the new weapon slot, create the witch's starting weapon:

1. **Name**—Witch Wand.

2. **Icon**—Double-click to pick the same icon you have for 025: Voodoo Rod.

3. **Description**—A slender wand of rowan wood.

4. **Animation**—019: Blow/Physical.

5. **Price**—900.

6. **Attack**—12.

Editing Armors   Now edit the armors in the same way. Click the Armors tab to go there and alter the following.

- **007: Feathered Hat > Witch Cap**—Change the description to "A conical hat covered in magic symbols." Change the icon to the purple hat beside the green one that it's set on already. Up Defense to 5 and in States to Resist, put a check next to Confusion.

- **015: Ring Mail > Leather Jacket**—Change the description to "Black leather jacket covered in studs." In Elements to Guard, put a check next to Slashing.

- **017: Chain Mail > Moldy Rags**—Change the description to "Long dusty bandages to wrap around your body."

- **018: Mystic Cloth > Trench Coat**—Change the description to "Tough long-hemmed coat that you can hide weapons under." Put a check next to Double EXP Gain in the Options area (this means that the wearer will get double experience whenever fighting in this armor).

- **019: Iron Armour > Iron Armor** (small spelling correction).

- **022: Dragon Mail > Mystic Bandages**—Change the description to "Tough reinforced bandages to wrap around your body."

- **025: Warrior Bracelet > Tough Bracers**—Change the description to "Thick metal bands woven to increase strength and protect against Darkness."

- **026: Magicians Bracelet > Witch Links**

- **027: Fortunate Necklace > Protective Amulet**

- **028: Fairy Shoes > Moonwalker Boots**—Change the description to "Magic boots that increase Agility and Evasion rate."

▪ **029: Life Ring > Scarab Ring**

▪ **030: Sage's Ring > Ring of the Magi**

Making New Armors   Create three new pieces of armor by clicking Change Maximum and raising the number to 33.

For your first armor, empty slot 031, you should alter as you see here:

1. **Name**—Sunglasses.

2. **Icon**—Double-click to pick the icon used for Blindness (looks like shades).

3. **Description**—Dark sunglasses that protect the user from bright light.

4. **Kind**—Accessory.

5. **Price**—750.

6. **Defense**—6.

7. **States to Resist**—Darkness, Sleep, and Paralysis.

8. **Options**—Put a check next to Double EXP Gain.

For empty slot 032, change the values below as you see them (Figure 4.12):

1. **Name**—Dracula Cape.

2. **Icon**—Double-click to pick the red cape icon on the right.

3. **Description**—An embroidered cape found in the wilds of Transylvania.

4. **Kind**—Body Armor.

5. **Price**—1500.

6. **Evasion**—3.

7. **Defense**—18.

8. **States to Resist**—Darkness.

9. **Options**—Auto HP Recover.

Lastly, for slot 033:

1. **Name**—Shock Ring.

2. **Icon**—Double-click to pick the ring icon.

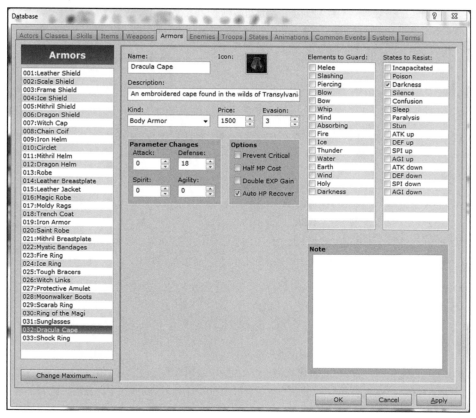

Figure 4.12
Create a new armor called Dracula Cape.

3. **Description**—A ring that protects from Lightning-based damage.

4. **Kind**—Accessory.

5. **Price**—1900.

6. **Elements to Guard**—Thunder.

Tip

If you find you have trouble inventing new names for characters, armors, weapons, or items, there is an application that can help. It is Zorns RM2K Tool, which can be downloaded from the RPG Crisis website at http://rpgcrisis.net/forums/files/file/33-zorns-rm2k-tool/. Zorns RM2K Tool was expressly created for RPG Maker 2000, so it's a little out-of-date, but it is still very useful. It is a generator that allows you to automatically come up with character names, weapons, items, equipment, and even skill names. Where it pulls the word combinations from are several text (TXT) files that exist in the tool's folder, and you can customize your word combinations by editing these TXT files.

Setting Restrictions for New Classes   Click on the Classes tab. Give the following classes the restrictions listed below:

- **Mummy**—Weapons: Bow, Wrapped Bow, Crossbow, and Repeater Bow. Armor: Moldy Rags, Mystic Bandages, Fire Ring, Ice Ring, Scarab Ring, and Shock Ring.

- **Stein**—Weapons: Bat, Mace, Axe, Flail, Morning Star, and Dragon Sword. Armor: Leather Shield, Dragon Shield, Iron Helm, Dragon Helm, Leather Jacket, Iron Armor, Fire Ring, Ice Ring, Tough Bracers, Protective Amulet, Scarab Ring, Sunglasses, and Shock Ring.

- **Vampire**—Weapons: Leather Whip, Flail, and Cat-o-Nine Tails. Armor: Circlet, Robe, Leather Jacket, Magic Robe, Trench Coat, Fire Ring, Ice Ring, Protective Amulet, Moonwalker Boots, Sunglasses, Dracula Cape, and Shock Ring.

- **Were**—Weapons: Iron Claw, Silver Claw, and Dragon Claw. Armor: Leather Jacket, Trench Coat, Fire Ring, Ice Ring, Tough Bracers, Protective Amulet, Moonwalker Boots, Scarab Ring, and Shock Ring.

- **Witch**—Weapons: Witch Wand, Staff of Ages, and Voodoo Rod. Armor: Witch Cap, Circlet, Robe, Magic Robe, Fire Ring, Ice Ring, Witch Links, Scarab Ring, Ring of the Magi, and Shock Ring.

Giving Classes Efficiencies   If you give a class an efficiency (besides the default C), it means you are setting the efficiency of states being inflicted on characters of this class.

- **A**—200% efficiency (does double damage).
- **B**—150% efficiency.
- **C**—100% efficiency (normal).
- **D**—50% efficiency.
- **E**—20% efficiency.
- **F**—0% efficiency (doesn't work at all).

Set the following efficiencies for each of your new classes.

- **Mummy**—Should be susceptible to Fire, so set Fire to A. Set his Piercing, Darkness (state), and Paralysis to E.

- **Stein**—Should have Fire set to B, because he doesn't like fire. He should have Thunder set to E, because he's good at getting shocked.

- **Vampire**—Set his Mind, Incapacitated, Sleep, and Stun to E and his Holy and Piercing to B. His Darkness should be set to F.

- **Were**—Should have his Melee, Slashing, and Darkness (state) set to D, and his Mind should be put around B for not being that bright.

- **Witch**—Needs her Melee and Blow set to B, because she's more delicate when it comes to close-up confrontations. Set her Poison to D, because you know she's tasted some poison in her life and received some immunity to it, and her Mind to E (Figure 4.13).

Giving Classes Skills to Learn   Last, but not least, you will have to give each class a set of skills they can learn (as they become more experienced, that is). For each skill, you also can set at what level the character has to be to learn that skill. This helps you monitor how fast and powerful actors can become over the course of the game. If you see that actors become too strong too early, you can come back here and raise the level limits for the skills.

First, you have to edit some of the preset skills. Click on the Skills tab and edit the following.

- **015: Poison Breath > Poison Bite**—Change Use Message to "uses Poison Bite!"

- **021: Supersonic > Supersonic Howl**—Change Use Message to "gives a Supersonic Howl!"

- **024: Sleep Pollen > Sleep Dust**—Change Use Message to "blows up the Sleep Dust!"

- **029: Warcry > Wolf Howl**—Change the Use Message to "howls!"

Click on the Classes tab. Give the following classes the skills listed below (Figure 4.14):

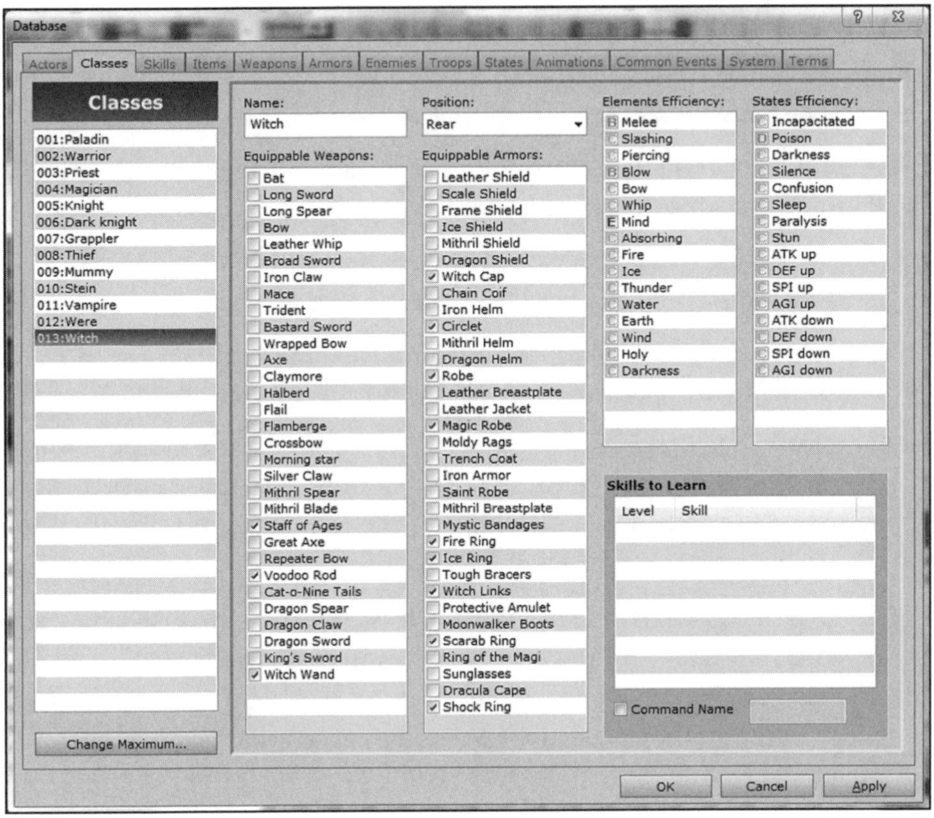

Figure 4.13
The Witch class's efficiencies.

■ **Mummy**—Slow Move: Level 4, Sleep Attack: Level 8, Gravel: Level 10, Sand Dust: Level 12, Meditation/Weak: Level 18, Sleep Dust: Level 22, Stone: Level 25, and Tornado: Level 30.

■ **Stein**—Quick Move: Level 4, Body Attack: Level 6, Thunder: Level 8, Raise: Level 10, Spark: Level 12, Thunder II: Level 16, Raise II: Level 20, and Spark II: Level 30.

■ **Vampire**—Slow Move: Level 4, Life Drain: Level 6, Spirit Curse: Level 8, Shade: Level 12, Uncanny Fog: Level 20, Vampirism: Level 22, Paralysis: Level 26, Weapon Curse: Level 28, and Darkness: Level 30.

■ **Were**—Double Attack: Level 4, Confusion Attack: Level 8, Triple Attack: Level 10, Self Recovery: Level 12, Howl: Level 16, Poison Bite: Level 22, and Supersonic Howl: Level 30.

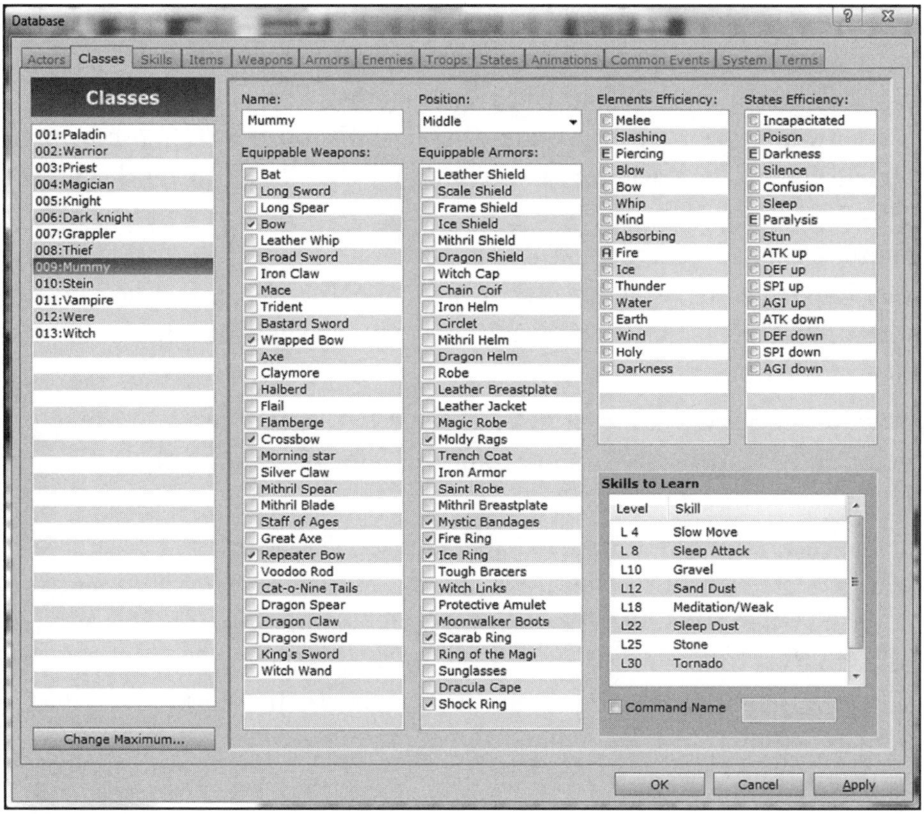

Figure 4.14
The Mummy class's skills.

- **Witch**—Fire: Level 1, Heal: Level 2, Flame: Level 4, Heal II: Level 6, Deadly Poison: Level 8, Temptation Song: Level 10, Silence: Level 14, Fire II: Level 18, Weapon Curse: Level 20, Mana Drain: Level 24, Flame II: Level 28, and Life Drain: Level 30.

Adjusting Actor Profiles

Click on the Actors tab. This is where we're going to play a little trick on the player. We want the game to center around a single character, named Vincent. He will start with one monster pet, a Stein named Freaky. Vincent will eventually gather other monster pets to help him on his quest, including each of the classes we just created.

To do this, we only have to create actors for each of the monster pets in the Database. Vincent won't do any fighting himself, because his monsters fight for him. This is all fine and dandy, but whoever is the first actor in the Database list is considered the player avatar, and the Character Graphic you choose for that actor is what your players will see on screen and what they control during the game. This is easy to fix, to fool the players. Create your monster pet actors, making sure that Freaky is in the 001 slot. Then, put Vincent's character in the Character Graphic, while using Freaky for the name, Face Graphic, Class, and so on. Don't worry if this sounds complicated. It's not. I'll show how to do this just after we've created our actors.

Freaky the Stein   Select your existing actors one-by-one and press Delete to get rid of them. Then, start with 001. Give him the Name of Freaky. Set his Class to 010: Stein.

Then double-click on MaxHP (under Parameter Curves) to enter the Parameter Curves dialog. Here, you can establish the amount of each stat the character gains per level. We'll use Quick Settings, because they're faster. For Freaky, set his MaxHP to Quick Setting A. Then click the MaxMP tab to go there and set it to Quick Setting C. Set his Attack to Quick Setting A, his Defense to Quick Setting B, his Spirit to Quick Setting D, and his Agility to Quick Setting D. Then click OK to leave the Parameter Curves dialog. Notice how each time you click the Quick Setting letter buttons, they will randomly generate a new curve. Also, be aware that what I did here was give Freaky a high health and Attack level, but I deliberately made his magic and Spirit low. This is a careful balance that will improve game flow.

For his Starting Equipment, give him 001: Bat for a Weapon, 001: Leather Shield for a Shield, and 025: Tough Bracers for an Accessory. This should come up in the drop-down lists for you, if you set up your Stein class correctly.

Now look at his Options section. Let me explain what each of these options does before we start enabling them.

- **Two Swords Style**—Gives the character an extra weapon slot and removes his ability to use a shield. Two-handed weapons cannot be used with any other weapon.

- **Fix Equipment**—Disallows the player from changing, adding to, or removing the actor's starting equipment. This is good for actors who only join the party for a short time or who have equipment that's important to the game narrative.

- **Auto Battle**—Makes the actor behave automatically in battle. The player can't make decisions for them, in other words. Good for helper allies.

- **Super Guard**—Makes the Defend battle command more effective for this actor.

- **Pharmacology**—Makes the use of recovery items (such as health potions) more effective when used by this character.

- **Critical Bonus**—Doubles the chance of a critical hit when this character attacks.

Freaky does not need any of these options enabled, but some of the other actors we create will.

Este the Witch   For 002, do the following:

1. **Name**—Este.

2. **Class**—013: Witch.

3. **Parameter Curves**—MaxHP: C, MaxMP: A, Attack: B, Defense: D, Spirit: A, and Agility: B.

4. **Starting Equipment**—Weapon: Witch Wand, Helmet: Witch Cap, Body Armor: Robe, and Accessory: Witch Links.

5. **Options**—Pharmacology.

Bonehead the Were   For 003, do the following (Figure 4.15):

1. **Name**—Bonehead.

2. **Class**—012: Were.

3. **Parameter Curves**—MaxHP: B, MaxMP: C, Attack: A, Defense: B, Spirit: D, and Agility: A.

4. **Starting Equipment**—Weapon: Iron Claw, Body Armor: Leather Jacket, and Accessory: Protective Amulet.

5. **Options**—Two Swords Style.

Toothy the Vampire   For 004, do the following:

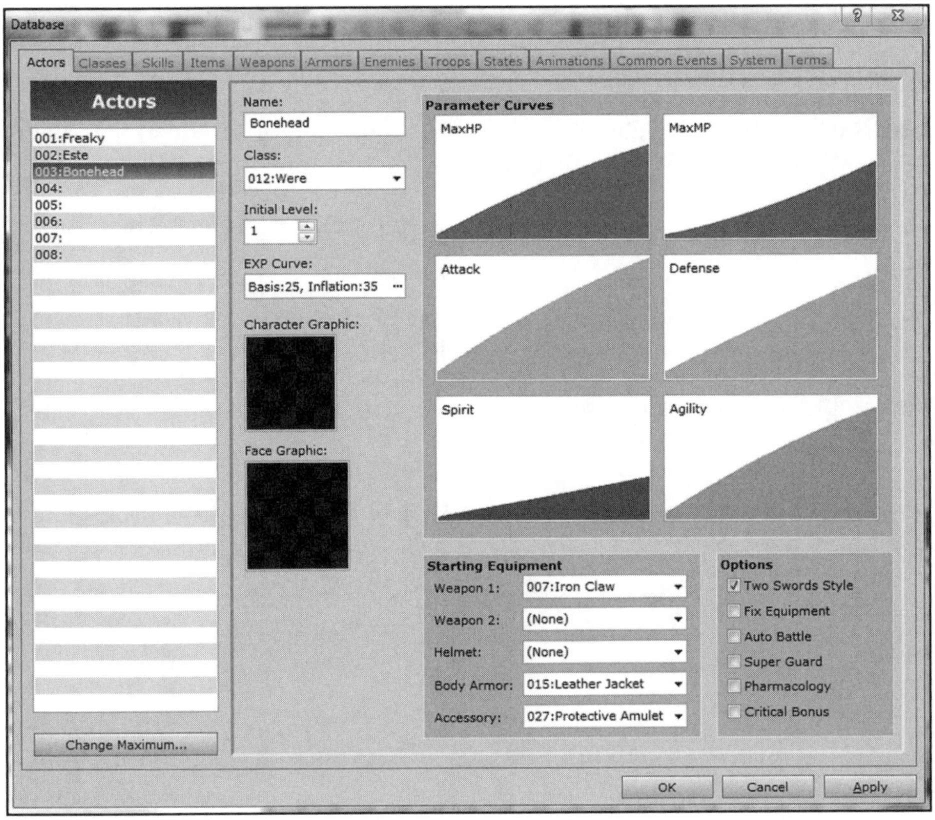

Figure 4.15
Bonehead's actor profile.

1. **Name**—Toothy.

2. **Class**—011: Vampire.

3. **Parameter Curves**—MaxHP: B, MaxMP: B, Attack: C, Defense: C, Spirit: B, and Agility: D.

4. **Starting Equipment**—Weapon: Leather Whip, Body Armor: Robe, and Accessory: Sunglasses.

5. **Options**—Critical Bonus.

Gus the Mummy   For 005, do the following:

1. **Name**—Gus.

2. **Class**—009: Mummy.

3. **Parameter Curves**—MaxHP: B, MaxMP: C, Attack: B, Defense: A, Spirit: C, and Agility: B.

4. **Starting Equipment**—Weapon: Bow, Body Armor: Moldy Rags, and Accessory: Scarab Ring.

5. **Options**—Super Guard.

Making Face Graphics for New Actors

To select a Face Graphic for an actor in the Database, you'd normally go to the Actors tab and select the actor you want to add a face to. Then, you'd double-click the image representation square below Face Graphic to open the Face Graphic dialog. You would scroll through the available face sets and click on one to become the face for your actor.

However, since you have made up your actors—and they are radically different than the ones displayed in the Face Graphic dialog—you will have to create your own. You will need to draw a separate face for each of the actors you've created: Freaky, Este, Bonehead, Toothy, and Gus. Plus, you'll need to make a sixth face for Vincent, our protagonist.

Exporting a Face Set   Exit the RPG Maker Database. Go to Tools > Resource Manager on the main menu (hotkey F10) or click the Resource Manager icon button on the toolbar; it's the button that looks like red, blue, and pink geometric shapes. The Resource Manager is the container for all the graphics and audio files you use in your game project. From here, you can import, export, and preview your files.

In the Resource Manager dialog, click on Graphics/Faces on the left and then click on Actor1 on the right. Click Preview so that you can see what a face set looks like.

To make a new face set, you must have the correct dimensions. A typical face set is 384 pixels wide and 192 pixels high and less than 200 kilobytes in total file size. Each face set is a single image laid on a grid, with squares for eight different faces. Click Close to exit the preview of Actor1's face set. Now, with Actor1 still selected, click Export. Save your Actor1.png image file somewhere on your computer where you can get to it. I often put files that are a work-in-progress on my Desktop until I am through with them.

You will need an image-editing program for this exercise. If you do not have one yet, refer to the list in Chapter 2.

At the time of this writing, there are roughly three different methods you can use to create a face set:

- Make one from scratch, using Actor1.png or one of the other face sets as a guide. This requires you knowing how to draw—especially how to draw anime characters. If you're a really good artist, you might want to take this route.

- Use the web-based program Moromagalabo. Moromagalabo is not that hard to use. You basically click-together the look of your character and then copy-and-paste the image into your image editor and arrange it just like Actor1.png shows you. On the downside, you will have to credit the creator of the program, and the character you can create is fairly limited.

- Download the itty-bitty FaceMaker program. FaceMaker is originally a Japanese program, so some of its language is still in Japanese, making it difficult to understand at times. However, you can randomly create faces or edit the features just like in Moromagalabo (but with far less limitations) and then save the faces from the program out to individual BMP or PNG files, which can then be copied-and-pasted into your image editor and arranged just like Actor1.png.

Using Moromagalabo to Make Faces   Go online to http://RPGVXstuff.Broke-Cat.org/Moromagalabo/Moromagalabo.html (Figure 4.16). The original site was created by Chu-Moroki/Margare and is in Japanese. But user Menda went through all the trouble and time to translate it into English for other RPG Maker users. Moromagalabo requires Firefox, Opera, or Internet Explorer 6+ to work, and you have to have JavaScript enabled.

Your image preview of "Moromaga" is in the upper-left corner. This is the female character you can edit. If you give her shorter hair, however, because of the way anime characters can appear androgynous, she will look like a boy.

To change her appearance, start by clicking on one of the tabbed categories at the top: Hair, Eyes, Clothing, Mouths/Eyebrows, Decoration, and Backgrounds. Subcategories appear beneath, which you click to activate. Once activated, fields of colored circles will come into view below the categories. Read a description of

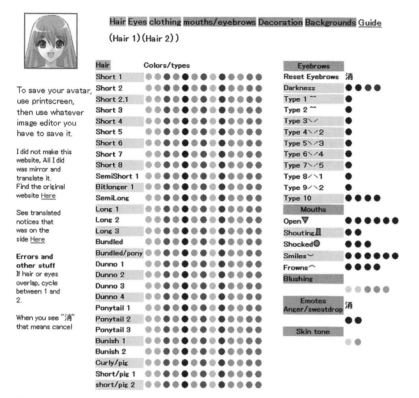

Figure 4.16
Moromagalabo.

what it is you are adding and click the colored circle in that same row to add it; the color represents the tint it will take on. When you see the Japanese character 消 it means "cancel."

Play around with Moromagalabo and see what kind of character face you can make with it. Make sure, under Backgrounds, to turn Border off (Figure 4.17).

When you're through, access the Snipping Tool found in Windows (Start > All Programs > Accessories > Snipping Tool) to click-and-drag your Snipping Tool's cursor over the preview in Moromagalabo and capture your face image to memory (Figure 4.18). Be sure only to snag the face and its square background, not the rest of the web page. If you don't have the Snipping Tool on your PC, you can use the Print Screen key on your keyboard to capture your screen image and then copy the face from it in your image editor.

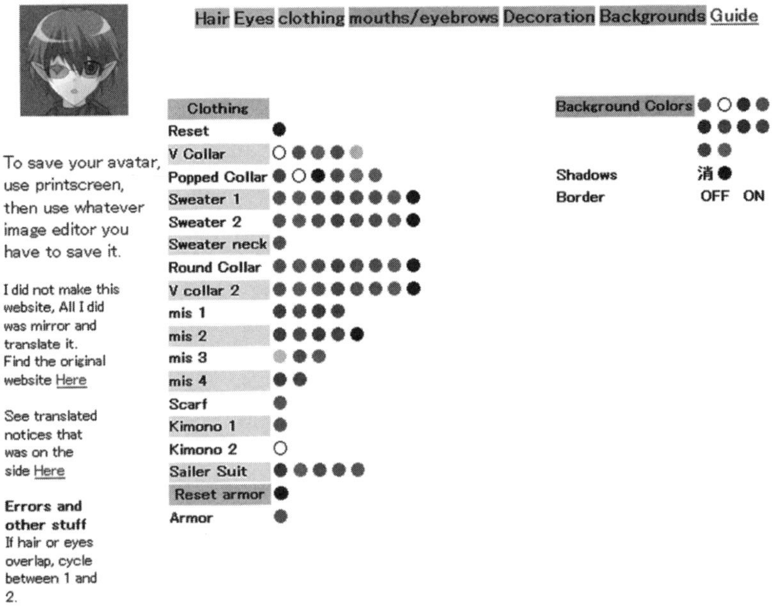

Hair Eyes clothing mouths/eyebrows Decoration Backgrounds Guide

Clothing

Reset
V Collar
Popped Collar
Sweater 1
Sweater 2
Sweater neck
Round Collar
V collar 2
mis 1
mis 2
mis 3
mis 4
Scarf
Kimono 1
Kimono 2
Sailer Suit
Reset armor
Armor

Background Colors

Shadows   消
Border   OFF   ON

To save your avatar, use printscreen, then use whatever image editor you have to save it.

I did not make this website, All I did was mirror and translate it.
Find the original website Here

See translated notices that was on the side Here

Errors and other stuff
If hair or eyes overlap, cycle between 1 and 2.

Figure 4.17
Make any face you want, but be sure to turn Border off.

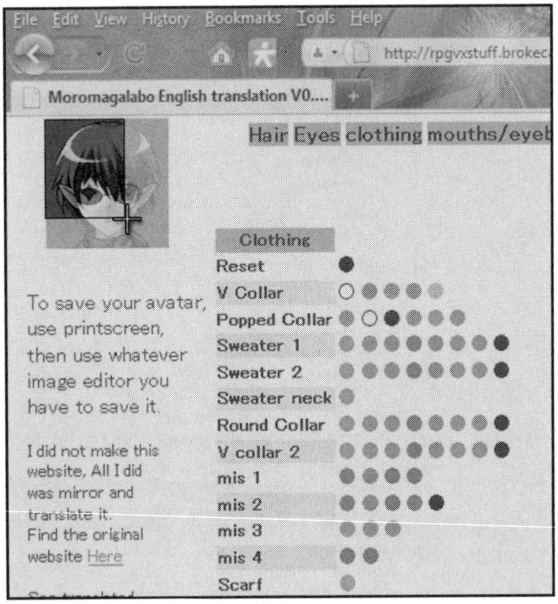

File Edit View History Bookmarks Tools Help

http://rpgvxstuff.brokec

Moromagalabo English translation V0....

Hair Eyes clothing mouths/eyeb

Clothing

Reset
V Collar
Popped Collar
Sweater 1
Sweater 2
Sweater neck
Round Collar
V collar 2
mis 1
mis 2
mis 3
mis 4
Scarf

To save your avatar, use printscreen, then use whatever image editor you have to save it.

I did not make this website, All I did was mirror and translate it.
Find the original website Here

Figure 4.18
Copy your face image using the Snipping Tool, if you have it.

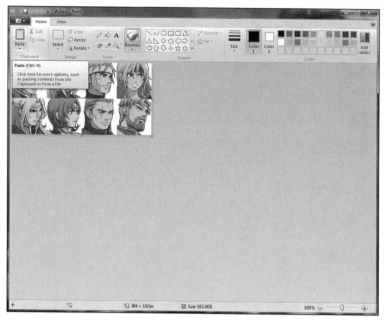

Figure 4.19
Paste your copied face from Moromagalabo into your image editor.

Now paste your copied face into your image editor. If you haven't picked an image editor yet, open Microsoft Paint (Start > All Programs > Accessories > Paint). Then open Actor1.png from wherever you saved it earlier. Click on the Paste button (Figure 4.19) or press Ctrl + V to paste your new face into Actor1.png. Arrange your pasted picture to cover the first tile in your face set. Only while the white anchors and dashed edges are apparent around your pasted picture can you move and stretch it.

Save your final face set (Figure 4.20) as something other than Actor1.png, because you don't want to accidentally overwrite the original face set. Then close Paint or whatever image editor you're using.

Using FaceMaker to Make Faces Download FaceMaker from the web at http://www.Mediafire.com/?mzmqjbdogyz. If you can't find it there, it might have been removed and you can do a Google search for it.

Once you download it, please note that you have a zipped folder. Unzip that folder using WinZip, WinRAR, Microsoft Explorer, or another unzipping utility.

Figure 4.20
An example of the face set after appending a new face into it.

Inside you will find the FaceMaker EN executable file in a portable folder you can take with you anywhere. If you run the executable, you will open the FaceMaker dialog (Figure 4.21).

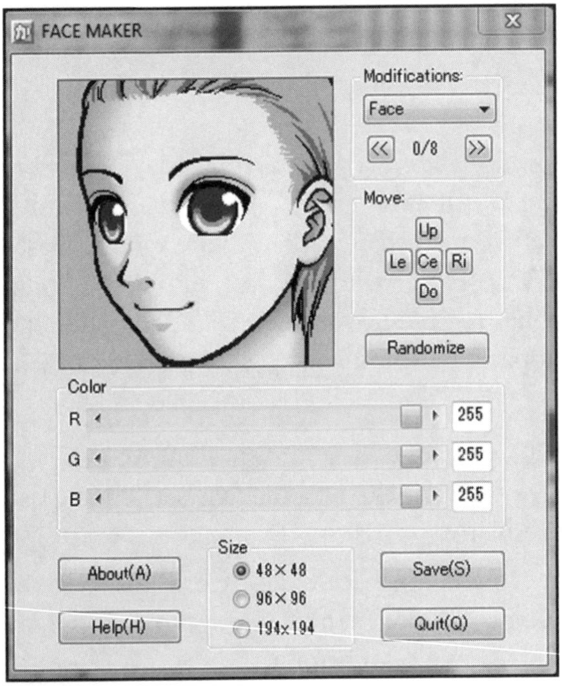

Figure 4.21
FaceMaker.

Figure 4.22
Freaky's face.

Some game artists click the Randomize button several times to create a random face, but this is not very precise.

Let's create Freaky the Stein in FaceMaker, just to get a feel for the program. Make the following adjustments. Your face should come out looking like Figure 4.22.

- **Face**—2 of 8. Color: R—178, G—255, and B—215.
- **Eyelashes**—19 of 32.
- **Eyes**—10 of 11. Color: R—35, G—255, and B—100. Tap the Move > Right button several times.
- **Nose**—4 of 11. Tap the Move > Up button a few times.
- **Mouth**—24 of 36. Color: R, G, and B—255.
- **Eyebrows**—9 of 14. Color: R—0, G—95, and B—124.
- **Upper Hair**—20 of 37. Color: R—0, G—95, and B—124. Tap the Move > Up button a few times.
- **Lower Hair**—8 of 36. Color: R—0, G—95, and B—124.
- **Shirt**—3 of 8. Color: R—0, G—50, and B—144.
- **Accessories 1**—2 of 6.
- **Accessories 2**—4 of 8. Color: R—216, G—249, and B—205.

Press the S key or click the Save button. Name your file Freaky, and save it as a BMP/PNG file type. (Instead of saving your face pic, you could simply use the Snipping Tool trick as you did with Moromagalabo, but that's totally up to you.)

Close FaceMaker and open your newly created file in your image editor. Select and copy the face. Then open your face set image (whatever you called your Actor1.png file from before). Paste your Freaky face into your face set. Scale and arrange him as necessary to fit within one of the squares. Then save your face set image, being careful not to overwrite the one before in case you need it as a backup. How simple is that?

Drawing Anime Faces by Hand   If you have even a smidgen of artistic talent, you could draw the faces by hand instead.

You could sketch them within a paint program using either a mouse or digital pen tablet (the pen tablet would be easier and much more professional-looking, nevertheless). Or you could draw and color the faces on paper and scan the pictures into digital files on your computer.

Any way you choose to do it, let me show you a few tricks to drawing anime faces. Why stick with the anime style? You do so merely because you are still affixing the premade characters in RPG Maker, and they are drawn in the anime style.

How to Hold Your Pencil or Pen   You might be thinking to yourself, "I already know how to hold a pencil or pen. I've been doing it for years!" That may be the case, but to draw takes a different holding style.

When first holding a pencil for drawing, most people adopt the writing position. They rest their hand on the paper and grip the pencil tightly in their fingers. This gives them a small controlled area and allows for sketching short lines and curves. It's more of a last step, or fine-detailing method. This is okay for writing notes, but it's not practical for broad sketching or coloring.

By lifting the hand of the paper you can work from your wrist and your fingers. A single line or curve drawn from the wrist can be two to three times longer than a line drawn from the fingers when the hand is resting on the table. Drawing from the wrist is more fluid.

Sit back in your chair with your hand still off the page. Try drawing a line from your elbow joint. This will give you even more freedom and you will be able to draw longer, free-flowing lines. You will have a much larger area for your hand and arm to sweep curved and straight lines from.

Try sketching lines in your sketch pad in the ways described above, working alternately from your fingers, wrist, elbow, and shoulder. Note how each way has its advantages and disadvantages.

You also get different pencil strokes from the way you hold your pencil. Hold it almost flat, with the side of the point resting against your paper, and create broad lines of value. This is an easy way to add thick shading to your work. Hold the pencil up in the air, just working from the tip of the pencil, and you will create fine thin lines. The amount of pressure you apply will also vary the thickness and weight of your pencil stroke.

Shading   The easiest way to make shapes appear three-dimensional is to add values, such as highlights and shading. Try adding lights and darks to your drawings.

All you need are three values: one for the basic tone of your object, one for the highlighted area, and one for the shaded area. Later, depending on your artistic style, you can add graduated tones, which make your subjects appear more realistic.

To decide the placement of highlights and shadows on an object, you first have to determine the direction of your light source. Highlights appear on objects on the sides and edges nearest to and facing the light source, while shade appears on the same objects on the opposite sides, facing away from the light source.

Here are four rules of thumb to remember when drawing shadows:

1. The higher the source of light, the shorter the shadow should be.
2. The lower the source of light, the longer the shadow should be.
3. The stronger the light, the darker the shadows.
4. The softer the light, the gentler the shadows will appear.

Pencils vary in degree of softness and hardness. You can vary the strength of shading by varying the pressure of your hand on the pencil (Figure 4.23).

Basic Shapes   All objects are made up of basic underlying geometric shapes (Figure 4.24). A drinking glass, for instance, is roughly cylindrical in shape. A basketball is a sphere. A wood crate is a cube. And so on. Even people are made up of various underlying shapes, including a sphere for the head, a beveled box

Figure 4.23
A lot of tonal variation can come about when pencil shading.

CIRCLE   CYLINDER   BOX

Figure 4.24
Basic shapes make up these objects.

for the torso, cylinders for the arms and legs, and so forth. The three most-used shapes are ovals, cylinders, and boxes.

Whenever you are drawing, you can start from the ground up by lightly sketching geometric shapes first. Then go over them with finer and finer details to work in the look of what you are drawing.

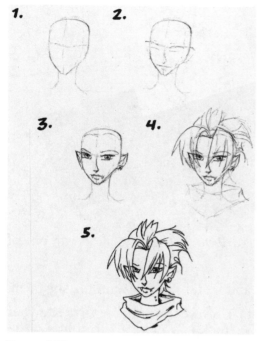

Figure 4.25
Drawing Tooth the Vampire, step-by-step.

Drawing Your First Face   Now put together what you've learned about drawing with drawing an anime character. Look at Figure 4.25 as you continue this exercise to draw Toothy the Vampire.

1. Draw a circle with guidelines for the face.

2. Sketch out some more details to the face.

3. Draw the details of the eyes, nose, and mouth for the face. It's ideal to draw the eyes first and then the rest, because the eyes are very important in anime.

4. Draw the hair. You can be as crazy and imaginative as you want when it comes to anime hair. Or you could use a hairstyling guide or magazine for inspiration.

5. Erase the guidelines you drew. Clean up your piece. Then add fine details and shading.

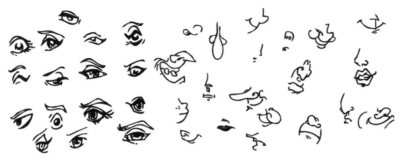

Figure 4.26
Some sample eyes and mouths you can draw.

Now draw your other characters, if you like. If you'd prefer to stick with one of the face-making programs, that's okay, too.

Figure 4.26 shows some examples of eyes and mouths, if you want to copy them.

Importing and Using Your New Face Set   However you choose to create your face set, you then need to import it to the Resource Manager in RPG Maker. Simply open the Resource Manager and click on Graphics/Faces. Then click the Import button and find your saved face set image to import to the Graphics/ Faces section. Close the Resource Manager when you're done. It's that easy!

Go to the Database and click on the Actors tab, if it's not already visible. Select Freaky from the left-side list and double-click on his Face Graphic. Browse until you find the Freaky face you made. Select it and return to the Actors list to preview it (Figure 4.27). Do the same with your remaining actors.

Making Vincent's Character Graphic

To select a Character Graphic for an actor in the Database, you'd normally go to the Actors tab and select the desired actor. Then, you'd double-click the image representation square below Character Graphic to open the Character Graphic dialog. You would scroll through the available sprite sets and click on one to become the sprite image used for your actor.

We have only one character that will need a sprite image shown on screen, and that's Vincent. As I said before, he exists in the narrative, but he isn't an actor that has a profile in the Database. We'll use Freaky, then, and put Vincent's

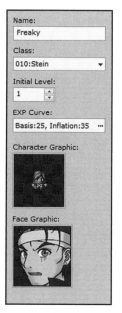

Figure 4.27
Freaky the Stein now has a face!

sprite in Freaky's Character Graphic spot. That way, the player avatar will show up as Vincent.

First, look at what sprites are already available. Open the Resource Manager and find Graphics/Characters in the list. Click on Actor1 and then on Preview. There's more than one character shown here. This is a sheet of character sprites that is 384 pixels wide by 256 pixels tall. Each character sprite is displayed in duplicate, three across and four down, making 12 copies of each character. Each copy shows the character in a different pose. The top row shows the character walking down the screen. The next row shows him walking left. Then right, and then up the screen.

None of the available graphic sprites fit the concept we have for Vincent, so you'll have to make one up. You could export the Actor1.png image and then open it in your image editor. You could then draw your character poses one at a time by hand. This is 100% acceptable, and many game artists do just that.

Thankfully, however, there's a web-based utility provided by Famitsu.com that's a breeze to use and will aid you in making custom sprites without going through that trouble. The only down side? The application is in Japanese. There are two different web pages you can use:

- **Girl characters**—http://www.famitsu.com/freegame/tool/chibi/index2.html

- **Guy characters**—http://www.famitsu.com/freegame/tool/chibi/index1.html

You could also use Google Translate to see a translated English view of these pages by typing the following in front of the URL:

http://translate.google.com/translate?hl=en&sl=ja&u=

Go to the male characters page (Figure 4.28). Scroll down until you see the character choices. The preview image of what your character will end up looking

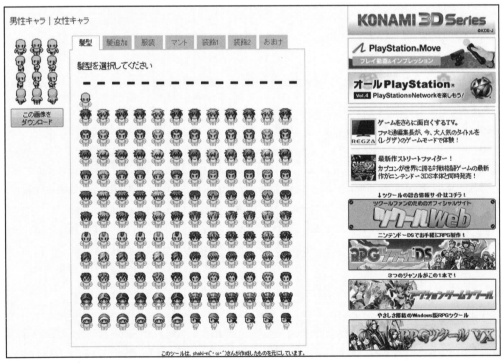

Figure 4.28
Famitsu.com's free game tool for creating RPG Maker VX character sprites.

like is on the upper left. All you have to do is click on an available image on the right, and it will be added to your preview image on the left. If you want to remove the item, you can click the small bald guy just above the image list.

The tabs, going across, contain the following.

- **Hairdo**—Hairstyles and head coverings.
- **Additional Hair**—Ponytails, ribbons, and more.
- **Clothes**—Basic outfits.
- **Cloak**—Capes.
- **Decorations 1**—Ties, facial hair, collars, scarves, and so on.
- **Decorations 2**—Masks, goggles, glasses, bunny ears, and the like.
- **Bonus**—Angel wings, devil wings, and fairy wings.

Make a Vincent character like you see in Figure 4.29. When you have your sprite completed, click the big gray button just below the preview image to save your work. You can save the PNG file to your computer. When you save the image, it is vital that you save it with a dollar sign ($) in front of the file name. Otherwise, when you import your graphic, RPG Maker won't recognize the file as an animated character sprite. For instance, you can save this image as $vincent.png.

Figure 4.29
The Vincent character sprite.

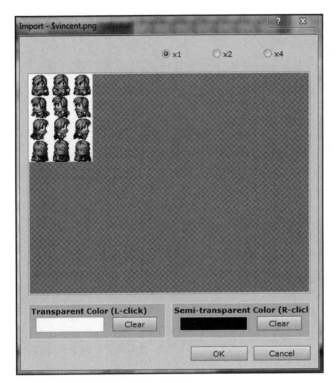

Figure 4.30
Importing the Vincent character sprite.

Now go to your RPG Maker project and open the Resource Manager. Go to Graphics/Characters and click on Import. Select the PNG file you just made. When you click Open, an Import dialog will open with options for transparent and semi-transparent colors. Left-click on the white background behind Vincent to add it to the Transparent Color slot below (Figure 4.30). Click OK, and Vincent will be added to your available sprites list.

Close the Resource Manager and open the Database. Go to the Actors tab, if you are not there already. Select Freaky from the actors list and double-click on the square below Character Graphic. Browse to the new sprite you just added. Click OK when you finish.

Save your game and test it. You should now see Victor strolling across the screen. When you get into battles, you will have Freaky, Toothy, Gus, and Bonehead to fight with.

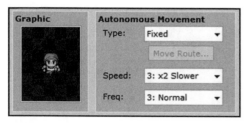

Figure 4.31
The Autonomous Movement panel.

Adding NPCs

To add an NPC to a game map is just like adding a transfer, door, or inn event. It starts by placing a new event into a square, editing the event's graphic to appear like a character, and giving it special event commands in keeping with what you want the NPC to be doing in-game.

Making an NPC Move

NPCs don't have to just stand around idle. You can make them walk around your map. There are different types of preprogrammed movement. All of them can be found in the Autonomous Movement section of the Edit Event dialog box (Figure 4.31).

- **Fixed**—Completely static movement. The sprite will remain in place.

- **Random**—The sprite will move in random directions around the map it's placed on.

- **Approach**—The sprite will chase after and keep in step with the player character. This is ideal for creating pets or a guide who must quickly approach the avatar.

- **Custom**—You can customize the movement the way you want.

For movement, you can also set the Speed, which is how fast the sprite event moves, and the Frequency, or how often it will move.

Let's create an NPC that moves.

Go to Candle Street. Right-click somewhere near the front entrance of the map and create a new event. Edit this event so that the graphic resembles a person.

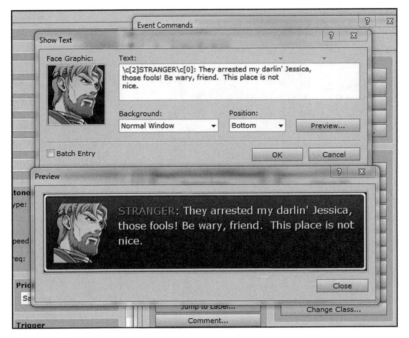

Figure 4.32
The Autonomous Movement panel.

Then set the event's movement type to Random. Double-click in the List of Event Commands and, in the dialog box that comes up, go to Tab 1 and click on Show Text. Type whatever text comes to your mind. I chose this:

```
\c[2]STRANGER\c[0]: They arrested my darlin' Jessica,
those fools! Be wary, friend. This place is not
nice.
```

Remember, putting \c[X] around words will alter the color of the text. In this case, the number 2 will change the word STRANGER orange (the 0 turns the text back to white). Be sure to keep whatever text you type within the arrows shown above the text box, or your words could be clipped. Click on Face Graphic to add a picture to this NPC dialog window. Attempt to always use a face that corresponds with the sprite image you are using. This avoids confusion. Finally, click Preview to see what your dialogue will end up as in-game (Figure 4.32). Click OK when you're satisfied with your dialogue.

You can set this behavior (the dialogue) to come up on touch or when the player is next to the sprite and presses Enter, by choosing Action Button or Player Touch in the Trigger panel. I usually set mine to Player Touch, because it can sometimes be a devil trying to approach a moving NPC and press the Enter key at the same time.

Save your game and test it. Now experiment with Speed and Frequency, to increase/decrease both. Save and test over and over to see what these values change about the NPC's path.

Next, let's change the Autonomous Movement to Custom. Once you do that, a button will appear called Move Route.

Click Move Route to open the Move Route dialog (Figure 4.33). Here, you can direct an entire movement path one step at a time, including slow-downs and stops, which is really important when creating animated cut-scenes for exposition in your RPG. Before you begin constructing a custom path, you must know what square your sprite event starts on and where you want him to go,

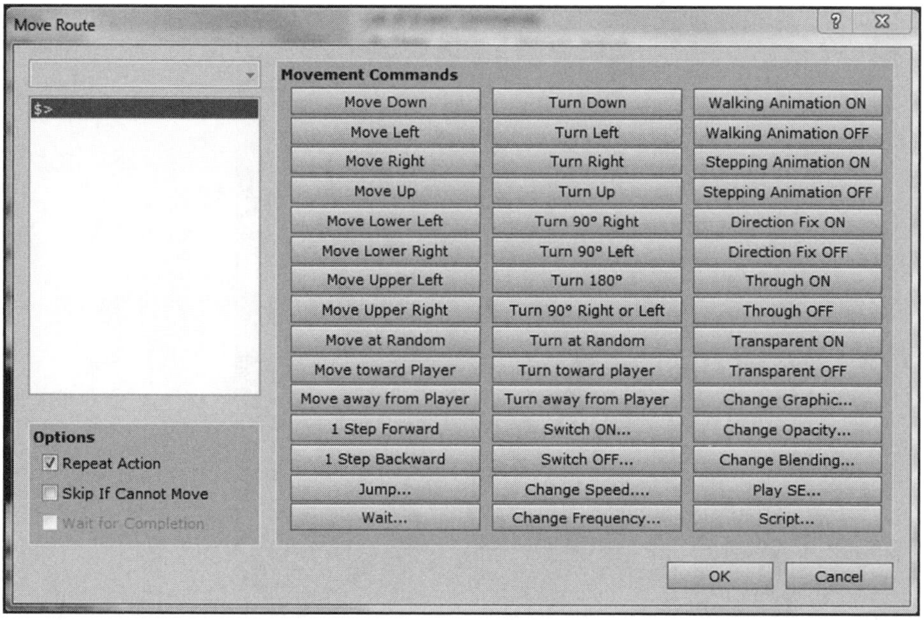

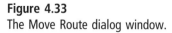

Figure 4.33
The Move Route dialog window.

square-by-square. This is easier to do on dual screens, or where you can minimize windows to see the Move Route dialog on one side and the map window on the other. Otherwise, you will need to pull out a notebook and take careful observations about positioning before customizing the Move Route.

For my NPC, I set him up so that he'd walk in a circle around the statue at the front entrance of Candle Street. You can put a check in the checkbox next to Repeat Action to have the sprite event repeat all the steps you make. He'll repeat them infinitely.

After customizing the NPC's movement, save your game and test it out (Figure 4.34).

Now let's have the player character talk back. Edit the moving sprite event again. Under the last line of the NPC dialogue in the List of Event Commands, double-click Pick Show Text. Now write what the player character, Vincent, would say back to the Stranger. Do it the same way you did the Stranger's text box. Only

Figure 4.34
Your finished NPC dialogue.

change the color of the word for Vincent's name (pick one color for each character in your game and try to keep with that choice throughout your game, for consistency's sake; I used the number 10, which is red) and his Face Graphic (select the face graphic you made to represent Vincent).

Now make as many mobile NPCs as you like. Some of them can give the player hints about how best to win at the game, or which direction he should take. Others may give more back story, telling the player what has occurred before his arrival at that location. Still others might spout riddles, gibberish, or tell them unrelated facts. It's your game, so make your NPCs as helpful or enjoyable as you like.

Giving the Player Dialogue Choices (a.k.a. Creating a Shop Event)

You have created more than one NPC that has dialogue. But dialogues can get a whole lot more complex than that. You can offer the player several choices to continue dialogue. This, in RPG development parlance, is what is known as a *dialogue tree*. In a dialogue tree, you start at the top and branch out into multiple avenues, depending on the player's pick of available choices, to reach a conclusion.

Create a new event called Shopkeeper in the Parlor map. Alter the Shopkeeper's graphic to look like a shopkeeper. Set the Autonomous Movement Type to Random and Trigger to Player Touch. Double-click on the List of Event Commands and pick Show Text from the command window. Give our shopkeeper a face and type a welcome from her (Figure 4.35):

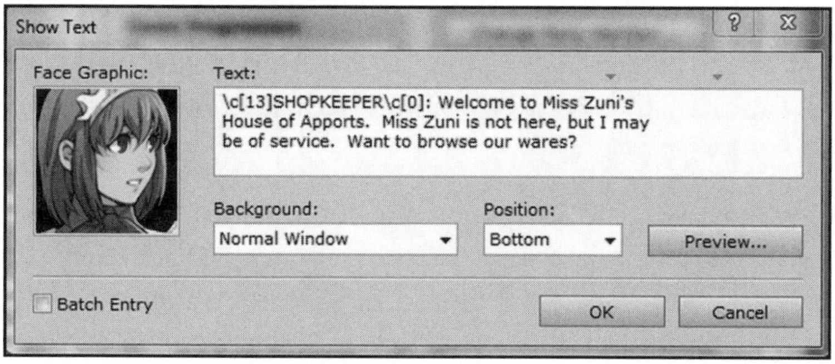

Figure 4.35
The shopkeeper's welcome message.

```
\c[13]SHOPKEEPER\c[0]: Welcome to Miss Zuni's
House of Apports. Miss Zuni is not here, but I
may be of service. Want to browse our wares?
```

Click OK when you're through.

Double-click again in the List of Event Commands, just below the show text part you just added, and pick Show Choices from Tab 1. In the Show Choices dialog box, you can set up to four different choices. When Cancel is your option to exit the choices altogether depending on which one the player chooses.

Set Choice 1 to say, "Sure." Set Choice 2 to say, "What's your name?" Set Choice 3 to say, "Not really. Goodbye." For When Cancel, click the radio button beside Choice 3. Click OK when you're done.

New lines of code have been added to your List of Event Commands. Double-click the line just below where it says "When [What's your name?]" and select Show Text. In the Show Text dialog, type the following (being sure to use the same graphic for your shopkeeper as before), and then close your Show Text dialog:

```
\c[13]SHOPKEEPER\c[0]: Me? Oh... My name
is Valerie. I work for Miss Zuni.
```

Back in the List of Event Commands, double-click the line just below where it says "When [Sure]." Pick Show Text. Use the same graphic, and type the following:

```
\c[13]SHOPKEEPER\c[0]: Great! Let me see...
I'll get some things for you to look at.
```

Press OK. It is now added to your List of Event Commands.

Next, double-click right after the last line of the text you just added and pick Shop Processing from Tab 3 of the Event Commands dialog. This starts our actual shop operation.

In the Shop Processing dialog, you can list goods and their prices. Double-click the first line and you will see a Goods dialog. Here, you can pick whether the goods in shop will be items, weapons, or armors. Miss Zuni's shop only sells items, which is selected by default for you. From the drop-down list, you can add any items that you like. Click OK after you pick one, and it will be added to the shop's list. The default price is set by the item description in the Database. You can add as many items as you want to Miss Zuni's shop.

If you put a check in the checkbox next to Purchase Only, it will restrict the player so that he cannot sell any goods but can still buy new goods. We don't want to restrict the player in Miss Zuni's shop, but there may be times when you want to later on.

Click OK when you're done, and you will return to the new event's dialog. Click OK to exit. Remember, it's a long way to travel to the Parlor, so if you want to cheat, simply move your player start position to the front entrance of the Parlor map (right-click somewhere in the Parlor and select Set As Starting Position > Player) before you save and test your game.

To test out the shop, walk up to the shopkeeper and, when she starts talking to you, choose the first dialogue option. In the shop, you can buy or sell items. Go to Buy, click Enter, and you'll see the list of items you created, like in Figure 4.36. Items are grayed out when your player doesn't have enough money to pay for them.

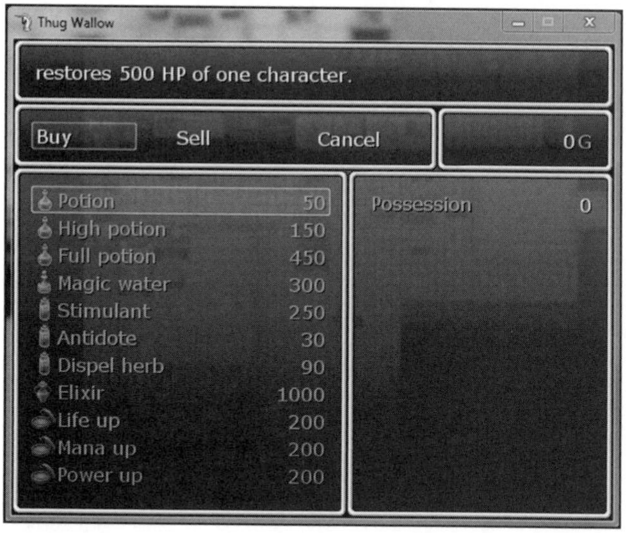

Figure 4.36
The shop menu.

When you're done testing, remember to move your player start position back to the World Map.

What's Next?

You've created the start of a grand game world for your player to search. You've given the player a party of attention-grabbing characters and some NPCs to talk to in that game world. The next step is putting into that game world some difficult enemies the player must overcome in order to make your RPG more challenging. This is a pretty easy task to accomplish in RPG Maker. We'll look at doing so in the next chapter.

CHAPTER 5

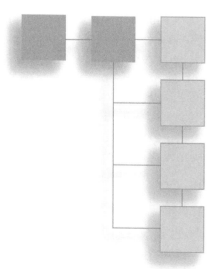

STAGING BATTLE ENCOUNTERS

In this chapter you will learn:

- How to make up terrifying monsters
- How to edit the RPG Maker enemies
- How to set up random encounters
- How to set up fixed encounters

The player characters and non-player characters (NPCs) are only one side of the coin when it comes to designing game characters. Remember that a video game has to have conflict, and one way conflict is portrayed in fantasy RPGs is for the player to have battles with ferocious monsters and other assorted enemies. Also, monsters are just plain cool. They're often one of the highlights of fantasy RPGs. Even *Pokémon* wouldn't be *Pokémon* without all the cute monster pets!

In this chapter, you will learn about what goes into making the perfect opponent, and how to create turn-by-turn combat scenarios in RPG Maker.

CREATING A MONSTER

Tip

"He who fights with monsters might take care lest he thereby become a monster. Is not life a hundred times too short for us to bore ourselves?"

— Friedrich Nietzsche

RPG monsters, especially the ones seen in video RPGs, are often terribly cliché. From the dwarf marauders to the orc warriors, they are more often than not pulled from mythology, legends, fantasy literature, and world religions. Some monsters have been a part of the RPG genre so long they are considered staples of the genre and are actually missed if not included in a new game. Others are just wild animals or giant insects. Few actually rely on the laws of physics to become manifest, the imaginary world of the RPG supporting them in ways only games of pretend can.

Players have come to expect these things. They want to be wowed by monsters that lurk in dungeons or under beds or in their own backyards.

The best way you can shake up a party of adventurers is to present them with a monster they don't recognize, even if it is one that has long been a genre staple but comes across as something of a novelty when they encounter it the first time. When something creeps up on a player that he can't identify, he will make mistakes trying to defend or attack it that will make the battle with that monster much more satisfying.

So do some thinking about your monsters. Don't strew them across your maps without adequate forethought.

Another thing: Monsters never just appear out of thin air! Natural monsters will have evolved to fill an ecological niche, and this gives them certain strengths and weaknesses within their domicile. Monsters bred or magically created by someone would have been made to fit a function, and this purpose will define their mix of abilities and flaws as evolution never could.

As the game's designer, you need to know the story of your monster. A creature built to guard a wizard's secret laboratory will appear very different from a predator evolved to feed on scurrying mammals in the rainforest. Consider the back story of every enemy you decide to include in your game carefully.

You could also use the trick of turning things upside-down. It works in most creative fields, but has been particularly successful in monster-making. Take the player's expectations and reverse them. Dumb monsters become smart, slow monsters become fast, and weak monsters gain surprising body weapons or poison attacks. Coupled with a decent back story, this gambit is a surefire way to create an interesting and less humdrum monster.

For instance, the film *28 Days Later* was one of the first zombie flicks to cast to the wayside the notion of slow, shuffling zombies and present them as ravenously fast, virulently vicious zombies. The film even had a viral excuse for why the creatures acted the way they did. If it weren't for such initial forays into quick-moving zombies, games like *Left 4 Dead* would not be nearly as suspenseful!

Subtypes of RPG Monsters

The common subtypes of RPG monsters are as follows.

- **Bug monsters**—If it crawls on more than four legs and appears particularly nasty or creepy, then it can become a monster. The common varieties include giant ants, centipedes, scorpions, spiders, and wasps.

- **People**—People can be monsters, too, especially if they don't have other folk's best intentions at heart. These enemies habitually include savages, bandits, barbarians, soldiers, dark knights, warlocks, and necromancers.

- **Legendary/folkloric monsters**—Monsters can be ripped straight from legends, fairy tales, myths, and religions. Others can be inspired by fantasy stories like the works of J.R.R. Tolkien or C.S. Lewis.

- **Undead monsters**—Part of our fear of death and the unknown, creatures that come back to life after passing the threshold of the grave often have a fascination for us.

- **Unusual/original monsters**—These monsters are colorful, unique, and often strangely funny. One of the most-used unusual monsters seen in video RPGs is the treasure chest that comes alive and tries to kill the hero. Or the mechanical automaton that looks like a steam-powered robot.

The RPG Maker Monsters

The default enemies that loads with RPG Maker (and can be edited at will) include the following. These can be found in the Database under the Enemies tab.

- **Slime**—Assumedly voracious blobs that ingest people much like amoebas would if they grew large enough.

- **Bat**—A vampire bat that swoops in to bite its prey.

- **Hornet**—A giant poisonous wasp.

- **Spider**—A giant poisonous spider.

- **Rat**—A starving, crazed rodent with a nasty physical attack.

- **Willowisp**—A floating ball of blue fire that can paralyze its enemy. It is presumably based on the folk tales of will o' wisp, or faerie fires, seen luring lone travelers into murky bogs at night.

- **Snake**—A small dinosaur with a physical attack.

- **Scorpion**—A giant poisonous scorpion.

- **Jellyfish**—A mutant tentacle-covered creature from the deep.

- **Plant**—A man-eating plant that can spray sleep-inducing spores on its victims.

- **Ghost**—A sepulchral visitor who can cast fire on people it doesn't like.

- **Skeleton**—The resurrected remains of a once-fierce fighter.

- **Orc**—A brutish misshapen creature with a powerful leg sweep attack.

- **Imp**—An ice-blasting demon creature from some nether region.

- **Gayzer**—A floating orb covered in eyeballs and leathery tentacles. It puts its victims to sleep and then sucks their blood.

- **Puppet**—A scary scarecrow that can ignite or rain rocks down on its enemies.

- **Zombie**—A slow-moving corpse brought back to life through dark arts.

- **Cockatrice**—A swift winged creature, part bird and part snake, that can paralyze people with its stare or cast whipping gales at them with its wings.

- **Chimera**—A cool customer who appears as part eagle and part lion. Not to be messed with.

- **Mimic**—A treasure chest that is not really a treasure chest. It has a large fanged maw where the lid and box meet, and it can confuse and dazzle its opponents.

- **Werewolf**—A wild beast with long sharp claws and poison bite.

- **Sahagin**—A merman who can raise tidal waves or summon curling fogbanks to silence his enemies.

- **Ogre**—A pudgy beast-man with a gnarled club and striking blow.

- **Gargoyle**—A European dragon with a paralyzing stare and flame breath weapon.

- **Lamia**—A sweet and luring snake-creature with a captivating voice and betraying attack.

- **Vampire**—A blood-sucking lord of the night.

- **Succubus**—A seductive but cruel beauty. She can drain a victim's life slowly or confuse him from attacking by weaving her illusions around him.

- **Demon**—A hideous ram-headed winged beast that can summon gouts of flame or beat its opponents relentlessly with its whip.

- **Darklord**—A terrifying dark magician who commands the elements and has a near indefensible blade attack.

- **Evilking**—The most deadly and notorious creature in all the realms, and definitely one of the hardest to defeat.

Editing RPG Maker Monsters

Tip

"You can't create a monster, then whine when it stomps on a few buildings."

— Lisa Simpson, *The Simpsons* (TV show)

You may want to edit the prefabricated monsters that come with RPG Maker, to call them something different or make them look or behave differently. To do so, simply open your game project. Go to the Database and the Enemies tab.

To show you how this is done, I want you to edit the enemies below in your Thug Wallow game.

Enemy Names

First, go to the Database and the Enemies tab. Then click on Snake. Since his name really doesn't match his picture, we want to change that. He looks like a

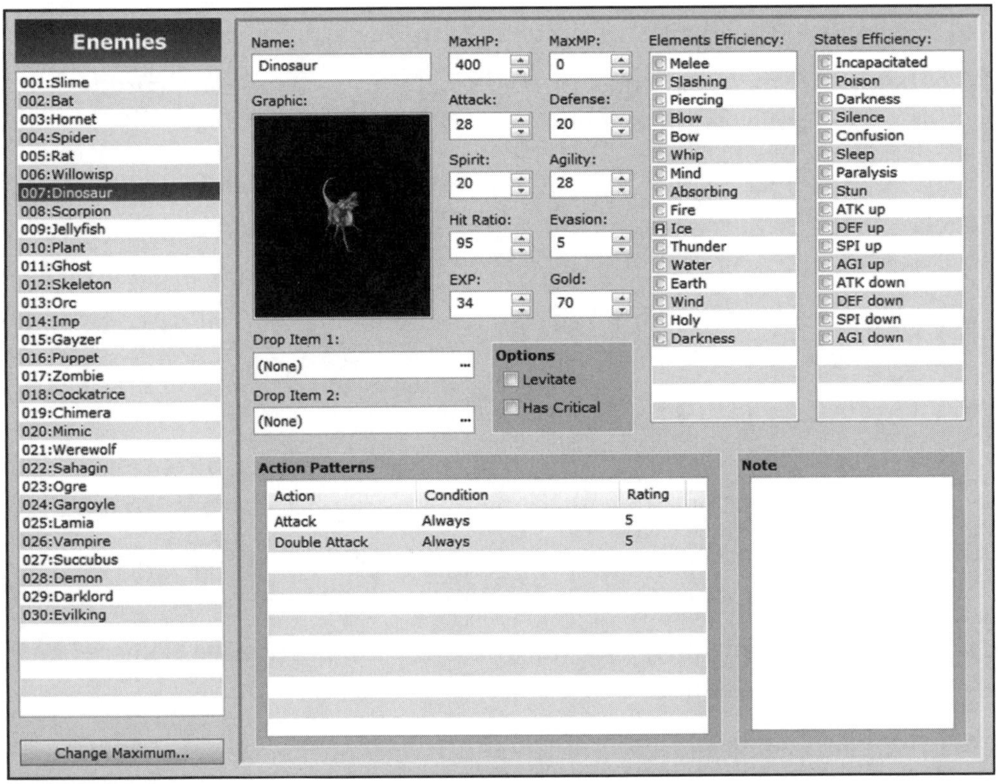

Figure 5.1
Change the name of Snake to Dinosaur.

frill-necked lizard or the dilophosaurus depicted in the *Jurassic Park* motion picture. In the middle window, put your cursor in the Name field. Highlight "Snake" and type "Dinosaur" in its place. The name will be automatically updated in the list on the left and in other areas of the Database (Figure 5.1).

Do the same with Puppet, naming it Scarecrow. Sahagin should become Deep One (a nod to horror writer H. P. Lovecraft), and Gargoyle should become Wyvern (another term used for a dragon). You can rename the other enemies, if you can think of more clever names for them.

Last but not least, rename Darklord as Korgan, as he'll be the boss enemy in Thug Wallow.

When you are through, click Apply to apply your changes.

Enemy Graphics

Slime, right now, is colored blue. The original inspiration for this creature, however, comes from the horror film *The Blob*, which was a pink creature. So let's alter the sprite image so that Slime appears pink instead of blue.

Open the Database and go to the Enemies tab, if you're not already there. Select Slime from the left-side list. Double-click on the Graphic image in the main window to open the Battler Graphic dialog window. Here, you can pick a different sprite image among the Graphics/Battlers list that has been loaded in the Resource Manager.

Don't pick another one other than the Slime image you already have. Instead, look at the bottom edge of the Battler Graphic dialog window, where you see a Hue slider. Click and drag the Hue slider handle. As you do so, notice the tint of your Slime image will vary. This Hue adjustment can be done to any of the enemy graphics, to give them dissimilar appearances.

I stopped at the fifth notch over, from left-to-right, to give Slime a pink tint (Figure 5.2). Click OK when you're done.

Try this again, making the Bat look indigo blue or almost purple in color and the Willowisp look brilliant green. When you're done, click Apply to save your changes to the Database.

What if you want to draw a brand-new enemy image, to replace an existing one? That's easy. Simply sketch it (on paper or in your art program). Color it in an image editor and save it, preferably as a PNG file with a transparent background. Then upload it to the Graphics/Battlers section of the Resource Manager. After it's safely in the Resource Manager, you can return to the Database and convert any enemy's Graphic to your brand-new sprite image.

Note

The Resource Manager contains both global and local resources. Global resources will have a blue dot in front of them, while local (often custom) resources will have an orange dot in front of them. When creating custom items you want imported into the Resource Manager, be sure to put those items into a file folder in or near your game project. If you import a PNG image file, you will be given prompts about giving the image a transparent background, which does not occur when importing other file types. Be sure to name all your custom items correctly, because if you give one

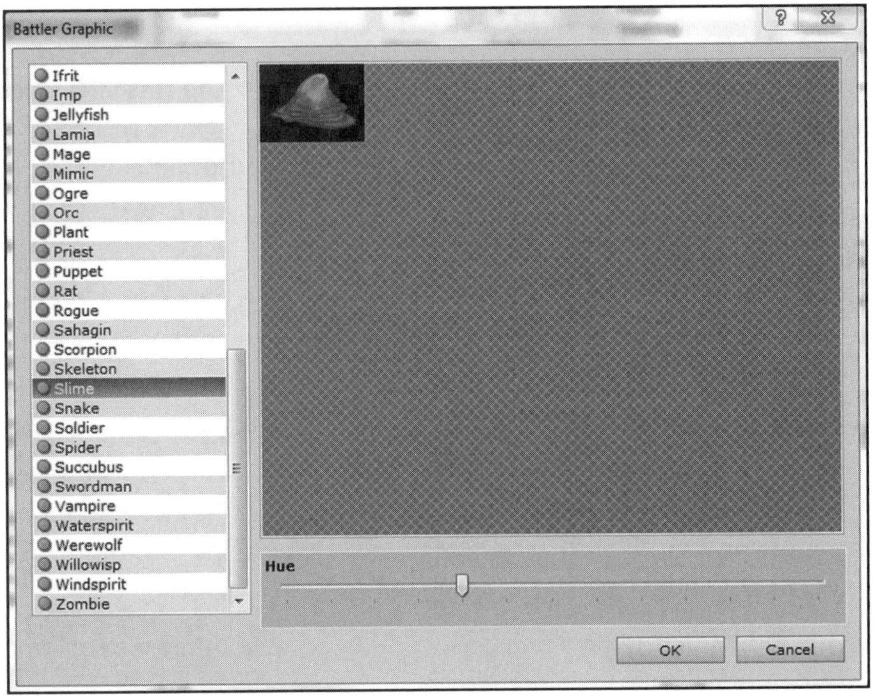

Figure 5.2
Make your Slime pink, like in *The Blob*.

> of them the same name as an existing, global resource, your Resource Manager will overwrite the existing file with your custom file automatically.

Enemy Stats

You can change a monster's appearance all day long, but to make it behave differently, you will have to adjust its stats.

Action Patterns   Select the Rat. Double-click the empty slot in the Action Patterns, just after Body Attack, to insert a new attack type. In the Action section of the Action dialog window, click the radio button beside Skill. From the drop-down list, pick 015: Poison Bite (which used to be Poison Breath before you edited it in the last chapter). This gives our Rat a poisonous bite attack.

Drag the Rating slider to 3 (Figure 5.3). Ratings govern how often an enemy uses a single attack. Of all actions the enemy has, the one with the highest rating (which is now set at 5) will be used the most, or given highest priority. An action

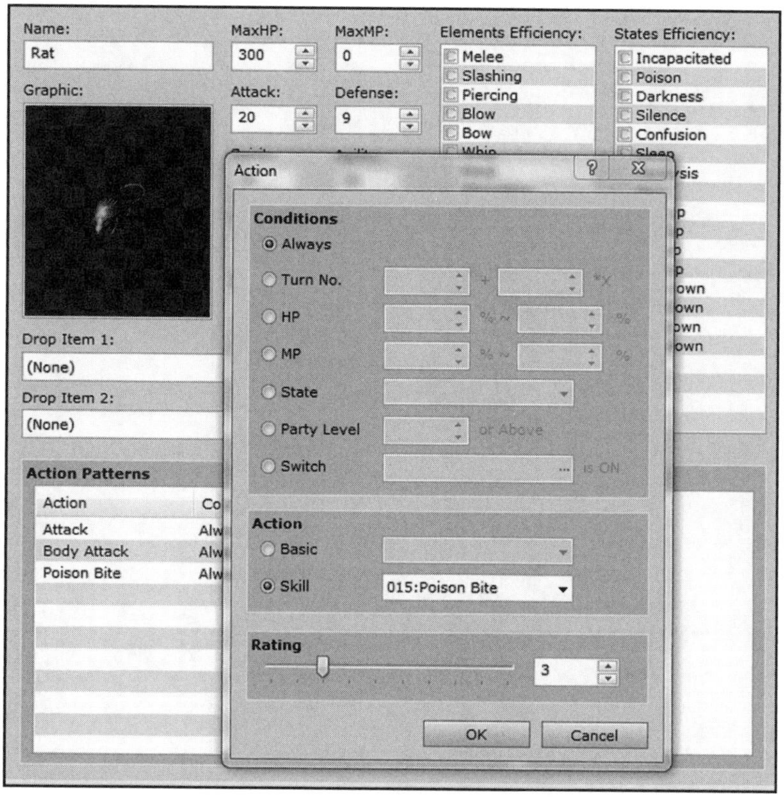

Figure 5.3
Give your Rat a Poison Bite attack with a Rating of 3.

that is one point away from the highest rating will occur roughly two-thirds of the time, while an action two points away will occur roughly one-third of the time. If you set the Rating at 3, this means the Poison Bite attack will only occur rarely, about one-third of the time. Since attacks are randomized, Ratings allow you to put restraints on their occurrence in battles.

Click OK when you're done.

Now that we've set Poison Bite to Rating 3, we might as well set Body Attack to Rating 4. Do that now.

Drop Items   You can also define what items a monster might drop after it's slain and what chance it might drop them.

Select Scarecrow from the left-side list. In the main window, click the browse button [...] beside Drop Item 1 to open the Drop Item dialog window. Click

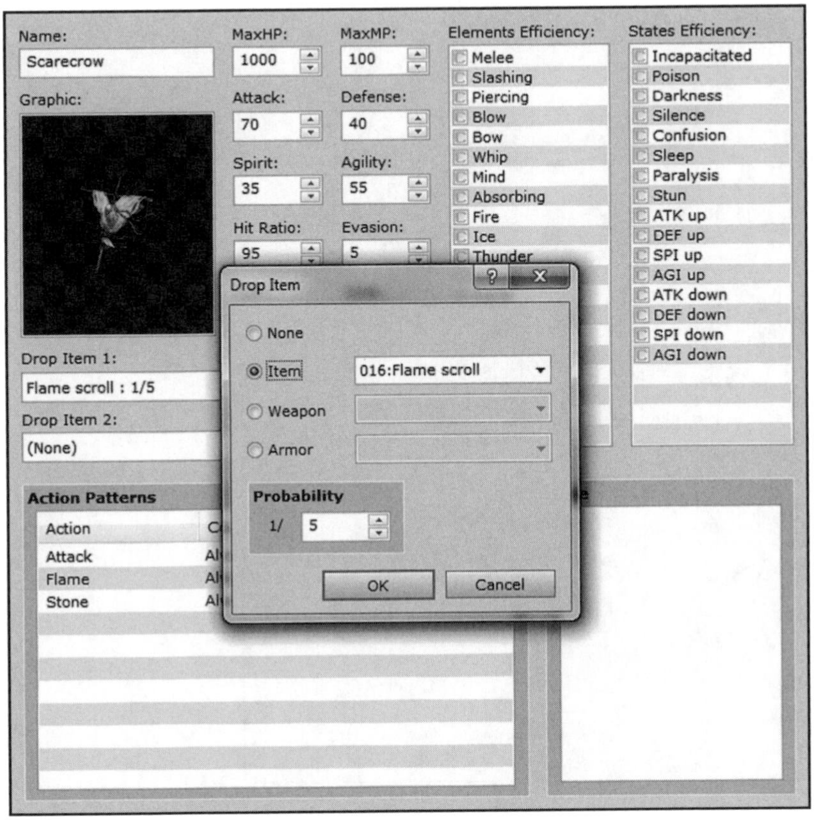

Figure 5.4
Give your Scarecrow a Flame Scroll for a dropped item.

the radio button next to Item and select 016: Flame Scroll from the items list. The default Probability for this action, you might note, is a one-in-one chance, which means always. You can raise the Probability. The higher the number is on the right, the less often the monster will drop this item. Set it to one-in-five (Figure 5.4), then click OK. This means that roughly every one in five Scarecrows the hero slays will drop a Flame Scroll, which grants the hero the chance to cast Flame at his opponents when in combat.

Of course, players will also be rewarded by gold, experience, or both after the successful completion of combat rounds (this is actually set by the stat fields EXP and Gold, just above where you see Drop Item 1). Dropped items such as the Flame Scroll are merely unexpected bonuses.

In a game of chance like the ones played in Las Vegas, people actually become obsessed in hopes of rare-but-not-unheard-of rewards they might win. They will keep putting money into machines on that slim off-chance that they will win it big. This is the same psychological mechanic dropped items give gamers who play RPGs. They may not get anything for a time while slashing and hacking monsters, and then suddenly they will hit the jackpot. When they do, it keeps the gamers playing in hopes they'll win it again—or find an even bigger reward!

Add more dropped items, if you like, to your other enemies. For instance, you might give Plant a Stimulant to drop, Ghost a Dispel Herb to drop, Lamia a Guard Up to drop, and so on.

Don't give one enemy an item it would never naturally be caught carrying, like the crows that drop gold or bullets in *Resident Evil 4*. Your rewards should make sense. Also, don't bulk up one enemy with too many powerful dropped items (unless he's a really difficult foe to beat). You don't want your game to be too easy.

Efficiencies   Just as player characters have element and state efficiencies, so, too, do monsters. If you don't recall, efficiencies are ways of rating how susceptible to a specific element or state a character is, on a scale from A (more vulnerable) to F (more resistant). As an example, Demon has a D in Fire and Darkness, becomes he comes from both and is therefore less hurt by them.

Go to your Deep One. His only efficiency, besides the average C that he has in almost all of them, is his B in Thunder. This means that he can be harmed more by thunder, lightning, and electrical attacks. This makes sense, because he is a merman and spends most of his time in or around water. Now let's add a B in Fire, because we want him to be hurt more by fire, which dries him out. And give him an F in Water. I mean, he spends all his time in the liquid substance, so why would it hurt him?

Take inventory of all your RPG Maker enemies. See what their efficiencies are and if any more of them need tweaking.

Creating a Custom Enemy

What if you decide you have a great idea for a monster, but it's not in the list? Simple: You add it! Let's do so now.

For Thug Wallow, you are going to add a creature called Darkling, which is a shadow-casting assassin who lives underground and in dark alleyways.

Click the Change Maximum button at the bottom of the Enemies section in the Database. Set the number to 31 and click OK. Select the new empty slot, 031, in the left-side list. You should see a blank slate appear in the main window.

Set Name as Darkling. Click on Graphic to set his sprite image to the Assassin, but give the image a purplish tint instead of brown by adjusting the Hue slider. For Efficiencies, give him an F in Darkness, a D in Earth, a B in Holy, and an A in Fire. Put a check in the checkbox next to Has Critical (found under Options in the middle of the window). Set his stats as follows:

- **MaxHP**—350
- **MaxMP**—20
- **Attack**—25
- **Defense**—30
- **Spirit**—30
- **Agility**—50
- **Hit Ratio**—95
- **Evasion**—5
- **EXP**—112
- **Gold**—175

For Action Patterns, add two more attacks: Double Attack with a Rating of 4 and Shade with a Rating of 3. For Drop Items, add two: Potion with a 1:3 chance and Speed Up with a 1:8 chance. Click Apply when you're done, to save your changes to the Database.

See Figure 5.5 for what your finished Darkling should look like.

Editing RPG Maker Troops

The Enemies tab of the Database is akin to a bestiary list. Monsters can attack singly or in groups. They're often more fearsome when attacking in groups. You organize combat formations in RPG Maker by use of troops. Troops are groups of enemies, although a single combatant can appear on his own. Troops can be found under the Troops tab of the Database. Go there now.

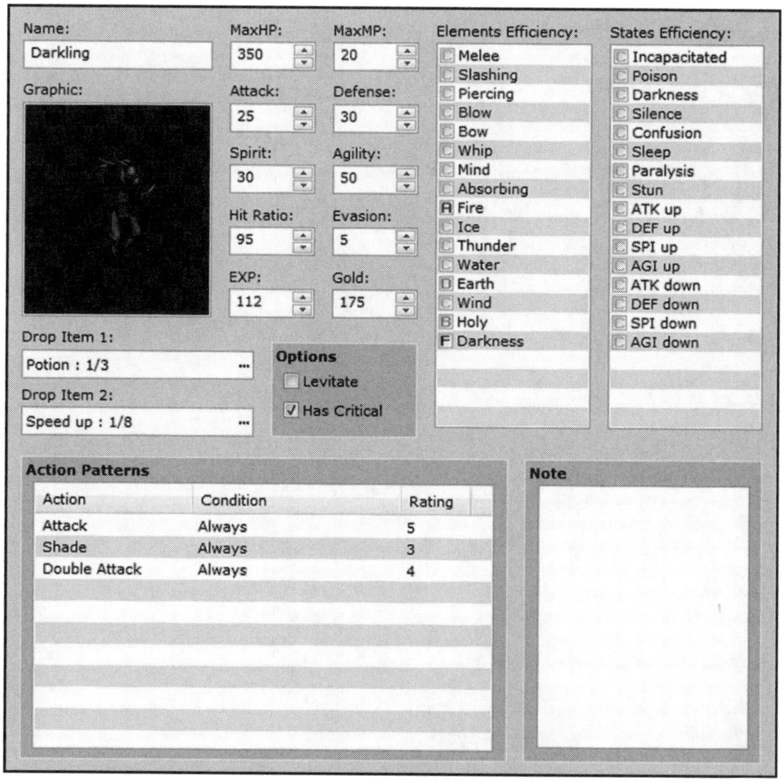

Name: Darkling

Graphic:

MaxHP: 350
MaxMP: 20

Attack: 25
Defense: 30

Spirit: 30
Agility: 50

Hit Ratio: 95
Evasion: 5

EXP: 112
Gold: 175

Drop Item 1: Potion : 1/3
Drop Item 2: Speed up : 1/8

Elements Efficiency:
- C Melee
- C Slashing
- C Piercing
- C Blow
- C Bow
- C Whip
- C Mind
- C Absorbing
- A Fire
- C Ice
- C Thunder
- C Water
- D Earth
- C Wind
- B Holy
- F Darkness

States Efficiency:
- C Incapacitated
- C Poison
- C Darkness
- C Silence
- C Confusion
- C Sleep
- C Paralysis
- C Stun
- C ATK up
- C DEF up
- C SPI up
- C AGI up
- C ATK down
- C DEF down
- C SPI down
- C AGI down

Options
- ☐ Levitate
- ☑ Has Critical

Action Patterns

Action	Condition	Rating
Attack	Always	5
Shade	Always	3
Double Attack	Always	4

Note

Figure 5.5
Your new Darkling enemy.

Troop Names

Click on Snake*2 in the left-side list and you'll see that it is a group of two Dinosaurs. Why didn't the name auto-update when we did our name change? Because you can name troops anything you like, just as you can enemies. See the button marked Autoname? Click it, and Snake*2 will become Dinosaur*2. Basically, this is how all the troops were originally created in RPG Maker. The name is independent of the enemies within the troop, however. So if you update the name of an enemy, you have to come to the Troops tab and update the names here, too.

On the other hand, you can name your troops whatever you like. For instance, you could name the Dinosaur*2 troop Couple of Dinosaurs, or the Rat*3 troop Pack of Rats. If you do change the name of troops, just remember what they are and how many enemies are in each one.

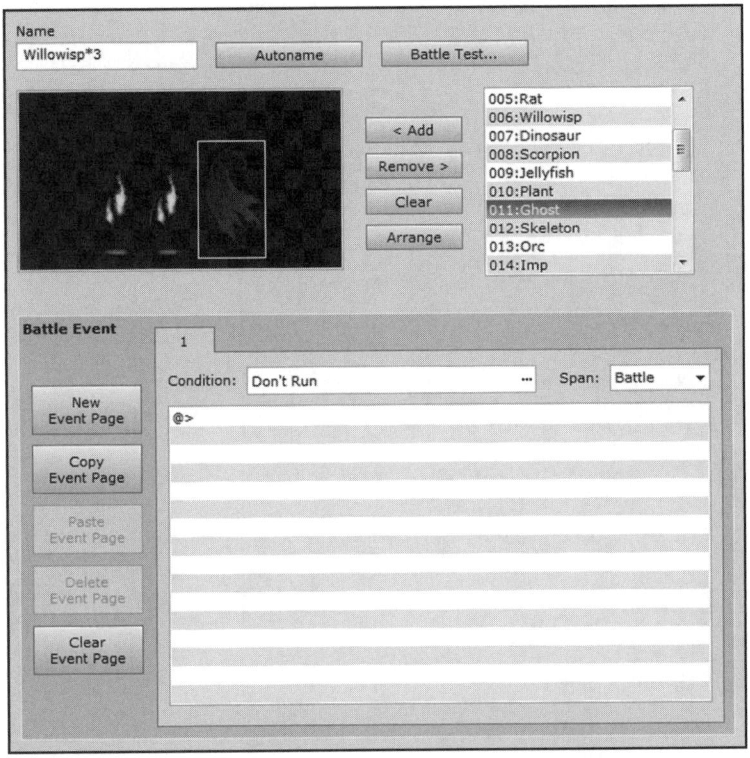

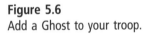

Figure 5.6
Add a Ghost to your troop.

For now, go to Puppet*2, Sahagin*2, Gargoyle*2, and Darklord (and any other enemies you might have changed the name of) and hit the Autoname button. Now that their names are correct, let's edit an existing troop.

Troop Formations

Click on Willowisp*3 and select the middle Willowisp in the graphic window. Click Remove> to delete him. Pick the Ghost from the right-side list and click <Add and you should see his sprite appear in the graphic window (Figure 5.6).

Move the Ghost near the middle of the graphic window and the Willowisps further out to the side, and then click the Autoname button. The name should change to Willowisp*2, Ghost (Figure 5.7). Click Apply to save your changes to the Database.

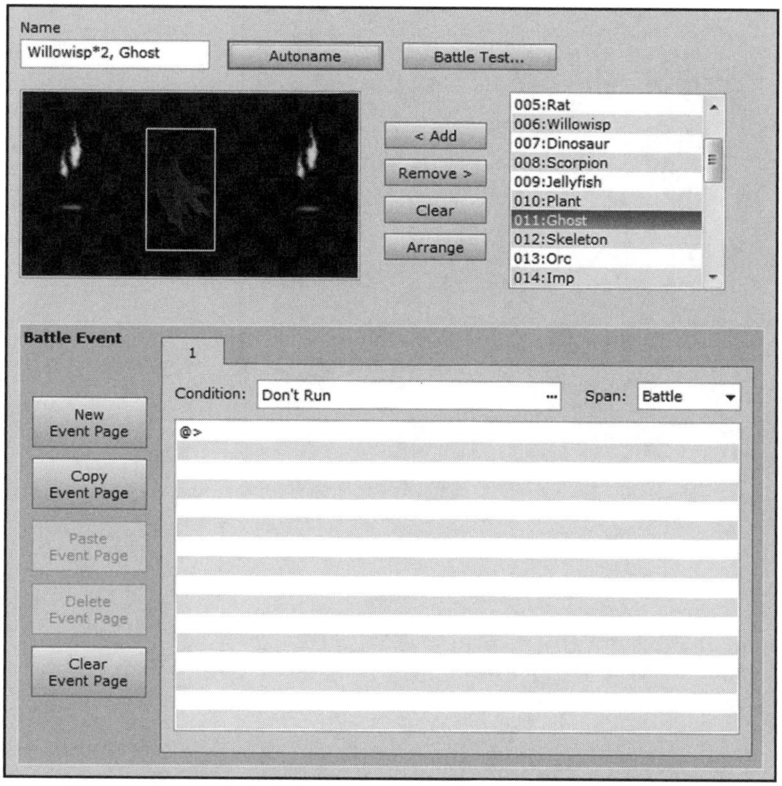

Figure 5.7
Move the Ghost and Willowisps around and then rename them.

Battle Events

When viewing Troops, the large field at the bottom of the main window is an event list called Battle Events. You can add events to battle sequences here, by writing or placing event commands in this field. This works similar to the List of Event Commands you see in editing regular events.

The most common Battle Event you might issue to a troop is a display message. Let's do that now.

Select Korgan from the left-side list (in the Troops tab of the Database). Double-click the first line in the Battle Events field. In the Event Commands dialog window that opens up, go to Tab 1 and click Show Text. Enter the following text:

Figure 5.8
Pick this face for Korgan.

```
\c[10]Korgan:\c[0] You can never defeat me,
you pathetic worms! I might as well put you
out of your misery.
```

Double-click on the graphic slot to add a face to this message. Select Monster from the list on the left and the face image at the bottom right for Korgan's face (Figure 5.8). Click OK twice to exit the edit mode and return to the Troops window. Your new Battle Event will appear in the list.

Click the top line of your new Battle Event to highlight and select the entire event. Above the Events field, click the browse button [. . .] beside Condition. In the Condition dialog window, put a check in the box next to Turn No. Make sure Turn No. is set to zero [0], as that means before the battle even begins. Then click OK.

Next, select Battle from the Span drop-down list, if it's not already selected. Span, when set to Battle, will make sure the event only happens once per battle sequence. You could, with some events, set them to recur every turn or moment using Span.

To see your Battle Event in action, click the Battle Test button at the top of the main troop window. A window will pop up, allowing you to configure the

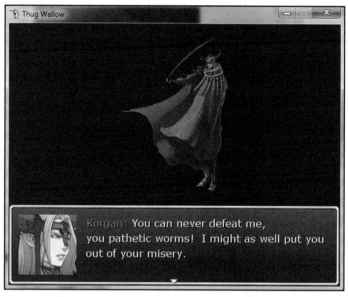

Figure 5.9
The fight with Korgan is on!

testing party. Leave the defaults in place and click OK. You will see a direct example of what will happen in-game if the troop Korgan is encountered (Figure 5.9). When you're done playing through the battle, which will be incredibly short-lived, because Korgan is the main boss of Thug Wallow and your initial party is all beginners, exit the window by clicking the X close button.

Back in the Database window, click Apply to save your changes to the Database.

Creating Custom Troops

Use the Change Maximum button to raise the maximum number of available troops in our list to 32. Select the first empty slot, 031, and use the <Add button to add two Darklings. Then click the Autoname button so that your troop 031 becomes Darkling*2.

For 032, add three Darklings and hit the Autoname button so it is called Darkling*3. You now have inserted two troops including your custom monsters. See how easy that was?

Click OK to save your changes and close the Database window.

States

We have not focused on this before, and so you might be curious. Just what are states, and how do they work? States are conditions that affect a character, be it a party member or enemy. States can temporarily change the amount of damage a character does per attack, drain his life, paralyze him so he can't move, increase his defense, and so on. Some states only take effect in battle, while others can still be in effect while the character explores the game map. The three most common states include:

- Incapacitated—The character is knocked out and cannot participate in the battle.

- Darkness—The character misses 75% of his physical attacks during battle.

- Poison—The character loses a little bit of life (HPs) every action he attempts.

Mapping Battle Encounters

Tip

"Who combats bravely is not therefore brave, / He dreads a death-bed like the meanest slave: Who reasons wisely is not therefore wise, / - His pride in reasoning, not in acting lies."

— Alexander Pope

Once you've created entities and developed troop and battle sequences, it's time to place encounters, which will lead the gamer to the battles. Encounters can be random or they can be triggered by a fixed event.

Random Encounters

Let's start by setting a random encounter in the World Map. In the RPG Maker editor window, right-click on World Map in your maps list and select Map Properties (or select World map from the list and press Spacebar) to open the Map Properties window. The Map Properties window can be used to name and set map dimensions, which we've already witnessed. You can also set random encounters here.

Double-click the first empty line in the field under Encounters. For Troop, add 001: Slime*2 and click OK. Add one more encounter type and make it 002: Bat*2.

That way we have one of two types of troops the player might wander upon while exploring the World Map. If you want the player to encounter one troop more often than another, you can add that troop a second or even a third time.

The reason you should choose the first two troops is because they're the easiest to beat, and they will be the first monsters the player encounters when they set out to explore your game world. That way, the player can beat a few monsters, raise his characters' stats, and be tough enough to face harder monsters later on. This is a method of ramping up the difficulty of the game, so the enemies the player faces are never too tough but just challenging enough to carry the gamer through.

Below the Troop field of the Encounters panel of the Map Properties window is a setting for Steps. This is the maximum number of steps the hero can take in the current map before initializing a battle encounter with one of the defined troops. The default here is set to 30 (squares), but our map is only 32 squares by 21 squares. Because the map is so small, we need to lower the number of Steps to 5 (Figure 5.10).

Test it out. Play through your game, saving your project first, and walk around the World Map a bit to strike up some random encounters. Also, notice the fade-in and way the battles commence. See how easy hacking up Bats and Slime is? Exit your play-test when you're through.

The following are two more maps you need to set up random encounters for:

- **Warehouse**—Darkling*2 and Darkling*3; Steps 5.
- **CVesper 1**—Spider*3 (twice), Rat*3 (twice), Skeleton*2, Ghost*3, Willowisp*2 + Ghost, Mimic, and Vampire; Steps 10.

Fixed Event Encounters

Let's place a fixed event encounter in one of our maps. This encounter will be with the main boss, Korgan.

Go to CVesper 2. Right-click on a square just in front of the throne and add a New Event. Name this event KorganBattle. Double-click on the Graphic window and select Monster from the list. Then select the bottom-right-most character sprite where he's facing down and click OK. For Trigger, set him to Player Touch, so as soon as the player brushes against him it will trigger the battle.

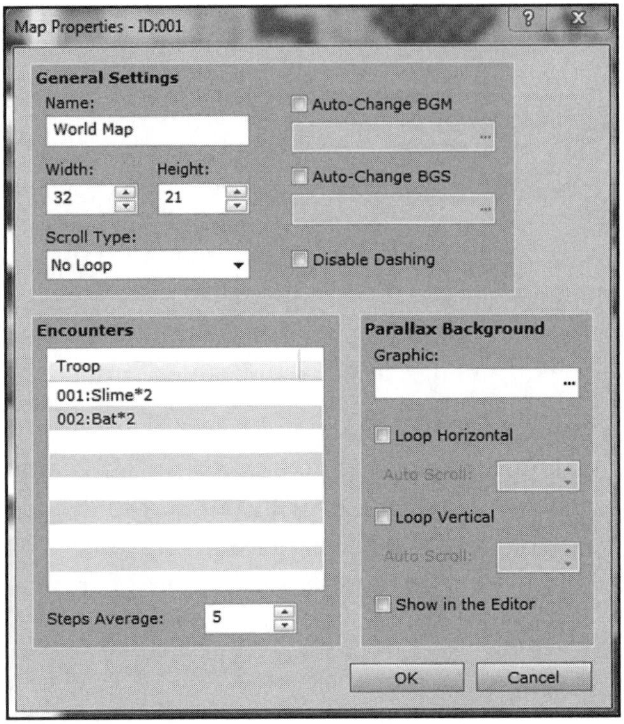

Figure 5.10
Create a random encounter where the player might face Slime or Bats at every 5 steps.

Insert a new command in the List of Event Commands. Choose Battle Processing from Tab 3. For Direct Designation, pick 029: Korgan. In the Battle Processing window, you can also give the player the chance to flee or to have the game continue even if the heroes all die (which is great for those plot-twists in RPGs, where even though the heroes don't win, the game isn't over yet!) by putting a check in the checkboxes. However, for this battle event, you don't want either option to be valid, so leave their boxes blank (Figure 5.11). Click OK three times to exit to the main editor.

To test this fixed event encounter, you need to right-click somewhere in CVesper 2 and choose Set as Starting Position > Player. Play-test your level, saving your game project first. When you walk up on Korgan, he should make his snide remark and then initiate a fight with you. Exit the play-test when you're through (or dead).

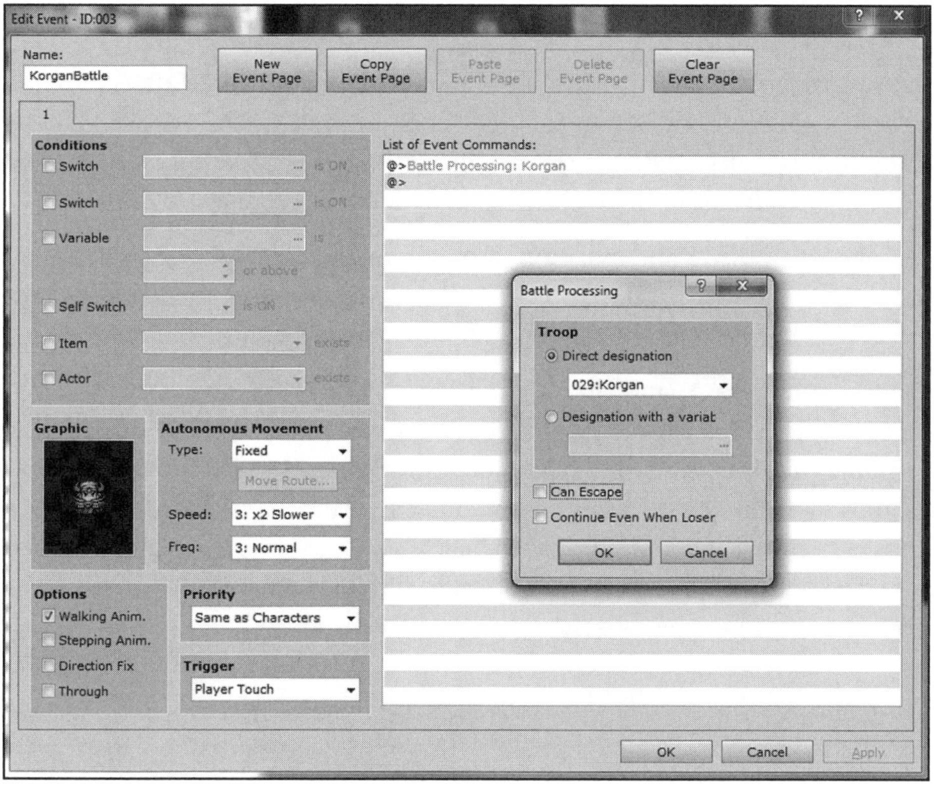

Figure 5.11
Set up Korgan so he will fight the player on contact.

Go to Timber Town and right-click near the front entrance of the town and add your player's starting position here, instead, as that is where the game will really begin. Save your changes to the Thug Wallow game project.

Tip

> In games like *Pokémon*, you might notice that within the same map, players get attacked more often on grass tiles than on pathway tiles. Feasibly, you could do the same thing. Create a new entity that is invisible (has no graphic). Place it on only those tiles where you want attacks to occur and set it to Trigger on Player Touch (Priority is Below Characters). The first event command you want to set is Control Variables, with a single variable you should name Attack Rate set to Operand at Random (some number between 1 and 5). Then add a Conditional Branch that checks to see if Attack Rate comes up 1 (odds of 1 in 5); if it does, call Battle Processing with whatever troop you desire. Then copy and paste this entity to all the other tiles you want, and you have just created dangerous areas within a map without setting random encounters for the whole map.

WHAT'S NEXT?

You should now understand how to add, edit, and customize monsters, define their battle formations, and set up combat encounters in RPG Maker. You've filled Thug Wallow for grand life-and-death adventure. Next you'll learn how to inject story into your game through the use of quest objectives.

But first, take some time and position some monsters into your own original game project. Remember to start off with easy monsters and then make them harder to defeat the further into your game your player gets.

A more advanced project, and one that would not truly be advisable for Thug Wallow, is to set up a side-view battle system as discussed at http://www .rmxpunlimited.net/forums/topic/5956-side-view-battle-system. If the discussion has moved from the RMXPUnlimited.net's forum, you might conduct a web search for "RPG Maker VX side view battle system." The tutorial written by Claimh requires more advanced coding and character sprites for each of the heroes, but the effects come closer to many of the modern sprite-based RPGs.

CHAPTER 6

QUEST DESIGN

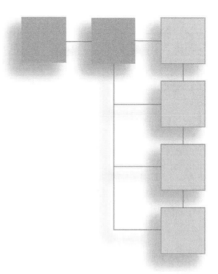

In this chapter you will learn:

- To immerse your gamers in narrative
- To find out your player's objectives
- The many types of game challenges you can use
- How quests are created for RPGs
- To build quests in RPG Maker with zero programming

Right now your game is almost a complete game, isn't it? So it would seem. You have avatars, NPCs, enemies, imaginative environments, and much more. But right now there's something very significant missing from your game. That something is purpose.

Without a purpose, your player is in effect wandering around, colliding with allies and enemies, and not accomplishing a whole lot. Players of RPGs need to have a mission, a reason for playing, and that reason boils down to questing.

A hero doesn't just wake up in the morning, eager to fight dragons. A hero must have a grander impetus. Usually, somebody is begging the hero to fight dragons. Or the dragons are attacking something (or someone) the hero loves and wishes to save from harm. This is ample motivation to make the hero *want* to fight dragons every day.

A quest motivates your gamers to want to explore your beautiful maps, talk to your NPCs, and vanquish your monsters. A quest puts a narrative touch on your whole game. In this chapter, we'll look at player interaction, why challenging the gamer is so important, and how to design proper quests for your fantasy RPG.

RPGS AND INTERACTIVE STORYTELLING

Face it: games are interactive. That's part of their playability. Games are not passive entertainment forms, such as watching a football game on the television or reading a good book. Games are active: they put you into the football field and place a ball of pigskin in your hands, or put you onto the page and in the middle of the action! They expect you to react.

RPGs are not like traditional stories at all. Stories are typically a series of facts that occur in time-sequenced order suggestive of a cause-and-effect relationship. In other words, a story plods from step to step in a linear fashion. A video game, on the other hand, has a lot of immersion to it, and players play it over and over again to explore new opportunities and avenues for expression. A story is relatively static, while an RPG is dynamic and constantly in motion!

Players don't want to be told a story; they want to tell or discover the story themselves. Listening to long-winded exposition, forced to watch long animated sequences, and even talking with characters should *always* be secondary to exploration, combat, manipulation, and problem solving. In other words, story is supplementary to interactivity.

Tip

LOUIS: Stay away, Arayam . . . You spell trouble!

ARAYAM: Sorry. Never learned my letters.

—Septerra Core: Legacy of the Creator

There is major significance to you, the designer, in providing a truly interactive RPG, one that does not lie cold. To do so, there are several steps to follow:

- Immerse your player
- Empower your player
- Keep your player entertained

- Provide reactive environments
- Challenge your player

Immerse Your Player

Have you ever played a game that kept you so focused that when your friend called or your parents interrupted, you realized with shock you'd been playing for hours straight? Have you ever been playing a game so intently you didn't want to stop? If the answer to either of these was, "Yes," then it's because you've discovered a key element of popular games: *immersion*.

Immersion makes gamers want to spend more time playing a game. It creates addictive game play by submerging players in the entertainment form. With immersion, you get so engrossed in a game that you forget it's a game! You lose track of the outside world (see Figure 6.1).

Different Depths of Immersion

The following are the different depths of immersion the gamer feels when playing a game:

Figure 6.1
This gamer has become so engrossed in his game he might not hear you if you tried getting his attention, because you're not part of his game world.

- **Curiosity**—The player feels a slight but fleeting interest in the game.

- **Sympathy**—The player is paying attention to the game but is still not personally motivated; he can put the game down if he wants.

- **Identification**—The player identifies with her character and suddenly has an invested interest in the game's outcome.

- **Empathy**—Even though the characters are make-believe, the player shares a strong emotional connection with one or more of them and wants to see the best ending to the game.

- **Transportation**—This is the "plenary state" or dream-like trance that you enter into whenever you are really intent in playing a game. The game becomes more real to the player than the room where he's playing it.

Perhaps to better understand how to make a game more immersive, it is first imperative to appreciate why players play games to begin with. What are a player's motivations?

What Are Your Player's Motivations?

Tim Schafer, designer of such games as *Grim Fandango*, *Psychonauts*, and *Brutal Legend*, once said that all games are about wish fulfillment. Whenever a player plays a game, he is put into a fictional scenario that he cannot experience in real life, and he can delight in the wonder, newness, and thrill of it all, at least for the duration of the game.

Simple wish fulfillment is a vague over-generalization of why players play games. There are many more factors that motivate people to play games. Let's take a look, briefly, at a few. As you read through these motives, consider what makes you want to play the games that you like!

- **Escapism**—One of the top motivating factors reported by gamers is escapism. After a long day of real life, it's nice for them to escape from the mundane world and enter an imaginative, sometimes "limitless," universe, where they can do whatever they want and have the approximation of control. This is known as *cathartic release* by doctors, and it's been shown to improve behavior in even the most stable citizen. Taboos often become okay in video games, for reasons of cathartic release.

- **Competition**—Lots of people play multiplayer online games, or MMOs, in order to compete with other players, either indirectly by gaining more tributes than other players or directly in player-versus-player, or PVP, confrontations. Do you find that the spirit of competition motivates you to play games?

- **Social Interaction**—All multiplayer games contain strong elements of social interaction, whether they are online, LAN-based, or multiplayer console games. Players can chat with other gamers over the Internet, even talk to other gamers by using headsets, and communication runs the gamut from taunts to strategy discussion. Some gamers band together in guilds, clans, or other social groups, often to team up together or to manage simulated worlds and societies. Some of these games have also sparked a micro-economy of gamers buying and selling in-game merchandise in the real world for real coin.

- **Creative Expression**—These games allow players to exhibit some form of creative expression. Games like *Dance Dance Revolution* and *Rock Band* allow gamers to express themselves musically (see Figure 6.2), while games like *Dungeon Keeper* and *The Sims* allow gamers to build original environments to be utilized as game environments. Then there are countless RPGs, sports games, and fighting games today that allow players to customize their characters in unique ways. All of these focus on creative expression factors.

- **Addiction**—A motivating factor that is difficult to clearly define is addiction, an intangible factor that results in an almost constant urge to play a game or type of game, without a rational explanation. Addiction works on a basic psychological level, consisting more of feeling than thought. Many people have criticized games for being addictive substances and game designers as being little better than peddlers of a narcotic agent, yet this scenario has always been overruled by psychologists who point that the same traits of game addicts exist in bookworms, who cannot put down a new book. Have you ever found yourself playing a game for no apparent reason? Was it difficult for you to tear yourself away, even if you wanted to?

Figure 6.2
Dance Dance Revolution allows gamers to express their rhythm (or lack thereof).

- **Therapy**—For some players, games can be a form of therapy. I do not mean cathartic release, as that is a part of escapism. Some doctors are beginning to prescribe games to their patients in order to relax them emotionally and to engage in eye-hand coordination for physical therapy. Patients who've had surgery to their fingers and hands are often encouraged to play console games, because they provide physical therapy for their recuperating digits, while at the same time removing patients from their misery by providing escapism. Psychologists have even used games to cure their patients' phobias.

Emotioneering

One of the premiere ways to inspire immersion in players, to gently sink them into your game world, is by getting them to care. Once a player cares about his or her character, the outcome of the game, or the game's story and/or

Figure 6.3
Marc Eckō.

environment, then you can get that player to make hard decisions and manipulate him through challenges you set up.

You will learn that making players care about what happens in a game is not always an easy task. A radical way game developers are approaching their trade is through *emotioneering*, where gamer emotions are used as buttons to make the experience more fraught, immersive, and riveting.

Fashion design guru Marc Eckō (shown in Figure 6.3) broke onto the video game world in 2006 with *Getting Up: Contents Under Pressure*, a game about a graffiti artist. Eckō called games "emotional entertainment products" because he considered games to be a form of entertainment unique in that it's the only form of entertainment that forces players to interact with it on a closely personal and emotional level. Emotions can be used to make players care about the games they play.

Eckō is not the only game creator out there who shares this viewpoint. Screenwriter David Freeman started the Freeman Group, which studies the many ways writers can put emotions into games. Freeman pioneered *emotioneering*, a cluster of techniques seeking to evoke in gamers a breadth and depth of rich emotions. These emotions not only create strong immersion, but they also generate control points for the designer to maneuver the player through the game.

Most emotioneering tricks are subtle triggers you can plant within your game's story, triggers that demand an emotional connection. Consider the following:

- Keep the plot twists coming. Remember: "Out of the frying pan, into the fire!"

- Have the other characters recognize or refer to one another as if they were real people.

- Give the player ambivalent feelings toward an ally or enemy character, like loving and hating them at the same time.

- Force the player to do something evil or otherwise violate their character's integrity.

- Have the player discover he's been tricked or betrayed by an ally.

- Set up incongruous events (like when the main character of Nintendo's *Chrono Cross* suddenly switches places with the main villain and has to gain new allies after losing all his old friends).

Conflict

One of the ways that games keep players involved is through the nature of *conflict*, which can be emotional for the player.

Chris Crawford once said, "Conflict is an intrinsic element of all games. It can be direct or indirect, violent or nonviolent, but it is always present in every game." He goes on to describe why: "Conflict implies danger, danger means risk or harm, and harm is undesirable."

Conflict in established storytelling is straightforward. The audience is introduced to a character, made to feel something about that character, and then shown a dilemma that character faces. Whether or not the character survives the dilemma or triumphs in the end is the suspense-building conflict the writers weave into the story. The writers know they have to keep the players on the edge of their seats in anticipation of the outcome.

Video games are not static. The player is often given control of a central figure in the game story. This puts the audience in direct control of the story, and gives them an abiding interest in the main character's future. The audience has a more intimate experience with the game story, because the story character is, in essence, them. But how do you create tension? What could threaten the player enough to inspire conflict within the game? Surely there will be objectives for the player, but what threats will the player face?

amazon.com

Your order of August 16, 2012 (Order ID 104-9232690-1625045)

Qty.	Item	Item Price	Total
1	**RPG Maker for Teens** Duggan, Michael --- Paperback (** P-1-E34F185 **) 1435459660	$23.08	$23.08

	Subtotal	$23.08
	Shipping & Handling	$3.99
	Order Total	$27.07
	Paid via credit/debit	$27.07
	Balance due	$0.00

This shipment completes your order.

Have feedback on how we packaged your order? Tell us at www.amazon.com/packaging.

Most video games feature "hit points" where, after getting hit enough times, the player's onscreen avatar expires. This is why so many games are slammed by the media for having too much violence, because the threat of danger is represented as bodily harm coming to characters in the game.

It is very important to know the difference between conflict and violence, because they are not one and the same. The gaming rating board ESRB has eight different definitions for violence. They are:

- **Animated Blood**: Discolored and/or unrealistic depictions of blood.

- **Blood**: Depictions of blood.

- **Blood and Gore**: Depictions of blood and/or mutilation of body parts.

- **Cartoon Violence**: Violent actions involving cartoon-like situations and characters; may include violence where a character is unharmed after the action has been inflicted.

- **Fantasy Violence**: Violent actions of a fantasy nature, involving human or non-human characters in situations easily distinguishable from real life.

- **Intense Violence**: Graphic and realistic-looking depictions of physical conflict; may involve extreme and/or realistic blood, gore, weapons, and depictions of human injury and death.

- **Mild Violence**: Mild scenes depicting characters in unsafe and/or violent situations.

- **Violence**: Scenes involving aggressive conflict.

Note that violence is "aggressive conflict," as opposed to being conflict in itself. Violence, therefore, is just one type of conflict that can be represented in games.

In the day and age of coin-op arcades, the loss of their quarters was enough to make players wag their heads in shame if they lost (Figure 6.4). Today's players are forced back to previously saved checkpoints or made to lose treasure or experience points they have gained as their punishment for losing. The penalty has to appear large enough to threaten players to seek greater rewards within the game, and one way to do that is through violence or implied violence.

Figure 6.4
Spending quarters to play video games was one way designers used to make games more intense.

What are some other ways to threaten players that do not include violence? If you think about it, almost all games have a penalty/reward system built in, where the player can get hurt (penalty) or gain something (reward). The simplest game is one where a player gains ambiguous score points for doing well in the game and loses the same score points for not doing well. That being said, the scoring methods and design of the game are up to you; as long as you impart that information to your player, your game will be fair. Therefore, you could have a completely non-violent game that does not upset anybody and still have a fun game.

Player Empowerment

Tip

"Our species can only survive if we have obstacles to overcome. You take away all obstacles. Without them to strengthen us, we will weaken and die."

—Captain Kirk, *Star Trek* ("Metamorphosis")

Putting the controls in your player's hands can sound scary for any game designer at first. You are handing over some of your power to allow the player to interact with the game you've provided. But without elevating your player to this status, you will never make a great fun game, because games are all about interactivity.

If you fail to empower your player with interactive control, you fail as a game designer.

Teach Your Player How to Play

First, you have to teach your gamer how to play your game.

Every game is slightly different in the way it is played. Games of the same genre are generally similar in their game play. You might notice that almost all classic fantasy RPGs have the same underlying mechanics, and RPG Maker uses those to its advantage as a game creation tool.

Tom Smith, once creative manager at THQ and now senior producer at Disney Mobile, says, "Communication is hard because players are not here to learn; they're here to play. But if they don't learn, they will never know how to play."

Things to think about when teaching players how to play your game include:

- Who is the player playing as in your game? What is his avatar?
- What can the player do in your game? What are the controls?
- Why should the player play your game? What are the goals and rewards?

Probably the easiest and most efficient way of telling the player how to play the game is to have a short briefing before the game starts. This requires players to have excellent memories, or for the controls to be so simple they're virtually intuitive. Or you could weave the instruction into the first level of game play, where short pop-up messages give the player hints about how to play the game, like: "Press A to jump over hedge." There are some games that use these pop-up messages as gates, blocking the player from moving on in the game until the player shows he understands the control system. Forcing the player to show he "gets it" is a neat way of reinforcing your message, but it can also make players feel like they aren't in control, robbing them of their entertainment, and on rare occasions it can reveal weaknesses in the game interface.

Of course, most shipped games come with short manuals that can help the player learn how to play the game, but most gamers these days pass over the manuals and jump right into playing the game, often assuming the designers have made some leeway in the learning curve.

Show your player the ropes and then step back and let him make the big choices governing the game's direction.

Give Your Player Important Choices to Make

Part of empowerment is giving the player choices. For your game to work, you must include the following:

- Difficult, not easy, decisions that have to be made by the gamer
- Tangible consequences for decisions the gamer makes

Tabletop RPGs like *Dungeons & Dragons* run on the imagination of the players, including the game master, in ad hoc fashion, starting with one suggested possibility and continuing open-ended. Computer RPGs do not have that luxury. In computer RPGs, the narrative has to be completely decided on and programmed before letting the player toy with it, so there are fewer chances for leaving anything open-ended.

Yet there is a joint partnership between you, the game designer, and your future gamer. You essentially must pass off partial control of your game and its contingent story to the gamer. Doing this is exciting. It is even more exciting when you are watching your testers playing through your game missions and observing how they make different decisions than you would.

When creating decisions for the player to make, you must remember a couple of rules:

- First of all, no one likes being "led by the nose," or feeling like he has no control over what happens.
- The choices the player is given should be reasonable ones. Don't ask her to go in a door marked "Great Stuff Inside" and then have a brick wall on the other side of it. Likewise, don't ask her to choose between getting a magnificent sword and a pile of junk, because she'll pick the sword every time.
- The choices the player is given should be real. Don't invent arbitrary decisions, like asking the player if he wants to go through Door A or Door B, when both doors lead to the same room. To the player, this is as bad as cheating. Also, the choices shouldn't be too obvious. If you ask the player if he wants to pick up a pile of gold, and there are no repercussions for him if he does, except that he gets richer, he will pick up

the pile of gold and shake his head at the stupidity of a game designer who would create such a hollow choice.

- The choice a player must make must never be an uninformed one. In other words, you must give the player enough knowledge to make a proper decision. If you leave out the fact that if he keeps the Sword of Eons, he will have to slaughter his only surviving sibling, you are sure to see a player throw a tantrum.

The best choices of all to present to your gamer are the difficult ones, especially if there is a perceptible tension surrounding the outcome of the decision.

For instance, say that the player has one onyx arrow, which he is led to believe might be the very last one because onyx arrows are extremely rare. The onyx arrow, he's been told, is the only weapon that can hurt Baron Bone Daddy. Now imagine you have scripted a scene where the player's ally gets hit with a poison gas cloud of a death mushroom and lies dying. The player is informed that the only antidote for the poison is an onyx arrow melted down and mixed with bitter root. The player is now faced with a dilemma: he can choose to save his friend and lose the only weapon he has to kill Baron Bone Daddy, or he can kill Baron Bone Daddy and lose his BFF.

This can be an extremely tense decision if you script it just right, with tangible results either way.

Keep Your Player Entertained

Tip

"Fairy tales do not tell children the dragons exist. Children already know that dragons exist. Fairy tales tell children the dragons can be killed."

—G.K. Chesterton

A story is about a decent fellow having stones thrown at him, and we, the audience, wait with baited breath to see what he will do. Video games, on the other hand, are unique, because we don't sit on our laurels and watch the action: we are that guy! And we decide what the guy will do when the stones are launched at him.

Figure 6.5
Journals, notes, taped messages, recordings, and so on are unique ways games use to impart back story.

There are three major ways story is told in most RPGs that weds narrative with game play. These are back story, cut-scenes, and in-game artifacts.

- *Back story* is the history of all events that have led up to the current action of the game. This can be as far-reaching as the creation myth of the world composing the game's setting, or the abduction of a perilous princess from her tower the night before the player's character wakes up and starts his quest. Back story is sometimes shown in a cut-scene before the game starts or through in-game artifacts, such as journals (Figure 6.5). It can also be information passed along through dialogue with NPCs.

- *Cut-scenes* are the short in-game movies that serve as the vehicle for exposition you find in other media. During a typical cut-scene, the player's controls are taken away from him, while he is forced to watch and listen to the onscreen action. Cut-scenes often reveal clues, reward the player, give the player a break to stop and breathe before continuing the action, and continue the game narrative.

- *In-game artifacts* are those objects discovered during game play that enhance or reveal story elements. They include talking to NPCs, reading journals and letters, and stumbling upon significant weapons, items, or landmarks. These items of information help divulge back story and current events of the game narrative.

So remember:

- Use narrative tools, such as setting and journals, to tell the story
- Accept that most of the actual story will have to be revealed in back story

Note

Where is the writer in a game studio? Sometimes the actual writing is outsourced when needed to develop the game story for a particular project. Often, due to the importance of game play and stable mechanics and great-looking graphics over narrative, traditional writers are not always in high demand in the game industry. This is unfortunate and might change as more developers attempt to integrate storytelling with game play for a more cohesive game experience.

Right now, it is not all that unusual for a game designer or director to write the story, or for the members of the design team to write the story and dialogue for their respective game levels or missions. There are only a few writers, such as Douglas Adams, Jane Jensen, or Clive Barker, who have forayed into the game industry and come back with a gem.

Provide Reactive Environments

The environment in video games must be somewhat reactive. Having *reactive environments* means that the game world responds to the player in logical and meaningful ways that help immerse the player in that game world.

This can mean that if the player sees a guy standing around as if he's waiting for something, the player's character should be able to walk up to and talk to the guy to find out some information about the location. Or if there appears to be a weak spot in a wall, a strong enough force from the player's character should be able to knock a hole through it. Or if the player sees a neat-looking door and wants to open it, he should be able to do so or you should let him know, "This door is locked. To open it, you must find a key." This empowers the player to explore the game's environment and to treat it as if it were its own real self-contained world.

The more interactive elements you can put into your game, the more "real" the game world will appear to your player. This takes time, trial, and effort, but the results can be uplifting. So when in doubt about whether to make the game background more interactive, always opt for the "yes" answer, although it usually means more work for you.

CHALLENGE YOUR PLAYER

Tip

"The very best games are the ones where you have to figure out what the object is. The trick is to provide direction subtle enough that it's not perceived immediately. Theme parks have that, too. When you enter Disneyland, you don't know the Sleeping Beauty Castle is your objective, but there's no doubt when you're in Town Square that you should be walking up Main Street USA. Just like in a great game, you always have an idea that you need to go this way or that way. Eventually you catch on to the themed worlds and the central hub."

—Danny Hills

A real game wouldn't be a game if it didn't offer the player a challenge. The types of challenges games offer vary widely, from the accumulation of resources to puzzles to self-preservation. Many challenges are staples of the game genres they belong in; others fit with the game play and are thus included.

Dennis Wixon who worked with Microsoft Games Studios in Redmond, Washington, says about challenges, "You're always trying to get the right level of challenge. You can't be too simple or it's not fun. [Nolan] Bushnell's famous quote is something along the lines of, 'A game should be easy to pick up and impossible to master.' We want that sweet spot where there's always another threshold to cross. In *Halo 1*, as we improved targeting, we found it was too intelligent and too simple. It was pretty straightforward for the Bungie team to fix that..."

Andrew Glassner calls this process the *game loop*, a cycle of repetitive steps your player takes to win at any given game challenge:

1. Player observes the situation

2. Player sets goals to overcome the challenge

3. Player researches or prepares

4. Player commits to plan and executes decisions

5. Player stops and compares the results of his actions to his original intention

6. Player evaluates the results

7. Player returns to step #1

Types of Game Challenges

Most of the time, challenges take the form of obstacles that must be overcome. These game obstacles, and the resulting types of game challenges, can be classified into these categories:

- Lock mechanisms
- Puzzles
- Mazes
- Monsters
- Traps
- Quests

Lock Mechanisms

Some of these challenges habitually appear as lock mechanisms, and players are used to them (and the standard manner in which the lock mechanisms must be unlocked). *Lock mechanisms* by their very nature fence the player in, preventing access to some area or reward in the game until that moment when the player beats the challenge and unlocks the next area or recovers the reward.

The simplest and most prosaic lock mechanism is a common lock: a locked door, a jammed gateway, or elevator without power stand in the way of the player getting to level three or three hundred. The player knows when encountering any aperture that is locked that he must find the key to unlocking it or else that area is completely off-limits to him (Figure 6.6).

Other lock mechanisms are more subtle. For instance, an overbearing guard standing at attention at the gate through which the player wants passage might just be overcome if the player bribes him with a peanut butter and banana sandwich.

And let's not forget blood locks. *Blood locks* are where the player is locked in a single locale (usually a room or arena) with lots of foes to defeat, and the exit from the locale will not appear until the player destroys all oncoming enemies. Blood locks can be seen in most third-person fighting and shooter games.

Whatever the lock mechanism you might use, it will be a powerful vital tool in your arsenal of game play devices, and it should be scripted with intelligence and creativity to work correctly.

Puzzles

The most noted use of puzzles in video games, aside from actual puzzle games like *Bejeweled* and *Tetris*, are the use of objects to further the story. If the player

Figure 6.6
The door is locked, which tells the gamer that this way is off-limits or that he needs to find a way around it.

does not know what key will unlock a specific lock mechanism to continue his quest in the game, he will have to find it.

Some puzzles are cryptographic or clue-driven in nature, where the player must supply a crucial bit of info, such as a password, key code, whodunit, etc., to pass by a guard, a locked door, open a wall safe, or close the case.

To figure out what the code/password/other is, the player must search for clues. These clues are often left lying around in convenient journals, computer e-mail messages, tape recordings, or found by talking to people. The player may have to figure out what something cryptic means in order to identify a clue, such as a cryptogram (a short encrypted text message) or rebus (a word puzzle that uses pictures or parts of pictures to represent words).

Mazes

Below-average gamers can get lost in standard game levels, so making the level more difficult to get through by adding in lots of twists, turns, and dead ends might quickly make for a player headache. On the other hand, if you use an in-game map or set up a trail of bread crumbs and some clever surprises along the way, a maze can become a wonderfully entertaining way to break the monotony of locked doors.

A maze can be one of the simplest ways to make a game more fun, as long as you don't leave the player completely in the dark on where to go. Besides, no one likes a straight-and-narrow game environment with nothing in it but blank space, so tinker with your game maps and make them thrilling to explore.

Monsters

Fighting games have progressive matches where the player must beat a tough opponent. Shooters have hordes of stinking zombies, war-time combatants, shielded androids, or other dehumanized monsters running at the player, which he must mow down with his fire power. RPGs have dungeons littered with monsters to tackle, and tackling them wins the player treasure or experience points.

Battles with monsters typify the combat system of these game genres. There is always something to be gained by overcoming the monsters in games, no matter how unlikely it might seem. Even killer crows tend to drop boxes of gold in *Resident Evil 4*.

Monsters should never get short shrift. They scare and titillate us on an instinctive level, and they make for fearsome foes, even if they are normal-looking humans in tanker gear. Either the monsters block the door to escape or they carry the key to the next level. Many games will ramp up the difficulty by using an evolution of ever-tougher monsters for us to fight. And the toughest of all are the "boss monsters" that guard the gates on the hero's journey (or at least the end of the level).

Traps

Traps, like monsters, have become a staple of popular RPGs ever since the days of pen-and-paper games like *Dungeons & Dragons*. One of the earliest video games to showcase traps was Atari's *Pitfall!* in 1982 (Figure 6.7). In it, the player character Pitfall Harry must leap or swing over tar pits, quicksand, water holes, rolling logs, crocodiles, and more.

Traps are a hodgepodge of suspense, scenery, and intrigue. Good traps can have whole stories behind them.

Figure 6.7
Atari's *Pitfall!*

A trap in a high cleric's abbey may appear and work very differently from a trap set in a demon warlord's dungeon. Traps reflect the places and people who built them, even if they do share a common goal: to stop trespassers or thieves. Use style to cater your traps to the game's locale. Consider adjusting traps according to their immediate surroundings, including terrain, special features of the land, and weather conditions.

Traps do not *have* to be lethal. Some may be designed to wound, harm, or hold a trespasser. Others may raise an alarm, scare off, or deter would-be invaders in other ways. Some traps may not have actually been designed to be traps in the first place but through age and disuse or negative natural conditions accident-prone areas may have developed. A typical example of such is a rickety bridge that, over the years, has planks that have started to rot and rope that has started to fray: a once-solid bridge may end up a death trap for our hero!

Quests

As we looked at in Chapter 1: What Is a Fantasy RPG?, quests are special sets of challenges that take place in both stories and games, linking narrative and play.

Quest games, like the *King's Quest* series, have quests that make up activities in which the players must overcome specific challenges in order to reach a goal, and when players successfully surmount the challenges of the quest and achieve the quest's main goal, the player's actions bring about or unlock a series of events comprising the game story.

Jesper Juul said in *Half-Real: Video Games between Real Rules and Fictional Worlds*: "Quests in games can actually provide an interesting type of bridge between game rules and game fiction in that the games can contain predefined sequences of events that the player then has to actualize or effect."

Types of Quests   Quests fall into three oft-used categories:

- **Clean-up quests**—Where the hero must wipe out an enemy or group of enemies skulking in a single area.

- **Fetch quests**—The hero must find and return with a particular item.

- **Escort quests**—The hero must protect or otherwise safely escort some helpless individual.

Players of RPGs are so used to quests such as these that they have become a staple of the genre. However, be wary in overusing them, or focusing on them to the exclusion of proper narrative or game play.

Questing the Hero's Journey   Game writers often cite Joseph Campbell's *monomyth* or "hero's journey" as a pattern for their quest games. In the "hero's journey" there are several legendary steps, which you can imagine as a staircase, where the first step starts with the hero in his own world confronted with a terrible evil threat requiring him to go where he's never gone before or do things he's never done before.

The monomyth, as described by mythologist Joseph Campbell in his *The Hero with a Thousand Faces*, includes the following steps, which are more like story suggestions that naturally follow one another in a chain of events and are common among most legends, fairy tales, books, and more.

- **Ordinary World**—This is the "fish out of water" concept, where you see the story's hero taken out of his ordinary space and time and landing in a strange, more challenging world or predicament he never imagined existing.

- **Call to Adventure**—The hero is presented with a problem, challenge, or quest, which will take him further away from everything ordinary he used to know. Often, he refuses the call until the ante is raised and the hero is further motivated to accept; if this happens, it is usually a self-sacrificing acceptance (not only has the villain taken over the kingdom, but now he's kidnapped the hero's girlfriend, too, and the hero won't stand for that!).

- **Supernatural Aid**—The hero encounters aid in the persona of an advisor or supernatural force. It is here that the hero often finds a map, a weapon that will smite the villain, or other useful tool to aid him in his quest.

- **Into the Woods**—Prepared for adventure, the hero crosses a threshold into a new and dangerous part of the imaginary world. His journey truly begins in earnest. Fraught with peril, this strange new world will test the hero's nerve.

- **Hero is Tested**—Once our hero has escaped the ordinary and advanced down a dangerous path on a noble goal, he will face many obstacles and tests. Along the way, the hero will gain new allies, artifacts, weapons, or knowledge to help him face the villain.

- **The Greatest Trial**—At the heart of the big nasty woods, the hero reaches the lair of the villain. Here he must face his own fears, deal with his own lingering doubts, and overcome adversity through a galvanizing ordeal that will lay his soul bare.

- **Hero is Rewarded**—The hero has beaten death, rose from the ashes a transformed, more heroic hero, smiting all enemies, and now gains that which he has sought so long—the pretty damsel, the golden chalice, the cure for a vile plague, or whatever the goal was in the first place—but is this The End?

- **Return to the Ordinary**—Danger is not out of the way yet, as the hero must now try to reenter the ordinary world. He may have more foes to beat, traps to escape, or death to outrace. Campbell likens this scene to rebirth and transformation, where the hero—like a phoenix—dies and is resurrected an avenging angel.

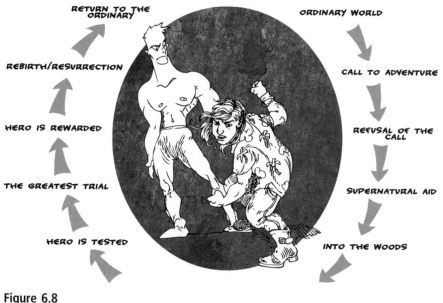

RETURN TO THE
ORDINARY

ORDINARY WORLD

REBIRTH/RESURRECTION

CALL TO ADVENTURE

HERO IS REWARDED

REFUSAL OF THE
CALL

THE GREATEST TRIAL

SUPERNATURAL AID

HERO IS TESTED

INTO THE WOODS

Figure 6.8
The hero's journey.

This mythic story structure forms the basis for the majority of our ancient legends and our current Hollywood story compositions. For a look at this pattern, you only have to watch *Star Wars* and *The Lord of the Rings*.

See Figure 6.8 for the outline of the hero's journey.

Make Your Quests Fraught with Peril   Quests would be very dull if they were uneventful.

If you told the player, "Go to Ornery Cave and bring back the Scepter of Sam," and the player went to the cave, conveniently marked for him on his map, and returned with the scepter, it would be very boring indeed.

Instead, you have the player go to the cave and fight or sneak his way past a gaggle of killer geese to get inside. Then when he does get the scepter, the walls begin to close in. When the player barely escapes Ornery Cave alive, he is beset by highwaymen intent on robbing him of the scepter. Eventually the player finishes his mission with a sense of fulfillment and pride.

This is the manner in which game storyline must be kept in pace with tension; anything less will end with the player scratching his head, wondering what the point to your game is supposed to be.

Interactive Storytelling with RPG Maker

Let's add some quests and get started adding real narrative to Thug Wallow.

In the Beginning

First, you want to teach the player how to play while doing your best to entertain him. So you need to add a cut-scene that does this.

Cut-scenes, of course, are those tidbits of inactivity where the player sits back and watches the onscreen events. There's usually some action and dialogue in a cut-scene that carries forward the game story. Cut-scenes are never very long, because if they drag on too long, the player might get bored or frustrated. Gamers want to game, not watch a sprite-based movie. Keep that in mind.

In our cut-scene, the hero Victor will enter Timber Town, wonder where everybody is, and make his way to Toad Inn. There, he'll meet the mayor of Timber Town, who tells him what's going on, and Victor will offer his assistance. Let's begin.

Your player start position should be near the front entrance of the Timber Town map. Right-click on a square somewhere off to the side of the start position and add a New Event. Name this event Intro Scene. Set the Trigger to Autorun, so that the event will start automatically and the player won't be able to do anything until the event ends.

In the List of Event Commands, the first event you want to add is under Tab 2 in the Event Commands window: Set Move Route. In the Move Route window, click the following in order:

1. Turn Up

2. Move Up

3. Wait (15 frames)

4. Turn Left

5. Wait (15 frames)

6. Turn Up

7. Wait (15 frames)

8. Turn Right

9. Wait (15 frames)

10. Turn Down

Click OK when you're done.

Add a Wait event command (found in the Timing panel under Tab 2 of the Event Commands window). Make it a 30 frames wait.

The next event to add is Show Balloon Icon, which is found in the Character panel under Tab 2 of the Event Commands window. In the Show Balloon Icon window, you can have word balloons pop up above a character's head to show a universal expression. In this instance, set the Character to Player and the Balloon Icon to Question (Figure 6.9), then click OK.

Add another Wait event command, also of 30 frames in duration.

The next event to add is Show Text, which is found in Event Commands window Tab 1. Type the following and add the Victor face that you created as part of your custom face set for the graphic.

```
\c[30]VICTOR:\c[0] Where is everybody? This
town looks deserted! Maybe we should try
the inn up the street...
```

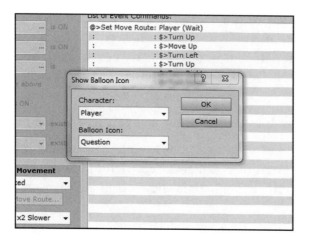

Figure 6.9
Show a balloon icon above the hero's head.

Note that I put the font color for Victor's name at 30. From now on, use font number 30, which is a violet color, for Victor's name. This will maintain consistency throughout the game. Click OK to include your text in the List of Event Commands.

Add another Set Move Route (Tab 2) that has Victor first Turn Up, then Move Up, and click OK to save your Move Route.

Now add the Fadeout Screen found in the Screen Effects panel of Tab 2 of the Event Commands window. This will darken the screen. Set a Transfer Player event command (Tab 2) that takes the player to a square near the middle of Toad Inn, facing right like he's about to walk over and talk to the innkeeper. Make a mental note of where you place the player.

Before going any further, we want to close this event so that it never returns. To do so, we'll add a self switch. A *switch* is based on something called Boolean logic and holds a yes/no or on/off status. There are switches local to a specific event that are called *self switches*, and there are switches that can be accessed anywhere that are called *control switches*. We'll be using both. For now, though, we need a self switch.

Add a new event command. Make it Control Self Switch, found in the Game Progression panel under Tab 3. Set the Self Switch to A and Operation to ON, if they're not already by default. Click OK to save your changes and exit.

Back in the Edit Event window, click the New Event Page button at the top of the window. You will now be presented with a blank List of Event Commands. This is a whole new page for event commands to appear on, separate from the first. In the Conditions panel on the left, put a check in the box next to Self Switch and set the status of A to ON. Don't add anything else to this screen. Return to Event Page 1. Your screen should resemble 6.10.

Click OK to save your changes to the Intro Scene event and exit its edit mode.

Switch to the Toad Inn map. Remember where you put the player character in the transfer event above? Add a new event three squares to the left of that square and name the event Mayor. Insert another event somewhere off in a corner and name this event Expo Scene.

In the Expo Scene's List of Event Commands, attach a Fadein Screen event command from the same place you got the Fadeout before. This will fade in the screen from black.

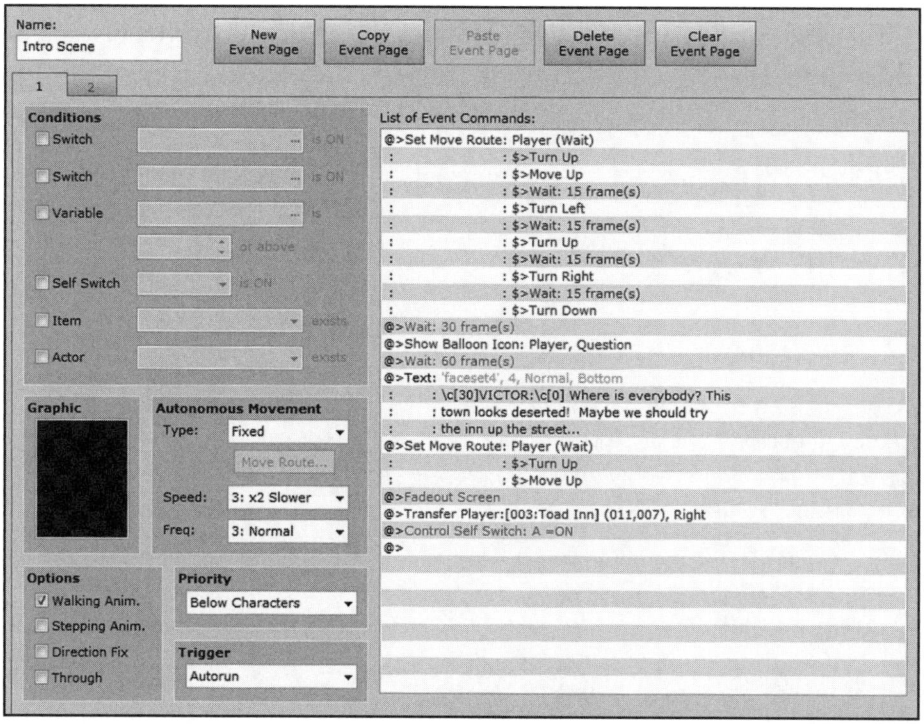

Figure 6.10
The Intro Scene event.

Add a Set Move Route (Tab 2) that makes Victor Move Right. Then add a Show Text with the Face Graphic of a friendly old man (found in the Actor2 face set) that reports the following:

```
\c[20]MAYOR:\c[0] Sir! I need to speak with
you, sir!
```

Place a Set Move Route and click Jump. When the options window comes up allowing you to move the player so far left and right in the jump, leave the integers both at 0 and click OK. This will let Victor jump in place. Affix a Wait event command of 15 frames. Place a Show Balloon Icon event command that is set to the Player and shows an Exclamation. Add another Wait of 15 frames. Then add a Set Move Route that has Victor Turn Left. Lastly, add a Wait of 60 frames.

The next event command you should add to the List of Event Commands is a Set Move Route, but this time, instead of controlling the Player, select the Mayor from the drop-down list. Tell him to Move Right.

Now we just need to add a bit of dialogue to move the story forward. For each of these, add a Show Text event command and append the correct Face Graphic for the character.

```
\c[30]VICTOR:\c[0] Yes?
\c[20]MAYOR:\c[0] You're a stranger to these
parts, yet I notice you carry monsters with
you as protection. You are not from Korgan,
I take it?

\c[30]VICTOR:\c[0] Who?

\c[20]MAYOR:\c[0] A bloodthirsty dark lord.
We don't know where he comes from, but he
has appeared in our fair town numerous times
- and each time he's hurt us!

\c[20]MAYOR:\c[0] Last time he was here, he
swore that when he next returned, he'd...
take my darling daughter!

\c[30]VICTOR:\c[0] That's awful! You live near
the city of Thug Wallow, don't you? Why not
appeal to the city Guard there?

\c[20]MAYOR:\c[0] The Guard is run by
Korgan's own henchman! There's nothing they
could do, except make us more miserable.

\c[20]MAYOR:\c[0] But perhaps you could -?
No! That's asking too much...

\c[30]VICTOR:\c[0] My monster friends and I
go where no sane man would... That's it! We
will find this Korgan fellow, wherever he lairs -
and stomp him out!

\c[20]MAYOR:\c[0] Oh, thank you, sir!
```

Insert two more Move Routes, after all this dialogue is through. First, have the Player Turn Down. Then, force the Mayor to Turn Left, Wait (30 frames), Move Left, Wait (60 frames), and Move Left again.

At this point, do the same thing you did at the end of the Intro Scene event. Add a Control Self Switch event command (A is ON), click the New Event Page to

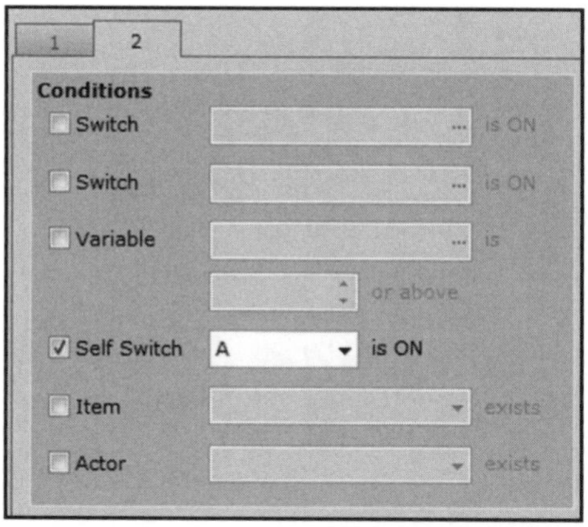

Figure 6.11
Set the Conditions of Event Page 2 to Self Switch A = ON.

add an Event Page 2, and on Event Page 2's Conditions, set Self Switch A to ON (Figure 6.11). This safely eliminates the Expo Scene event, so that it won't come up again.

Return to Event Page 1. Your screen should resemble Figure 6.12. Click OK to save your changes and return to the main editor.

Save your project and then play-test your game. If you positioned any of the characters in the wrong spots, or missed a step, you should see it. Otherwise, your mission briefing should go off without a hitch, and play actually starts now in Toad Inn, where you can raid the treasure chest in the corner and head off in search of adventure!

The Middle

The player now knows he or she must find Korgan's location and strike him down before Korgan does anything more dastardly to Timber Town. As the designer, you can work backward to help set up the clues.

We know, for instance, that Korgan resides in Castle Vesper, which is the castle ruins on the other side of Thug Wallow. Victor will have to go to Thug Wallow and find someone who knows where Korgan is and how to get there. That someone will be Gaspar, a sorcerer who used to work in Thug Wallow until Korgan put his minion in the Guard. Gaspar will live in the Hut map, which is underground beneath the Warehouse map.

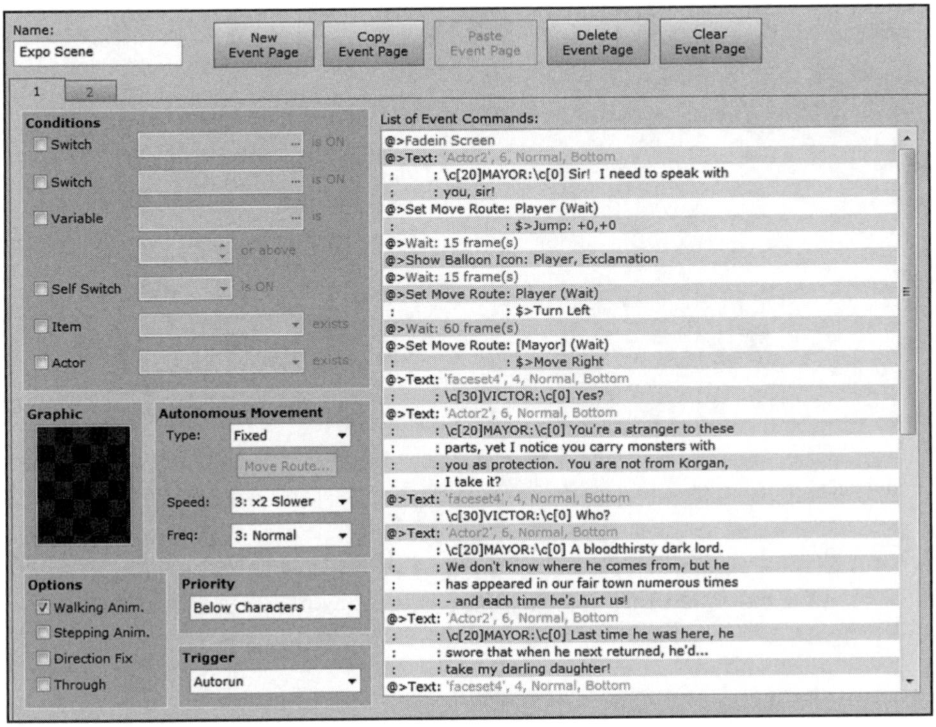

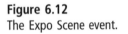

Figure 6.12
The Expo Scene event.

Gaspar also knows of a teleport scroll that will take Victor to Castle Vesper. The teleport scroll belongs to the pirate Jam Beard, who stays at the Black Lobster. To get the teleport scroll from Jam Beard, Victor will have to give him a shiny pearl stolen by a Lamia.

That gives us enough material to start with and is, in effect, a locking mechanism that prevents the player from going directly to Castle Vesper to defeat Korgan. It also makes sense, at least in the context of the game story.

First, we need a Lamia. Go to the Market Street map. Right-click on a square in the top-right corner and add New Event. Name this event Pearl Thief. For Graphic, choose the female in the Monster character set, facing down. Set the Trigger to Player Touch.

The first event command to add is Show Text. Pick the corresponding Face Graphic for our monster. Then type the following message:

```
\c[5]LAMIA:\c[0] Ssssay, ssssailor... Would
you come classser and help me?
```

Add another Show Text, this time with Victor speaking:

```
\c[30]VICTOR:\c[0] What ... ? I'm not a
sailor!
```

Next, have Gus the Mummy speak (being sure to insert his Face Graphic):

```
\c[25]GUS:\c[0] Careful, Vic! She's not a
human lass. In fact ... She's a Lamia!
```

Insert a Show Balloon Icon event command. Set it to This Event and the icon to Anger, so it makes it look like the Lamia is getting mad.

Lastly, have the Lamia say:

```
\c[5]LAMIA:\c[0] He isss right ... Now you all
mussst die!!
```

Now we're ready for a fight. Insert a Battle Processing (Tab 3) event command with a Direct Designation set to 025: Lamia. Make sure the player cannot escape this fight.

Similar to the other events you've closed out, use a Control Self Switch (Tab 1) with A set to ON. Then click New Event Page, and on Event Page 2, set the Conditions where Self Switch A is set to ON. Be sure that there is no Graphic on Event Page 2, because you want Lamia to appear to vanish after the battle.

Exit the event editor by clicking OK.

We want the battle to end and the player to receive Shiny Pearl. To do this, we have to edit the Database. In the Database, go to Items. Change the maximum number of items to 21. In the new empty slot, name your item Shiny Pearl. For Graphic, pick the glass ball sprite icon as you see in Figure 6.13. For description, type "A pretty bauble that looks like it came from the islands far away." Set its Scope as None, its Occasion as Never, and its Price as 0 (we don't want the player to trade this item). Everything else should be left blank or at defaults. Click Apply.

Go to the Enemies tab and select Lamia from the list (Figure 6.14). For Drop Item 2, force the Lamia to drop the Shiny Pearl 1/1 (or every time Lamia is beaten). You might also, while you are here, change Lamia's stats so he appears

Figure 6.13
Choose the glass ball sprite icon for the Graphic.

weaker than he is by default. Put her Max HP at 1000, her Attack at 60, and her Defense at 45.

Test the Pearl Thief out. Temporarily set a player start position a few squares away from her position and play-test the game. You will immediately notice if there's anything you missed.

Now that we have a Shiny Pearl, let's set up Jam Beard. Before leaving the Database, go back to the Items tab and raise the maximum number once more. The new item will be named Teleport Scroll and should look like a scroll. Its description should read, "This item, when read, can transport the holder to Castle Vesper." Like the Shiny Pearl, set its Price to 0 and Consume to No (Figure 6.15).

Unlike the Shiny Pearl, we are going to add an event that happens whenever the player uses the Teleport Scroll. Under Common Event, pick 001, which is blank

Figure 6.14
Now select Lamia and give her the Shiny Pearl as a drop item.

for now. Go to the Common Events tab and select the 001 slot. Set the Name to Teleport. For the event commands, first place a Flash Screen (Tab 2) with the settings left at defaults and then add a Transfer Player. Set the teleport destination to the World Map, just beside the Castle Vesper entrance.

You can test the Teleport Scroll item to see if it works. The way to do so is to temporarily add a treasure chest event in front of your player start position, which should still be near the Pearl Thief event. Tell the treasure chest to give the player the Teleport Scroll item. Then you can play-test your level. After opening the treasure chest and pulling out the Teleport Scroll, you can press Escape to enter the game menu. Go to Items, select the Teleport Scroll, and press Enter to use it. You should immediately see a flash of white light and then the screen will fade to black as the player is teleported to outside Castle Vesper.

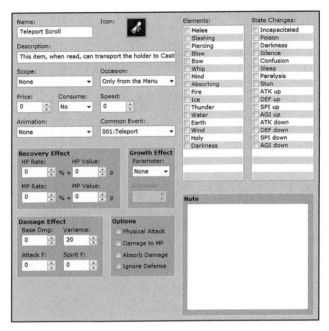

Figure 6.15
Create a Teleport Scroll.

When you're through play-testing, exit the play-test window and delete the treasure chest event containing the Teleport Scroll.

Go to the Black Lobster map. Create a new event named Jam Beard that looks something like a pirate. A pirate can be found topmost right in the People 3 character set. The first event command should be a Show Text with Bonehead the Were.

```
\c[12]BONEHEAD:\c[0] Vic, are you sure we
should approach this fellow? He smells like a
fish.
```

Then add a Show Text from Jam Beard. Set the Face Graphic to that of the pirate.

```
\c[14]JAM BEARD:\c[0] Name's Jam Beard and
I still have ears, furry one! What be ye want-
in' with old Jam Beard?
```

Now we'll set a conditional branch. Conditional branches change the path of events based on predetermined settings, such as values, switches, or existing

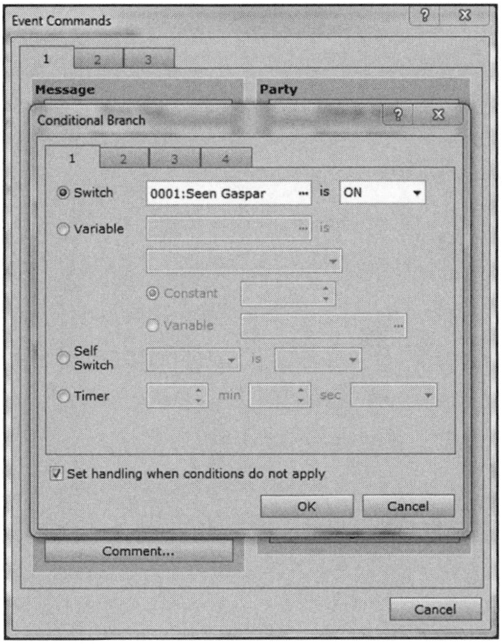

Figure 6.16
Set your condition to see whether or not Seen Gaspar is ON.

inventory. We'll use a new switch, one that checks to see if the player has visited Gaspar first and learned that Jam Beard has a Teleport Scroll that could be of use to the player.

Double-click the next empty event command line and choose Conditional Branch (found in the Flow Control panel of Tab 1). In the Conditional Branch window, you want to leave Switch selected but click the browse button [...] beside Switch to open the Switch window. At the bottom left is a name field. Name this field Seen Gaspar and click OK to return to the Conditional Branch window (Figure 6.16). Click OK to return to the event editor. You should now see multiple lines have appeared, first checking to see if the Seen Gaspar switch is ON, and if not, then running a separate event (under Else).

The main event, if Seen Gaspar is ON, is highlighted by default. Double-click the empty slot and add a Show Text that has Victor saying:

```
\c[30]VICTOR:\c[0] Gaspar told us you have
a Teleport Scroll that can get us outside the
city.
```

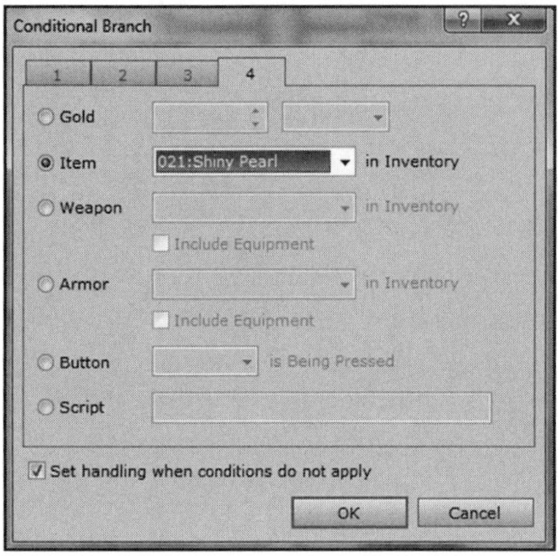

Figure 6.17
Set your condition to see whether the player has the Shiny Pearl in his inventory.

Have Jam Beard reply:

```
\c[14]JAM BEARD:\c[0] So I do ... I might
part with it if you can find who stole my Shiny
Pearl, my precious, and bring her back to me.
Could you find yourself doing that for me?
```

Set another Conditional Branch. This time, in the Conditional Branch window, go to Tab 4, select Item, and use the drop-down list to pick Shiny Pearl (Figure 6.17). Click OK. You now have a new if/else conditional branch nestled within your other one.

In the event line right under Conditional Branch: [Shiny Pearl] in Inventory, add a Show Text that displays Victor saying:

```
\c[30]VICTOR:\c[0] Is this your Shiny Pearl?
```

And have Jam Beard say:

```
\c[14]JAM BEARD:\c[0] That's it! Oh, my
precious! ... Here, for your trouble, take this
Teleport Scroll. I have no use for it ...
```

Now insert something new called Change Items, which can be found under Tab 1 of the Event Commands window. Select Shiny Pearl from the drop-down list of Items and select Decrease. Leave the default number to decrease by at 1, since we only have 1 Shiny Pearl in inventory (Figure 6.18). Click OK. Add another

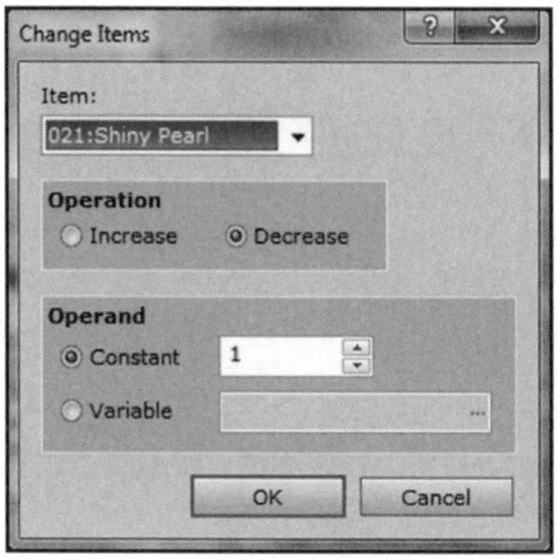

Figure 6.18
Take away the player's Shiny Pearl.

Change Items and increase the player's inventory by 1 Teleport Scroll. This is a simple enough exchange, one Shiny Pearl for one Teleport Scroll, and is a major accomplishment for the player!

Just beneath that event command, insert a Control Self Switch of A being ON, then create a new event page where Self Switch A is ON. Add the pirate graphic here, set his Trigger to Player Touch, and add a Show Text event that has Jam Beard say:

```
\c[14]JAM BEARD:\c[0] Thank ye for finding
me precious Pearl!
```

Return to Event Page 1. In the conditional area where it checks to see if the player has the Shiny Pearl in his inventory, go to the Else statement. We've already set what will happen if the player does have the Shiny Pearl, but if he doesn't, we need to set up a brief event. So add a Show Text where Victor says the following just after the Else line:

```
\c[30]VICTOR:\c[0] Looks like I don't have
much choice. OK, I'll do it!
```

That ends that entire branch. If the player has seen Gaspar and learned that Jam Beard has a Teleport Scroll, he asks about it and Jam Beard offers the scroll in exchange for the pearl. If the player has the Shiny Pearl, the exchange is made and then Jam Beard is basically through talking to the player. If the player doesn't have the Shiny Pearl, he offers to find it and can return later to go through this same rigmarole with Jam Beard.

Now we have to set the events that occur if the player hasn't seen Gaspar. At the bottom of the List of Event Commands, you should see an empty Else section for the first conditional branch that checks to see if switch Seen Gaspar is ON.

Set a Show Text that has Victor saying:

```
\c[30]VICTOR:\c[0] Nothing ... Sorry to
bother you.
```

Now we need to set up a conversation with Gaspar that turns the switch Seen Gaspar to ON.

Go to the Hut map and insert a new event named Gaspar on the right side of the map, near but not in his living quarters. Find an old man character for the Graphic and in the Autonomous Movement panel, set his Type to Random and Speed to x4 Slower (Figure 6.19). Set the Trigger to Player Touch.

The first event in the List of Event Commands should be a Show Text where Gaspar says:

```
\c[33]GASPAR:\c[0] Who ... who are you,
young man, to barge in on my solitude and
surround yourself with monsters?
```

Have Este the Witch say:

```
\c[24]ESTE:\c[0] Who are you calling monster
old man?
```

Continue the conversation as follows:

```
\c[33]GASPAR:\c[0] I meant no disrespect,
dear Witch. I am used to being alone and
unused to having company, I'm afraid. But
what have you with an old man like me?
```

```
\c[30]VICTOR:\c[0] We are looking for a
way to stop Korgan, before he destroys
Timber Town and takes the Mayor's
daughter!
```

```
\c[33]GASPAR:\c[0] Oh dear ... dear, dear
me ... Well, Korgan was once my pupil. But
he became too ambitious and vain for his own
good. I did not realize he ruined lives.
```

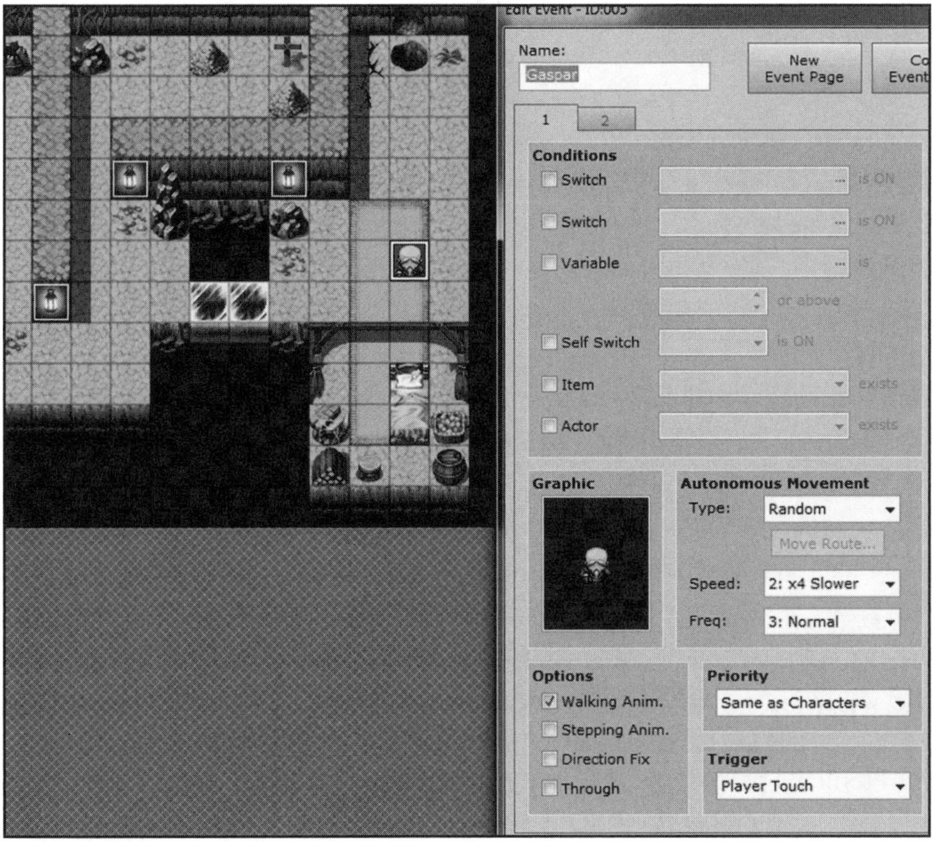

Figure 6.19
Place the old man Gaspar in the Hut map.

\c[33]GASPAR:\c[0] You can find Korgan in the ruins of Castle Vesper, outside the city. You cannot reach the ruins without a Teleport Scroll, however.

\c[33]GASPAR:\c[0] No, but there is a pirate named Jam Beard who does. You can find him most often at the Black Lobster tavern near the wharf.

\c[24]ESTE:\c[0] Thank you, kind sir! Vic, let's go get that Teleport Scroll and kick Korgan's butt!

\c[33]GASPAR:\c[0] Wait, there's one more
thing ... Korgan is weak against electrical
attacks. If you can find him, use this ...

Use the Change Items event command to give the player one Thunder Scroll.

\c[3]FREAKY:\c[0] Thunder's my specialty!

\c[30]VICTOR:\c[0] Thank you, old man.
Team, let's go ... !

Now insert an event command of Control Switches where Seen Gaspar is ON. Lastly, add a Self Switch where A is ON, and add a new event page. On Event Page 2, set Self Switch A to ON and add a graphic of the old man. Have him say something like:

\c[33]GASPAR:\c[0] Have you finished your
task so soon?

Be sure to set the Gaspar on Event Page 2 to walk around randomly x4 Slower with his Trigger set to Player Touch, too.

There! Now all you have to do is add some random NPCs around Thug Wallow that hint that an old man named Gaspar might be able to help the player and where he might be found (in or under the old abandoned warehouse in Clog Street). You can also set up street signs that help the player find the names of streets and advertisements posted on walls that help the player find the Black Lobster and the Parlor, where they can buy items to help them. These little touches are not essential but certainly make the game more enjoyable and easier to navigate.

The End

The last thing you have to plan for is the meeting with Korgan in Castle Vesper.

First, let's add a short cut-scene when the player enters Castle Vesper. Go to CVesper 1's map and, close to the entrance, add a new event named Into Vesper. Set its Trigger to Autorun. Insert a Set Move Route that has the player Move Up twice. Wait 30 seconds. Then, add a Show Balloon Icon with the expression set to Sweat. Wait 60 seconds. After that, place the following Show Texts:

\c[12]BONEHEAD:\c[0] So are we ready to
face Korgan?

\c[25]GUS:\c[0] I believe we are! Korgan
has got to be hiding around here somewhere.

`\c[24]ESTE:\c[0] Let's stop wasting time and`
`go get him!`

Then add a Control Self Switch where A is turned ON. Add a new event page where the Self Switch (under Conditions) is set to A is ON and leave it blank. This will safely close out the cut-scene.

Go to the Database and Enemies tab. Select Korgan from the leftmost list and set his Thunder Elemental Efficiency to A, so that what Gaspar said about Korgan being weak against electrical attacks is true. Also, go ahead and halve most of his stats (including Max HP, Max MP, Attack, Defense, Spirit, and Agility) so that he's not so tough and in his Action Patterns remove the following attacks:

- Flame II
- Spark II

Your screen should resemble Figure 6.20. Click OK to save your changes to the Database.

Back in the main editor, go to CVesper 2 and right-click on the KorganBattle event you placed there earlier to edit it. Double-click on the Battle Processing event command line to add a Show Text above it, and insert the following conversation.

`\c[10]Korgan:\c[0] I have been waiting for`
`you imbeciles. Who are you to come into my`
`lair and defeat my minions like you have?`

`\c[30]VICTOR:\c[0] We won't let you harm`
`the folks of Timber Town any longer, Korgan!`

Insert an event command just after Battle Processing that is Game Over (found under Tab 3 of the Event Commands window). This way, as soon as the party defeats Korgan, the game is through, because they've won!

Before you finish, there's one more thing. Add the player start position back to the front entrance of the Timber Town map, before you forget.

What's Next?

You have given the player a purpose in your game world: to find and defeat the dark lord Korgan, who has been terrorizing Timber Town. You have set up a lock mechanism whereby the player has to find out where Korgan is and how to

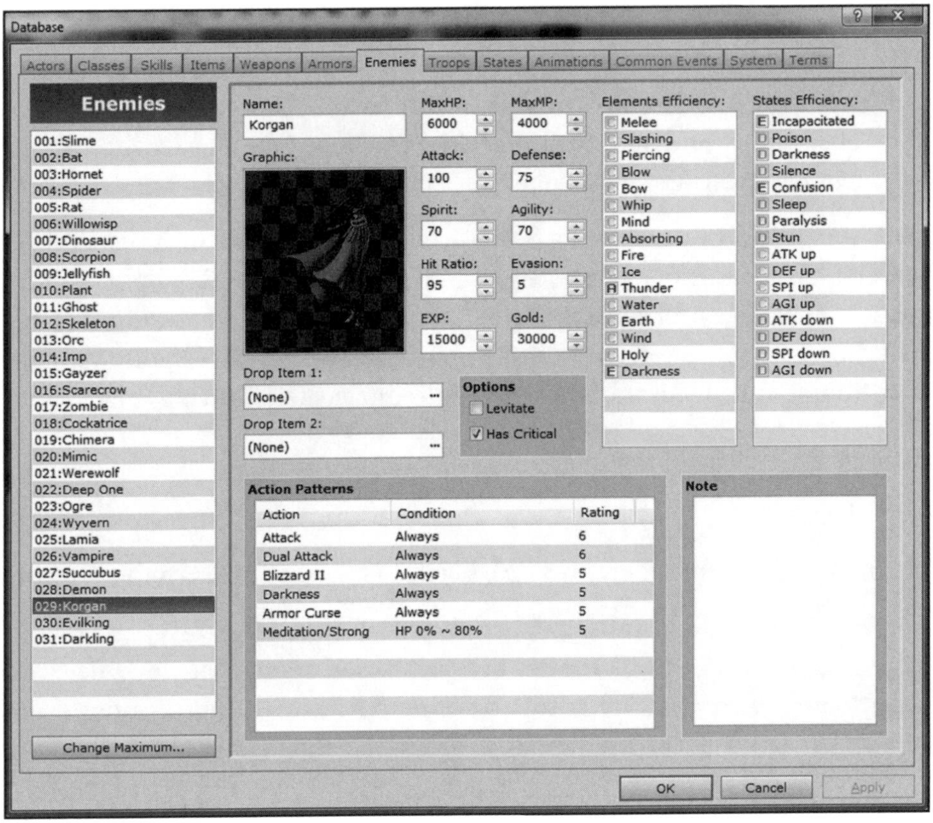

Figure 6.20
Adjust Korgan and his traits so that he's not so tough.

get there before he can actually defeat Korgan, and you've left a tidy trail of breadcrumbs to help the player to do so. First, you have the player look for the old man Gaspar, who sends him to Jam Beard, who will trade a Teleport Scroll for a Shiny Pearl, and these steps are filled with entertainment and sub-questing. You can make the trail of breadcrumbs more complex if you like, but for our purposes, this is all Thug Wallow needs.

Now take some time to add quests to your own original RPG Maker project. What are the player's objectives in your game? What quests are they going on? Work backward to set up breadcrumbs to lead your gamer through the mission you've developed for them. And do so with creativity and flair and nearly no programming involved!

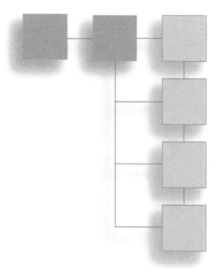

CHAPTER 7

FINAL TOUCHES

In this chapter you will learn:

- To add spectacular effects to your game
- To alter the look and feel of your game's main menu
- To add sound (music/SFX) to your game
- To make your party members' faces visible in battle

Thug Wallow, as well as your original game creation, should be almost done. However, there are just a few more items to add to make them truly polished-looking RPGs. In this chapter, you will put the finishing touches to your games and make them look like they truly belong on the game market.

LAST-MINUTE MODIFICATIONS

Tip

"It is a bad plan that admits of no modification."

—Publilius Syrus, 1st Century B.C.

Your game will look much better with some minor adjustments. Mostly, these adjustments are for aesthetic reasons, which is why they have not been covered before now.

These amendments include:

- Lighting and weather conditions in your game maps
- Adding some enemies who will really surprise the player
- Switching out the title and/or game over screens
- Altering the terms used throughout the game, including menu options
- Changing the title music and adding background music and sound effects to your maps
- Revealing the party members' faces in the battle sequences

Lighting and Weather Conditions

Tip

We knew we would go out and try our best. It was fun to get first place. We tried to forget about the weather.

—Jess Yates

Create a new event in the Timber Town map somewhere. Name this event Stormy Weather. Do not give this event a picture but do set its Trigger to Parallel Process. Create a conditional branch that checks a new switch you're going to call Outdoors. If the player is outside, or this Outdoors switch is ON, then add two event commands:

- **Set Weather Effects**—Found in the Picture and Weather panel under Tab 2 of the Event Commands window. Set it to Storm at Power 7.
- **Tint Screen**—Found in the Screen Effects panel under Tab 2 of the Event Commands window. Set it to Red –119, Green 0, Blue 0, and Gray 68 with no wait.

If the Outdoors switch is OFF (the Else section of the conditional branch), add a Set Weather Effects event command which is set to defaults (no weather) and a Tint Screen event command set to defaults (all zeroes).

This event should loop continuously. All we have to do now is turn the Outdoors switch on and off throughout game-play.

First, go to the Intro Scene event and edit it. Double-click on the topmost line in the List of Event Commands to add a new event command. Make it a Control Switches one. Turn Outdoors to ON. Go to the bottom of the List of Event Commands, and double-click on the Control Self Switch to insert a new event command above it. Make it another Control Switch, but this time turn Outdoors to OFF.

Now go to the Toad Inn map and edit the transfer events at the door of the inn, so that if the player goes outside, Outdoors switch is turned ON. Go back to the Timber Town map and edit the transfer event at the front door of the inn so that it turns Outdoors to OFF if the player goes inside the inn.

Go to the World Map and select the transfer event in front of the Castle Vesper ruins. Edit that transfer event so that it, too, has a Control Switch that turns the Outdoors switch to OFF as the player enters CVesper 1.

The last switches are at the city of Thug Wallow. At the outside of Thug Wallow on the World Map, edit its transfer event to turn the Outdoors switch to OFF. Also, we're going to add a color tint to all of Thug Wallow, so let's get it set up starting now. Add another Control Switch and point to a new switch you'll call Gloom. Turn Gloom's switch to ON as the player enters Candle Street (Figure 7.1). At the front bottommost entrance to Candle Street, edit the transfer event to turn the Outdoors switch to ON and the Gloom switch to OFF.

Move to the World Map and select the transfer event in front of Castle Vesper's ruins again. Edit it to turn Gloom to ON when the player enters Castle Vesper.

Go to the Candle Street map. Affix an event somewhere within that map, preferably somewhere the player won't be going, and name the event Gloom Light. Just as you did with Stormy Weather, make this event's Trigger a Parallel Process. You're going to set a conditional branch, but this time the condition will rest on the switch Gloom, and whether it's set to ON. If it is ON, set it up to do a Screen Tint. Set the Screen Tint to Red –85, Green –102, Blue –102, and Gray 85 with no wait.

Test it out if you want to see how dark the screen will get (Figure 7.2).

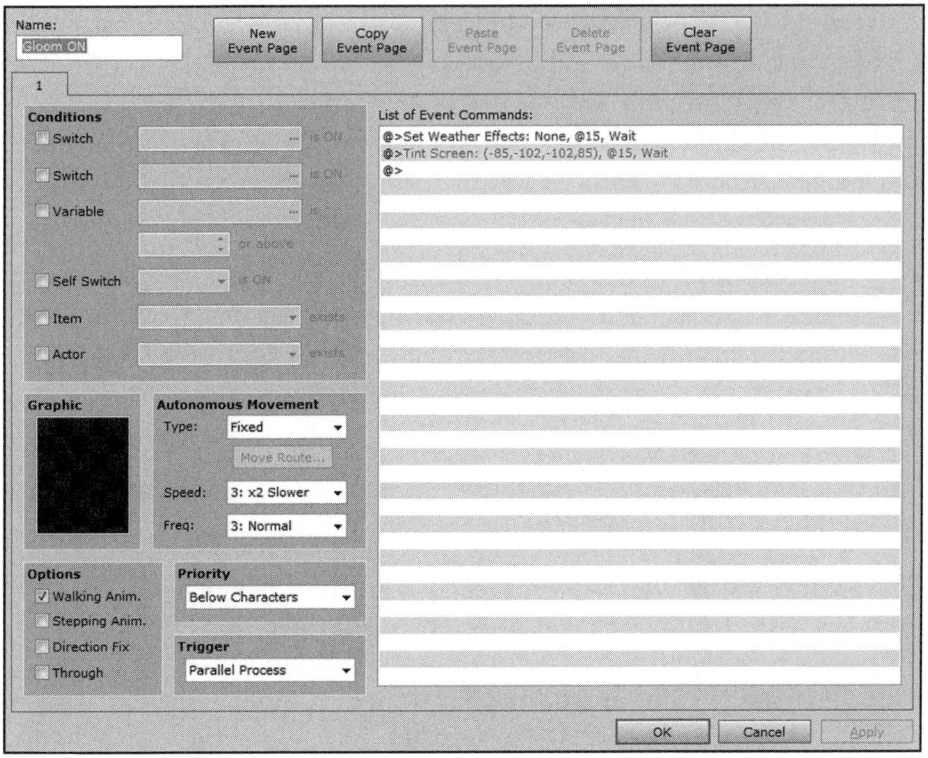

Figure 7.1
Set the transfer events to turn the Gloom switch ON or OFF as needed.

Some Nasty Surprises

> **Tip**
> _____
>
> "Yoiks!"
>
> —Shaggy, *Scooby-Doo Where Are You?*

Let's add muggers on the streets of Thug Wallow. In the Candle Street map somewhere, add a new event and name it Thief. Set the Trigger to Player Touch, the Type (Autonomous Movement) to Random and the Speed to x2 Slower. For the graphic, pick the hooded guy in the tunic found in the Evil character set.

Figure 7.2
The dim-lit screen of Thug Wallow's city streets.

Give this event a Show Text that says something along these lines, with the same hooded guy from the Evil face set affixed to the message:

`\c[7]THIEF:\c[0] Give me all your valuables!`

Then add a Battle Processing event command that summons a battle with the Darkling*2 troop. When you've done that, a new conditional branch will appear in your List of Event Commands, with a win condition and escape condition. Double-click the line in the win condition and add a Control Self Switch that turns A to ON. Then add a new event page that has as its Conditions that A be ON. This will remove the Thief event after the player has beaten the Darklings.

If the player successfully escapes, you might want the Thief to take the player's valuables. So add an event command of Change Items to the escape condition and set it to deduct a variable amount of Gold (Figure 7.3). Click OK to save your changes and return to the main editor. Copy and paste duplicates of the Thief event in each of the Thug Wallow street maps. This should reflect the dangerous nature of the city.

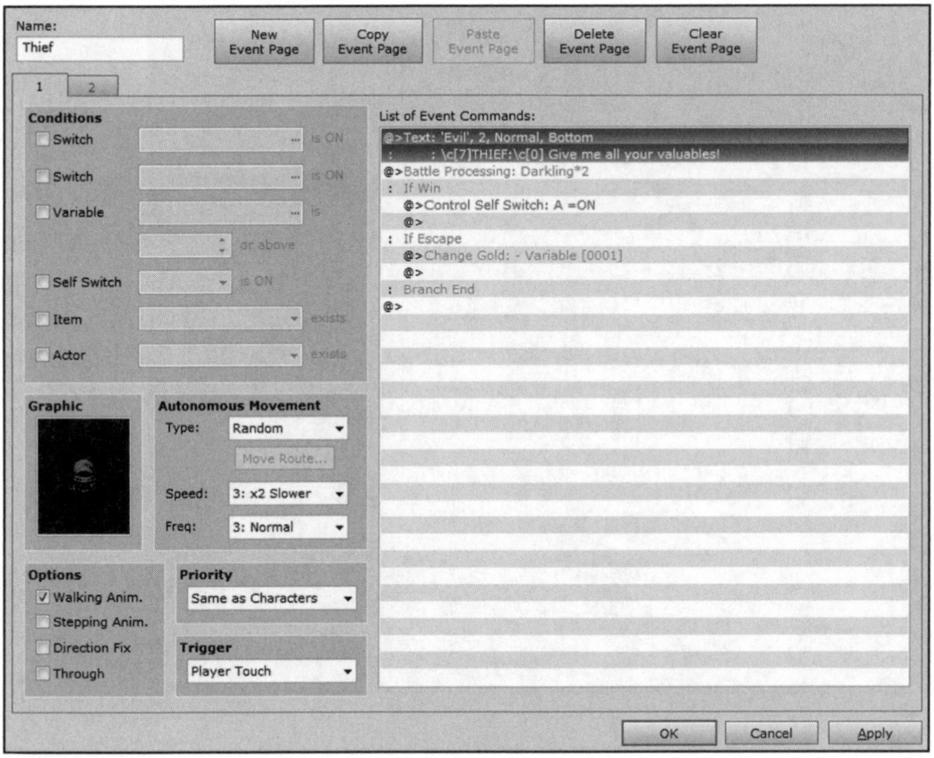

Figure 7.3
Have the Thief steal the player's Gold if he escapes from battle.

Title and Game Over Screens

To overwrite the existing title and game over screens is fairly simple. You create an image file for each, naming one Title.png and the other GameOver.png. Then you go into the Resource Manager and import them into Graphics/System. The local, newer images will overwrite the existing ones.

Let's try it now with Thug Wallow's title screen. First, go to the main editor of your game project, if you're not there already, and open the Resource Manager. Browse to the Graphics/System section. Select Title from the list and hit the Preview button to see what the title screen looks like now (Figure 7.4). Click Export and save your Title.png file somewhere where you can find it again shortly.

Minimize your Resource Manager for now and open your image editor. For this exercise, I will use Picnik, which you can, too. Picnik is a free web-based photo

Figure 7.4
The original RPG Maker title screen.

editing program found at http://www.Picnik.com. When you get there, click the Get Started Now button in the center of the screen. Wait for the program to launch in your browser window. When it finishes, click the Upload Photo button and browse to find the Title.png file you just saved. It will appear in the editor (Figure 7.5).

Click on the Colors button and set Saturation to −59 and Temperature to −30. Then click OK. Click on Exposure and set the Exposure to 2 and Contrast to 8. Then click OK. Now that the basics are done, click on the Create tab near the top of the window.

Click on Effects in the horizontal menu bar to display picture effects on the left-side panel. In the Effects panel list, click Vignette to add a dark fuzzy border around the edges of your picture, then click Apply. Click on Cross Process in the Effects panel list and set its Fade to 50% before clicking Apply (Figure 7.6).

Click on Text in the horizontal menu bar. Type the words "Thug Wallow" in the empty field in the upper-left corner of the Text panel. Choose the font named Sabonete, or another font to your liking, and click the Add button. In the Text Properties panel that appears, change the color of your text to one of your liking. Set the Fade to 20% and Size to 76. Click and drag the text that has appeared over your image somewhere in the upper-left area, so that it won't be covered up

Figure 7.5
The Picnik editor.

by your title menu options (Figure 7.7). If you want, go ahead and add another line of text that says "By…" and your name, to show ownership.

Click on Stickers to open the Stickers panel on the left side of your browser window. Scroll down the list until you see the Dingbats > Iconian Stickers. Click on Iconian Stickers to expand the list. Scroll down to the Imaginary Forces section and click to select the dragon with the wide wingspan and spiral tail. It will come into sight on top of your image in the main window.

Use the Sticker Properties panel that pops up to set the sticker's color and then set its Advanced Blend Mode to Darken. Change its Fade to 40%. Now you can click-and-drag the dragon around your image to find the perfect placement. You can also grab one of the corner handles of your sticker and drag it with your cursor to resize it.

Last, but not least, right-click on your dragon and from the options list, choose Send Backward. All items so far that have been added to your image are done so

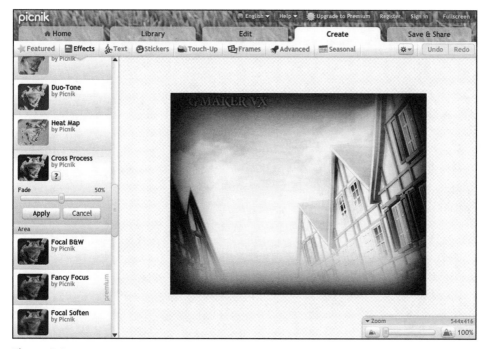

Figure 7.6
Add a Cross Process to your image.

in layers, and Send Backward moves the dragon sticker back one layer, just behind your text, because the text was the last item created before you added the dragon sticker. If you add more than one item of text to your image, you might have to select Send Backward again, until your dragon sticker is all the way behind the text (Figure 7.8).

Click the Save & Share tab at the top of your window. You will see a preview of your finished image. Make sure the file name shows up as Title, but change the Format to PNG (Best for archiving). Click Save Photo and save it to your game project folder. When it has finished saving, close Picnik and return to RPG Maker.

In RPG Maker, open the Resource Manager and browse to the Graphics/System section if you're not already there. Click Import and browse to find your new, revised Title.png file. Close the Resource Manager and play-test your game, saving your game project first. Note how the opening title screen looks now (Figure 7.9).

Figure 7.7
Move your text below where it says "RPG Maker VX" but above the area where menu options will become visible.

Terms Used in the Game

Tip

"It is clear enough that you are making some distinction in what you said, that there is some nicety of terminology in your words. I can't quite follow you."

—Flann O'Brien

Since we just altered the title screen, let's go ahead and adjust the title screen options. The way we do that (and so much more) is through the Database. In RPG Maker, open your Database and go to the Terms tab. This section of the Database is where you can change what all the common game elements are called, offering you even more customization options.

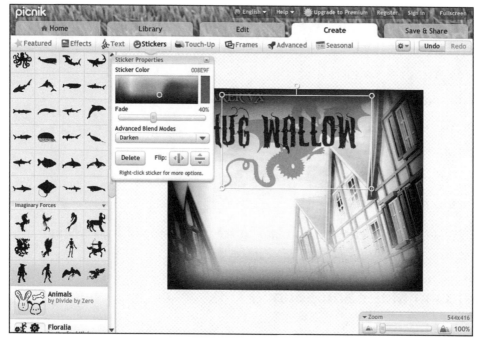

Figure 7.8
Place the dragon sticker behind your text.

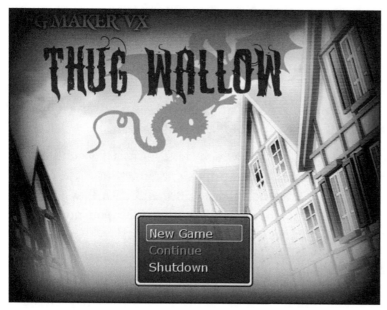

Figure 7.9
What your final title screen should look like in-game.

For your Thug Wallow game, adjust the following elements:

- **Level (Abbr.)**—LVL

- **Body Armor**—Armor

- **Skill**—Ability

- **Guard**—Defend

- **Shutdown**—Quit Game

- **To Title**—Main Menu

- **G** (under Currency)—Gold

You can play-test your game, if you like, to see what some of these changes will look like in-game.

Background Music and Sound FX

Tip

"I'm a musician, and I'm fascinated with the effects of sound, and tone, and pitch and melody and all that sort of stuff. It's the first thing I have to solidify whenever I'm coming up—not 'coming up' with the character, because I never come up with them, the writer does that—whenever I get into a character. The first thing I need to get sorted out before I can then move forward, before I can feel any confidence whatsoever, is the voice."

—Guy Pearce

Melodies and other audio used in your game projects are governed by the System tab of the Database. Go there now to see what I mean.

Click the browse button beside Title BGM, which stands for background music, because I'm sick of hearing the same start-up music, aren't you? Pick Theme3 from the list. Raise Volume to 100% and Pitch to 50% and click Play to hear a sample of the music (Figure 7.10). Then click Stop and OK. You now have a brand-new piece of music to listen to when your game starts!

There are 10 different pre-generated pieces of background music for battles that you could set your game to, and two victory songs. Select Battle10 for the Battle BGM for now. You can fiddle with the rest of the music options all day long. But let's move on. Click OK to save your changes and exit the Database.

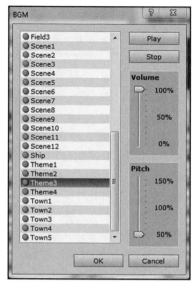

Figure 7.10
Amend and preview the Theme3 song.

In the main editor, right-click on Timber Town in the left-side list and select Map Properties from your options. In the top-right corner there are two toggles for music: The first one says Auto-Change BGM, and is for setting map-specific background music; and the second, Auto-Change SE, is for setting map-specific ambient sound effects. You can do neither, both, or either one.

For Timber Town, you want to set a sound effect so that, when the player is visiting Timber Town, it sounds like it's storming. So put a check next to Auto-Change SE and click the browse button to open the BS (background sounds) window. Select Storm from the list. Put your Volume just above 50% and your Pitch somewhere between 50% and 100% (Figure 7.11) before you click OK. Go to the World Map and add the same Storm sound to its Map Properties, too.

Make the changes below to each of the maps' Map Properties.

- **World Map**—BGM: None; BGS: Storm 50% Volume, 75% Pitch.
- **Toad Inn**—BGM: None; BGS: Drips 50% Volume, 100% Pitch.
- **Candle Street**—BGM: Scene11 100% Volume, 50% Pitch; BGS: None.

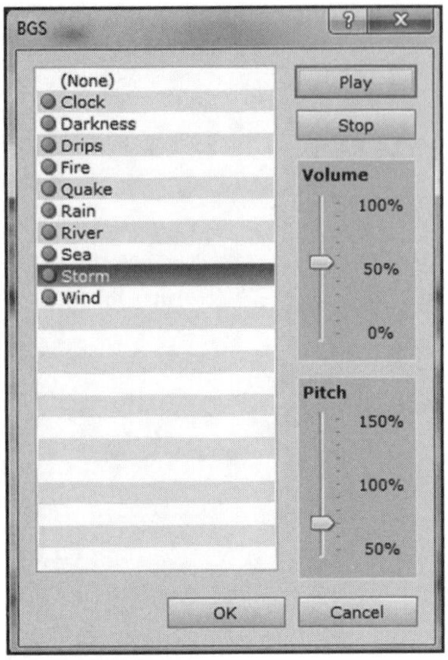

Figure 7.11
Give Timber Town an ambient Storm sound effect.

- **Clog Street**—BGM: Scene11 100% Volume, 50% Pitch; BGS: None.
- **Anchor Street**—BGM: Scene11 100% Volume, 50% Pitch; BGS: Sea 50% Volume, 75% Pitch.
- **Market Street**—BGM: Scene11 100% Volume, 50% Pitch; BGS: None.
- **Black Lobster**—BGM: Scene4 100% Volume, 75% Pitch; BGS: None.
- **Parlor**—BGM: Town1 75% Volume, 100% Pitch; BGS: Clock 75% Volume, 100% Pitch.
- **Warehouse**—BGM: Dungeon6 100% Volume, 100% Pitch; BGS: None.
- **Hut**—BGM: None; BGS: Drips 75% Volume, 100% Pitch.
- **CVesper 1**—BGM: Dungeon5 100% Volume, 100% Pitch; BGS: None.
- **CVesper 2**—BGM: None; BGS: Darkness 75% Volume, 75% Pitch.

You can easily import your own audio files to customize the game, too.

If you don't want to make your own sound effects, you can find lots of resources online for download. Here are just a few websites that can help you:

- **Acoustica**—www.Acoustica.com/sounds.htm
- **Flash Kit SFX**—www.Flashkit.com/soundfx/
- **Freesound Project**—http://www.Freesound.org
- **SFX Library**—http://Sound-Effects-Library.com

Another great site, but one that contains copyrighted music from many different kinds of games, is the Video Game Music Archive (www.VGMusic.com). You can browse by platform and alphabetically to find downloadable music used in many top industry games. A related, but separate, site is OverClocked Remix, sometimes just called OCRemix (Figure 7.12), which has remixes people have made of popular video game music ready for download. It can be found on the web at http://OCRemix.org.

Try these sites when you have time and incorporate their sounds or tunes as desired.

Figure 7.12
The OCRemix website.

Battle Faces

Tip
_____

"Not everything that is faced can be changed. But nothing can be changed until it is faced."

—James Arthur Baldwin
_____

If you get tired of not seeing your party members during battles, there's a simple way to fix that, thanks to a script written by Yanfly. Yanfly's script can show up to four different statuses, besides HP and MP, the character face graphics for each of the party members, and even the character sprites of the party.

There are four sections you can customize within the script. They are as follows:

- **SHOW_ALLY_FACE**—Set this to true to show the face graphics in the battle window. Set it to false if you don't want them appearing at all.

- **ALLY_FACE_OPACITY**—Set the opacity or how see-through the faces of the party members are, on a scale from 0 (invisible) to 255 (fully opaque).

- **SHOW_ALLY_SPRITE**—Set this to true to show the party member's character sprites in the battle window. Set it to false if you don't want them to appear at all.

- **MAX_STATES_SHOWN**—This value determines the maximum number of status effects displayed, up to four. You can set a value higher than 4, but if you do, it will overlap statuses and not look right.

To add Yanfly's script, go to your RPG Maker project, Thug Wallow. Open the Script Editor (it's the icon that looks like writing on paper). Scroll down the left-side list until you see Materials. Click the empty slot, and some instructions will appear in the main window area. Highlight and delete those instructions and start typing the following.

I am assuming, for the purposes of Thug Wallow, that we want the faces to appear at 150 opacity, but we don't want the character sprites showing up, since the only character sprite we're using in Thug Wallow is Vincent's. I am also setting the maximum number of visible states to 2.

Name your script module Battle Faces.

```
#==================================================
#
# Yanfly Engine RD - Display Party Data
# Last Date Updated: 2009.02.23
# Level: Easy
#
#==================================================

$imported = {} if $imported == nil
$imported["DisplayPartyData"] = true

module YE
module BATTLE

module DISPLAY

# This changes what will and will not be shown. If you choose to show
# the actor's face graphic, you can choose its opacity. 255 means it's
# fully visible while 0 means it's completely transparent. For the
# number of states shown, do not exceed 4 unless you want the states to
# overlap into the next actor's data window.

SHOW_ALLY_FACE = true
ALLY_FACE_OPACITY = 100
SHOW_ALLY_SPRITE = false
MAX_STATES_SHOWN = 4

end # end module DISPLAY
end # end module BATTLE
end # end module YE

#==================================================
# Don't touch anything past here or else your computer will explode
# and you will be a very sad person.
#==================================================


#==================================================
# Window_BattleStatus
#==================================================

class Window_BattleStatus < Window_Selectable
```

```ruby
alias displaypartydata_initialize initialize
def initialize
displaypartydata_initialize
@column_max = $game_party.members.size
@spacing = 0
end

def draw_item(index)
rect = Rect.new(index * 96, 96, 96, 96)
rect.width = 96
rect.height = 96
actor = $game_party.members[index]
fo = YE::BATTLE::DISPLAY::ALLY_FACE_OPACITY
draw_party_face(actor, 96 * index + 2, 2, fo, 92) if YE::BATTLE::DISPLAY::
SHOW_ALLY_FACE
draw_actor_graphic(actor, 96 * index + 72, 48) if YE::BATTLE::DISPLAY::
SHOW_ALLY_SPRITE
draw_actor_state(actor, 96 * index, WLH * 1, 24 * YE::BATTLE::DISPLAY::
MAX_STATES_SHOWN)
draw_actor_name(actor, 96 * index + 4, 0)
draw_actor_hp(actor, 96 * index + 2, WLH * 2, 92)
draw_actor_mp(actor, 96 * index + 2, WLH * 3, 92)
end

def update_cursor
if @index < 0
self.cursor_rect.empty
else
self.cursor_rect.set(@index * 96, 0, 96, 96)
end
end

def draw_party_face(actor, x, y, opacity = 255, size = 96)
face_name = actor.face_name
face_index = actor.face_index
bitmap = Cache.face(face_name)
rect = Rect.new(0, 0, 0, 0)
rect.x = face_index % 4 * 96 + (96 - size) / 2
rect.y = face_index / 4 * 96 + (96 - size) / 2
rect.width = size
```

```
rect.height = size
self.contents.blt(x, y, bitmap, rect, opacity)
bitmap.dispose
end

end # end Window_BattleStatus

#==============================================================
#
# END OF FILE
#
#==============================================================
```

Go ahead and test it, to make sure you got it right. Click OK to close the Script Editor and return to the main editor window. Go to the World Map and set your player start position somewhere just outside Timber Town. After the game starts, move around a little bit until a battle commences, and you should now be able to see the faces of your party members, like in Figure 7.13.

When you're done testing, remember to move your player start position back to the front entrance of your Timber Town map.

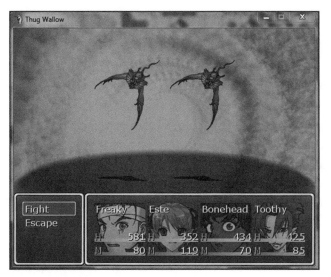

Figure 7.13
Your party members finally have a face!

ADD MORE AS YOU LIKE

You can put in additional NPCs, interactive items, enemies, and other details as you like—to both Thug Wallow and your original game creation. The more you include in them (as long as you don't get carried away and overburden your maps with so many features you confuse the whole point of the game), the better reception your games will receive from players.

Also, there are some great online community sites, where you can share what you've done so far and find tutorials and scripts made by other users of RPG Maker. The top sites you should investigate when you have time include:

- **RPG Maker VX Community**—www.RPGMakerVX.net
- **RPG Crisis**—http://RPGCrisis.net

These are excellent places to let somebody see your work-in-progress and get together with like-minded folk who might even contribute art and/or other resources—or who might like *you* to help *them* on their game projects. If you are eager to collaborate, or just have a few quick questions, go ahead and register on these sites and browse around them. You never know what you might find.

WHAT'S NEXT?

Your Thug Wallow game, for all intents and purposes, is complete. Now I will show you how to get people playing it. That is what the next, and final chapter, is all about.

While you are preparing to move on to that chapter, however, take a moment to complete your own private project. Put the right finishing touches to it, so you will make it the very best game you can. Keep in mind, though, that (as many game industry professionals have said before) your first few games won't be as great as the ones you make once you have the right amount of practice and experience under your belt. So after you make these two games, make many more, and pretty soon you will be a top-notch RPG maker yourself!

CHAPTER 8

WHERE TO GO FROM HERE

In this chapter you will learn:

- Why editing is important in polishing your work
- How to burn your finished game to disc
- How to take screenshots of your game
- How to put your game on the Internet for download
- How you can make money selling your game

Finally! You have finished Thug Wallow and it is now a complete (albeit short) RPG. The game has one overarching quest and a few sub-quests. To make Thug Wallow a longer game, you could add more maps, NPCs, enemies, sub-quests, and so on. However, you don't want your game to be too lengthy or it will become burdensome and fewer people will want to play it. You are catering, after all, to both RPG lovers and casual gamers alike. So put in some effort, with the time you have, to really add your own personal touch to Thug Wallow.

Don't neglect your private RPG either. After all, your own, original game is another project that deserves your attention. You should complete these two games to your best ability before reading this chapter.

In this chapter, you will learn how to edit and publish your game. After publishing it, you can put your RPG on disc or on the web and really get players' attention.

EDITING YOUR GAME

Just as with writing a story or filming a movie, some of the best work a designer does is in editing. Making a video game is iterative development, so you do a lot of editing on the go, but even the best-planned video game will require careful analysis, review, and touch-ups. What you can do is, just after finishing a game, wait several days and then return to it with fresh eyes and a clearer perspective.

Have you ever been playing a game and then fallen outside the game world and caught a glimpse of the underlying geometry? Or passed through an object you weren't supposed to be able to pass through? Or got stuck in one animated state for an indefinite period of time, unsure how to get out of it? Or suddenly lost the audio track the game was supposed to be playing? These are all software defects also known as bugs. In game design, testing is supposed to help discover and remove irritating bugs for the purposes of quality control. No designer wants to make a game that is difficult to play, frustrating at its worst, or filled with glitches. Every game a developer makes should be one that players desire to play.

Every game company has a set of testers who put each game through its paces. Testers spend laborious hours searching and looking for bugs in video games. Often, a tester will study one particular map or section of the game over and over, measuring nuances and recording everything that he finds so developers can amend, repair, or cut parts of the game that aren't working as smoothly as they should.

Testing is done procedurally to every conceptual game build that comes out of the developers' work room. The following is standard procedure for testing:

1. **Identification**—Incorrect program behavior is analyzed and identified as a bug.

2. **Reporting**—The bug is reported to developers by use of a defect tracking system.

3. **Editing**—The team member responsible for the bug, be it an artist, programmer, or other developer, checks the program for the malfunction and attempts to correct it.

4. **Verification**—The program is tested again to see if the bug has been fixed or if there is something else to be done to it.

Most game companies rate bugs based on an estimate of their severity, from A to C:

- **A Bugs**—A bugs are critical errors that prevent the game from being shipped. They must be nailed head-on, because if they are not the game itself will be totally unplayable.

- **B Bugs**—These are crucial problems that need attention. However, the game itself may still be playable. But if you get a large cluster of B bugs, they become equivalent to an A bug.

- **C Bugs**—C bugs are minor issues. In fact, many C bugs are small, obscure problems or may actually be biased opinions or random suggestions. They are not critical, but if the game company has time, they'll handle them.

Many people who want to get into the game biz actually seek out jobs as testers first, because game companies are more likely to hire testers who don't have direct experience with shipping out a triple-A title.

Unfortunately, you don't have access to a large pool of testers. You will have to count on yourself—and who you know—for quality-assurance when it comes to your RPGs. If you have friends or family members you respect, you might ask if they will play-test your game and give you some feedback. Ask them what they think, if there are any glitches or holes in your game, or if the story is too difficult for them to follow. Listen to what they're saying and what they're not saying. Create a list of possible bugs based on what they've told you. Rate those bugs you've listed from A to C. Tackle the A bugs first, the B bugs second, and the C bugs if you have time left.

Go back to your game project and check for possible malfunctions, and if you find any, correct them. Then double-check to see if you edited your game correctly, or if you need to do more to it. If you know you're not hassling them, go ahead and ask your friends or family members to double-check your work, too. The more eyes you have on a single game project, often the better chances nothing will slip your notice.

You do this because you don't want to send your game off into the world with even the slimmest possibility that someone out there will point out its flaws—especially glaring flaws.

Tip

"Games testing is sometimes referred to as 'Getting paid to play games' and from that, it sounds like an awesome job. After all, most (if not all) aspiring testers play games every day, why not get paid to play them? The reason is because the quote is wrong, testers are not being paid to play games, they are being paid to test them and that is the crucial difference."

—Steven Yau, Parabellum Games

PUBLISHING YOUR GAME

Once your game is ready for publication, it is not that hard to set it up to share it with the rest of the world. However, the end user must have a machine and computer operating system that is compatible, and they must have the Run-Time Package, or RTP, to be able to play your game. They can download the RTP themselves from Enterbrain's website, or you can publish your game as a standalone package that includes the RTP. The most advisable course of action is the latter.

Let's publish Thug Wallow. Open it now in RPG Maker, and go to File > Compress Game Data.

The Output Folder field gives you a choice of where to put your published game. For now, select a target folder apart from your project folder. Select a destination by clicking the browse button, and then type at the end of your chosen destination a subfolder to put your published game into, such as Finished Game (Figure 8.1).

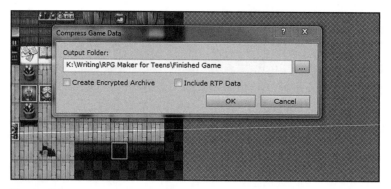

Figure 8.1
Put your final game into a subfolder that is easily identifiable.

See the two checkbox options beneath Output Folder? Create Encrypted Archive is a great option if you are making regular backups of your project and don't want anyone to see what you're creating, because you can block attempts by others to read your project. We want to leave this unchecked for now. Include RTP Data will add the necessary RTP data to your project, so that your game will be standalone and won't require the user to download RTP separately. Check this box.

Click OK and wait as the compression commences. You will see all data files being stored and compressed in your final project folder. At any time, you can click the Abort button to stop the compression of game data. If you do, you will have to start the compression over again, as there's no way to resume from where you left off. It usually won't take compression very long to finish, but the larger your game project is, the longer the compression will take.

When you see a message that says "Successfully compressed game data," you may click OK to close the window. Now you can test your finished game. Go to the folder where you compressed your final game data, and you should see a single executable file accompanied by a blue gem icon (Figure 8.2). If you click it,

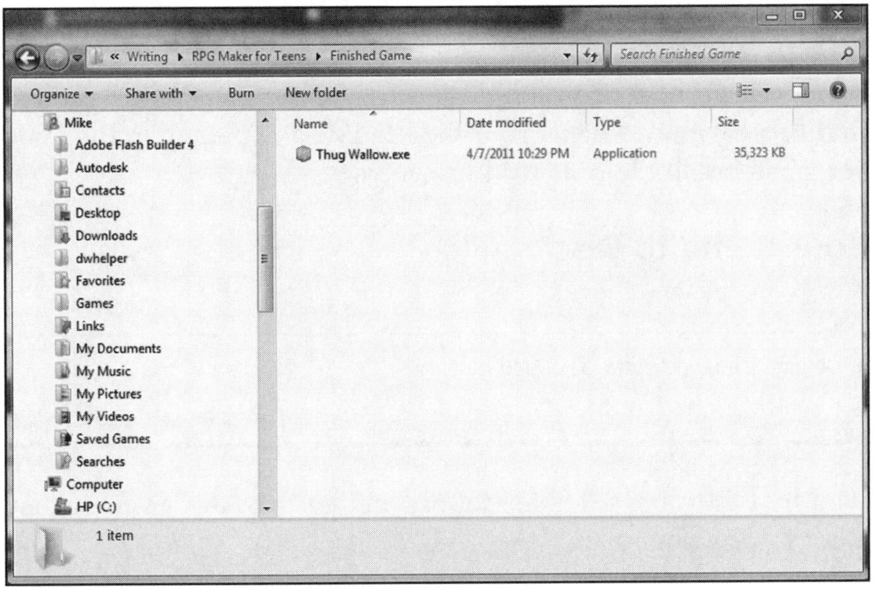

Figure 8.2
Your finished game install file.

it will ask you where you want to extract your game. This is exactly what you want your player to see, because he or she can install your game from this single executable file.

The downside to game publication is the total file size. If you look at Figure 8.2, my final Thug Wallow game was just over 35,000 kilobytes, which is equivalent to 34.2 megabytes. This isn't very much overall, not when you compare it to games that have a much larger digital footprint, but Thug Wallow is a rather small RPG comparatively. Gamers aren't likely to complain about the file size, especially when you point out to them that your game is completely portable—that they can play it on their computer, laptop, USB thumb drive, or other device—but it will make Internet distribution a little more difficult.

Creating a ReadMe File

Now that you have an install file, it wouldn't hurt to share a few words with your player about the file, how to install the game, or even how to play the game. Anything you want to say to your player that was not said in your game should be stated in a ReadMe file. ReadMe files are so commonplace nowadays that few program users actually bother reading them unless they find themselves stuck and needing help. Even so, it doesn't hurt to include one with your game.

In Windows, go to Start > All Programs > Accessories and click on Notepad. Start typing. You can pronounce whatever you feel is essential. When you are through, go to File > Save As to name your file ReadMe and place it in the same subfolder your game install file resides in presently.

Burning Your Game to Disc

Tip

"You gotta live and learn, you gotta crash and burn..."

—Darius Rucker, *Learn to Live*

One option you have is to burn this file to disc and give the disc to friends or people you want to play your game.

You can burn to CD or DVD direct through Windows. The software does not offer many options, but for creating a basic installation disc, it suffices as a simple solution. In Windows, go to Start > All Programs > Accessories > Windows Explorer. Open the DVD burner tray on your machine and insert a blank DVD or CD. Close the tray. Navigate to the hard drive that holds your compressed game file, such as the Thug Wallow.exe application file shown above. Click and drag this file to the DVD burner drive icon in Windows Explorer.

Select File, then "Write these files to CD." Ensure that both the install and ReadMe file that needs to be written to CD or DVD shows up in the temporary file list in Windows. The CD writing wizard will open. Follow the prompts to complete the wizard. Remove your CD or DVD when it's finished burning and write your game's name on the front of it or apply an appropriate label. Close the drive tray.

If you want more options and a fancier installation package (Figure 8.3), there are several programs on the market that can help you. Some of them are even free. Here are a few to check out:

- **Inno Setup**—www.jrsoftware.org/isinfo.php

- **InstallJammer**—www.installjammer.com

- **InstallSimple**—http://installsimple.com

- **Nullsoft Scriptable Install System**—http://NSIS.sourceforge.net

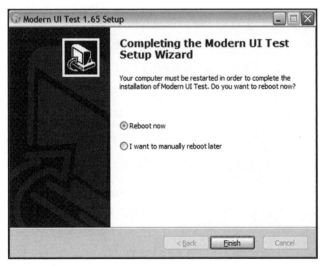

Figure 8.3
An example of a fancier software installation package at work.

Putting Your Game on the Web

You can put your game on disc and give the disc to your nearest friends and family members, but that is still very limited. In today's technological environment, it's a simple task to put your RPG on the web for anyone and everyone to enjoy—and you can receive more recognition for it in the process!

To put your game on the web, the first thing you have to do is compress (which should be already done). Then you can make a ReadMe file, which is optional. Lastly, add your files to a compressed or archived file format, such as ZIP or RAR. You can make a ZIP file easily in Windows.

Your Thug Wallow executable file and ReadMe file should already be in a folder named Finished Game or something similar. Go up one hierarchy and right-click on the folder Finished Game (or whatever you might have named it) and select Send To > Compressed (zipped) folder. The zipped folder icon should look like a folder with a zipper running up the side of it. As soon as you do this, a new zipped folder file, or ZIP file, will be created. Rename it something that will make better sense, if applicable, such as ThugWallowGame.zip.

Now you have a completely transportable file you can distribute over the Internet. You can, alternatively, share your executable (EXE) file by itself, but you might notice hesitancy on the part of different web and email filters that don't take kindly to executable files. This is because some executable files floating around the Net are actually viruses and not tolerated. Therefore, placing your executable file into a compressed, or zipped, folder is recommended.

Once you have a zipped file folder, you can upload it to the Internet. Where and how is another question.

Taking Screenshots

Most people expect to see visuals of your game. Screenshots are a big selling tool and means for you to promote your game without having to say much about it.

The easiest way to take screenshots of a game you've made with RPG Maker is to use the Windows' Snipping Tool, which you can find by going to Star > All Programs > Accessories. Open the Snipping Tool after you've begun a play-test of your game. At first, when the Snipping Tool launches, it will blur out the screen and give you a target cursor to click-and-drag over any area of the screen

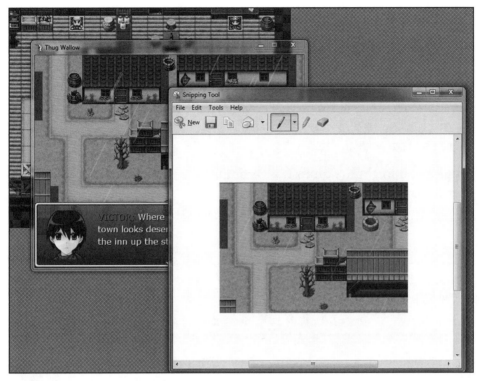

Figure 8.4
The Snipping Tool will display a preview of your capture, which you can save or start over.

you want captured. You will see your selection take place in real time. The Snipping Tool, by the way, will pause your RPG Maker game while you do this, which is very handy for capturing animated objects.

After you've clicked-and-dragged over an area of your screen you want to capture, the Snipping Tool will show you a preview of your capture (Figure 8.4). If you do not like it, you can click the New button to take another capture. If you do like it, however, you can click the Save button and save your image.

The two file formats you'll want to save screenshots as are PNG and JPG; these are web-ready image file formats.

Using Social Networks and Forums

One kind of place you can share your distributable game is on a social network. A *social network* is a social structure made up of individuals who are connected by one or more specific types of interdependency, such as friendship, kinship, common interest, financial exchange, dislike, or relationships of beliefs, knowledge, or prestige.

There are two very popular social networks that you can take advantage of, if you haven't already, and they are Facebook and Myspace. There are others, but these two are the titans of social networks online, meaning they have the most members registered with them.

Another place you might look into is a community forum. There are specialized forums for RPG Maker users.

Facebook

Tip

"How on earth did we stalk our exes, remember our co-workers' birthdays, bug our friends, and play a rousing game of Scrabulous before Facebook?"

—*Entertainment Weekly*, December 11th 2009

Facebook is a very popular social networking website that allows anyone to sign up and have a free account. Unlike other social networking sites, Facebook caters to individual networks so that a person can connect with others in his or her college, university, high school, company, or geographical location.

Facebook began in 2004 and was founded by Mark Zuckerberg and his college roommates and fellow computer science students Eduardo Saverin, Dustin Moskovitz, and Chris Hughes. At the outset, Facebook was limited to Harvard students, eventually expanding to other universities. Today it is open to anyone over the age of 13. Here is how you can create a Facebook account.

Open your web browser. Go to www.facebook.com and look on the right (Figure 8.5). You will see a section that says Sign Up: It's free, and always will be. (If you don't see this screen come up, it may be because the computer you're on is already logged into Facebook. If so, log out.)

Enter your first name, last name, a valid email address, a password that you'll remember (write it down, though, just in case!), your gender, and your birthday. Make sure that all the information you enter is valid and correct before you click the Sign Up button. Enter the captcha if prompted. A captcha is a way that

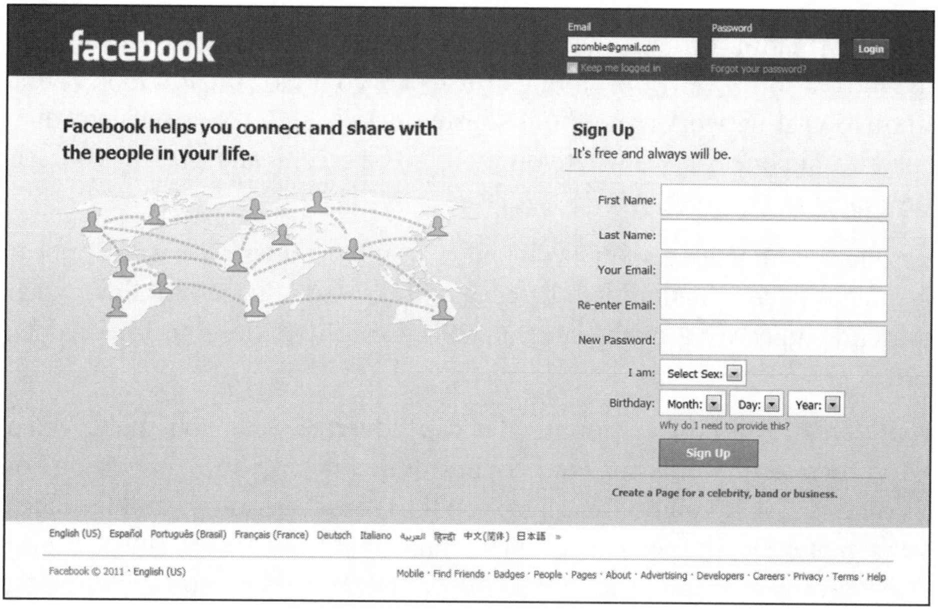

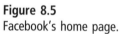

Figure 8.5
Facebook's home page.

Internet forms can tell if you're really a human being filling out the data on a form or another computer program, such as a virus. No one likes a virus!

Confirm your account. Accept some friend requests if people have invited you to join Facebook. You can also find some of your existing friends by providing your password to your email or AIM accounts. Facebook will not share your user name or password on any email/AIM accounts, so feel free to browse your existing contact lists to see who is already on Facebook. However, this step is optional and can be skipped if you feel uncomfortable sharing this information with Facebook. Even if you do share it, you can still change your passwords after you take this step just to ensure your privacy.

Fill out some of your profile information, such as what school you go to and the city you live in, and try to join the local network. You can skip this step, but joining a network can help you find friends and help others find you.

If you want, share information about yourself, such as what video games you like to play and what your preferred movies are. This is optional, but it gives viewers a close approximation to your personality and character.

Keep your information professional. Future companies who might want to hire you could look at this. Even your family or teachers could log on and look at this information. Social networks are about sharing details about yourself, but they are not private; anyone can see what you write, so be careful and present yourself in the best light at all times.

Your personal home page displays your news feed, current status, and applications you might have joined/added. Later, it will display other useful links, such as your friends' upcoming birth dates, notifications, invitations to join events, and so on.

Once you have a Facebook account, you can advertise that you make video games. And then share a link for your friends to download your game in one of your status messages. If you do this right, you'll have fast responses and feedback about your game. Do this with each new game that you make. You can also upload screenshots of your game (which you've taken with Windows' Snipping Tool) to foster visual interest.

Myspace Myspace (originally MySpace) became the most popular social networking site in the United States in June 2006, a position it held until 2008, when its main competitor, Facebook, brooked more unique visitors per month.

Go to https://www.myspace.com/signup to set up an account (Figure 8.6). As Step 1 will tell you, you have just three steps to take, and the entire sign-up process should take you less than 60 seconds to get started. First, select your Account Type to be Personal. Then fill out the sign up form. Enter the captcha as displayed on your screen. When you click the Sign-up free button at the bottom of your screen, you will be taken to Step 2.

In Step 2 (Figure 8.7), you will be asked to post a photo. You can add a photo of yourself—or video game brand logo you create yourself, or even a screenshot of your RPG, if you prefer—by clicking on the Browse button, finding the image file on your computer you want to use, and clicking the Upload button. If you don't want to add a profile picture for now, or want to do it at a later time, click the link below that says Skip for now. You can always add an image to your profile later.

You can also change your Myspace URL to something easier for people to remember. If that URL is available, you will be allowed to alter the URL to reflect

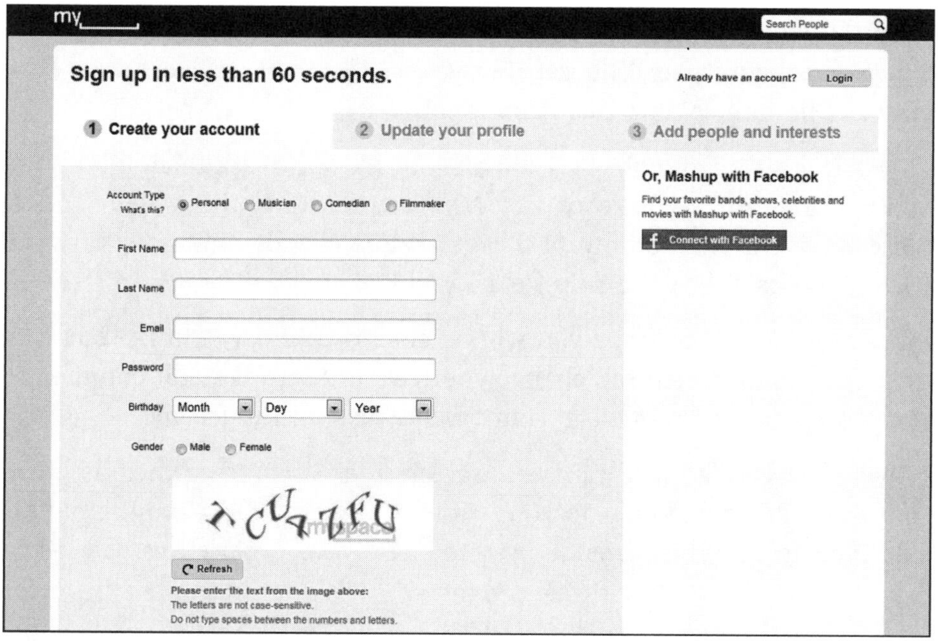

Figure 8.6
Step 1 of creating a Myspace account.

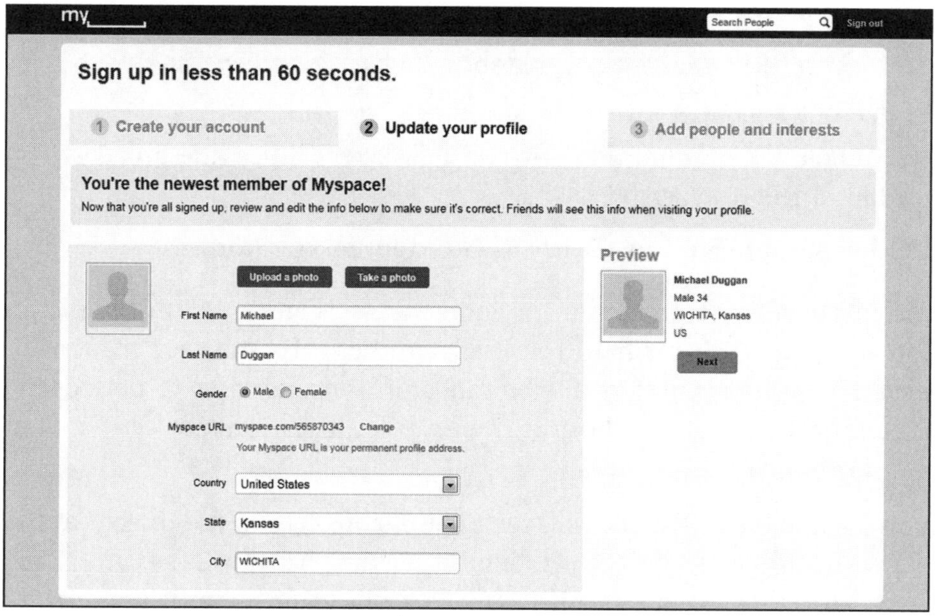

Figure 8.7
Step 2 of creating a Myspace account.

your changes. If you are under the age of 18, you do not need to tell anybody on the Internet where you live. You can list your City, then, as Nowhere. This reinforces your privacy. Again, this is optional.

The next task (Step 3) is to send emails to all your friends to ask them to sign up for Myspace. If they already have existing Myspace accounts, they will be added to your Friends list. If you don't want to sign up any friends right now, or want to do it later, you can click the Skip for now link.

From your Myspace editing page you will be able to do many things. You can edit your profile, upload pictures, change your account settings, edit comments, check your Myspace inbox, manage your Friends list, and much more.

Just like with Facebook, you can add screenshots of your game, describe your game, input download links to your game, and write a blog about building your game. This is a fast and friendly way to share your experiences with RPG Maker.

RPG Maker Groups   There are sites exclusive to the RPG Maker community where you may want to join and/or advertise your games. The most popular group and community forum sites particular to RPG Maker at the time of this writing are as follows.

- **RMN**—http://RPGMaker.net (probably the best for advertising your games!)

- **RPG Maker VX Community**—www.RPGMakerVX.net (the broadest base for all RPG Maker users)

- **RPG Revolution Forums**—www.RPGRevolution.com/forums

RMN, listed above, is a great site for indie RPGs (Figure 8.8). Visitors can download and play RPGs for free. The RPGs on the RMN site were made with RPG Maker. The site also offers a wide range of useful services to developers, such as tutorials, free game hosting, critical feedback on projects, and a discussion forum.

To submit a game on RMN, click on the Submissions tab on the toolbar at the top of any RMN page and select Submit Game. You will be given the opportunity to create a game profile. Demo or full game submissions require at least one paragraph-long description explaining what your game is all about.

Figure 8.8
The RMN home page.

Your game must meet certain standards of quality. These standards are fairly subjective and arbitrary, but in general, your game should contain proper spelling and grammar, demonstrate understanding of game play and mechanics, and be free of any obvious bugs (namely Type A bugs).

You cannot add a game download until your game is approved by the RMN staff. You are also required to upload at least three screenshots of each game.

To add screenshots after submitting your game, click on the Submissions tab and edit your game profile. Then go to the image section and upload screenshots there. Click the Add Image button. Click Choose and browse to where you've saved your screenshot and select it. Click Submit and you should see a message similar to "Your game image has been added successfully!" Edit the image to enter a title for the image, such as (Scene 1 of Thug Wallow). Title screens, splash screens, map art, or character art do not count toward your screenshot total but are certainly allowed.

Once your game is available for download at RMN, you can add links to it on your Myspace or Facebook profiles, so that your friends and family (and anyone else who explores your profiles) can play your game.

File Sharing Sites

Besides RMN, you can also upload your game to the web in other ways. One of those ways is to find a file sharing site that will accept a large zipped file. Below are the top file sharing sites you can use.

- **4shared** (www.4shared.com)—4shared has been around since 2005 but is just now starting to get noticed. Users can register for a free account that gives them a maximum storage space of up to 15GBs and file uploads of 2047MBs per file. It is the file sharing site I prefer.

- **Box.net** (www.Box.net)—Popular for its simple interface and large feature set, Box.net provides users 1GB of free storage space. Unfortunately, Box.net's biggest drawback is the free version's 10MB file size upload limit—especially when many RPGs are over 10MBs!

- **MediaFire** (www.MediaFire.com)—Users loved unlimited file storage, which is what MediaFire offers. There's no sign-up and it's free. The downside? The files you upload must be 100MBs or smaller in file size.

- **Rapid Share** (www.RapidShare.com)—The Rapid Share site has been around a long time and has several outspoken supporters. Users must register an account with Rapid Share to upload and share files. The maximum size for a free account's upload is 500MBs per file with a 10-file limit. Free uploads remain on Rapid Share for a total of 30 days before being automatically removed.

- **Windows Live Sync** (www.FolderShare.com)—A Redmond service that's quickly gaining notice is Sync, which used to be known as SkyDrive. It works as a folder/file syncing program. Individual uploads are limited to 50MBs or less.

Constructing a Website

These days, the easiest way to self-publish is to build a website, something that anybody can do for little or no cost.

There's no question that the Internet has profoundly changed our society. People from all over the world instantaneously share information in ways humans never considered possible before the birth of the web. In this day and age, "I found it online," has become a household refrain.

The Easy Way If you feel completely out-of-place trying to code your own website by yourself, or you would prefer whipping something together with very little effort and don't have to possess the most amazing or customized site, you can make use of one of several free online web builders.

Some of these kits create websites for you on a trial basis, asking you to pay money for adequate hosting or maintenance, while others are free if you agree to use their hosting service. Be sure to read the fine print of any web builder that says it's "free," because too many people have been disappointed before from using them because of banner ads, pop-ups, and other ways companies try to profiteer off of offering "free" resources.

- **DoodleKit**—http://DoodleKit.com
- **Handzon Sitemaker**—www.Handzon.com
- **Moonfruit**—www.Moonfruit.com
- **Wix**—www.Wix.com (Figure 8.9)
- **Yola**—www.Yola.com

The More Advanced Way Of course, if you know how to program, you can build your own website from scratch. To do so requires a reserved web host or hosting server and knowledge of HTML, XHTML, and CSS. You can use even more scripting languages (such as PHP, Java, ASP, and more) to add further functionality to your website, but at the very least you need to know these.

Finding a Web Host It all seems very simple. You click, and a new page appears on your screen. But where do these pages live while they're not being looked at? Where are web pages stored?

Websites and their pages are stored on special computers called servers. A *server* is a computer that is hooked up to the Internet 24/7 and might have one or more websites stored on it at any given time. The number of sites and pages that can reside on a single server depends on the server's memory capacity. When you enter a web page address in the address bar of your browser, the server responds by sending a copy of that page to your browser.

Figure 8.9
The Wix home page.

To publish your website, you don't need to set up your own personal server. You can borrow someone else's server to put your files on. This type of server is called a *web host*. There are countless choices in finding web hosts: some are free, and others cost. Following is a list of free web host services:

- **110 MB**—www.110MB.com

- **AtSpace**—www.AtSpace.com

- **Byet Internet Services**—www.ByetHost.com

- **Freehostia**—www.Freehostia.com/hosting.html

- **Webs**—www.Webs.com/free-website-hosting.jsp

When choosing free hosting, go with a reputable host. Some free hosting sites add bulky code to your page, which increases the loading time at which your page displays. Others place advertisements on your page. Avoid these types of hosts if you can.

Web Programming   Think of your website as a neighborhood. In that neighborhood, you'll need to put stuff, such as houses, trees, and sidewalks. Just as a city planner would, you will want to have a clear concept of what kind of stuff you want to include in your site before you start building it.

If you decide you really want to publish your games on the web, however, there are whole books devoted to that topic you should really read. A few I'd suggest from Cengage Learning include the following:

- *Web Design for Teens*, by Maneesh Sethi
- *Principles of Web Design, 4th Edition*, by Joel Sklar
- *Web Design BASICS*, by Todd Stubbs and Karl Barksdale
- *PHP for Teens*, by Maneesh Sethi

Once your site is constructed, you use your web host's cPanel or FTP (file transfer protocol) connection to upload your site's content to the web.

Search Engine Submission   When you have some cyber real estate and you're confident in your overall design, it's time to open the doors wide and let web browsers in. In order for them to find you, your first step is to submit your site to search engines so that it can be indexed with them.

Pages are published to the web by their domain owners or contributors, and just as easily, they can be changed or taken off the site. Thus, a page may be there one week and gone the next. This makes the web an ever-shifting environment. Humans can compile directories of web links that point to subjects of interest, but if these same people don't check their links on a regular basis, they may quickly turn into dead ends. This is why we've developed other methods for searching the web for the content we want: search engines.

A *search engine* is a web program that searches the web for specified keywords and phrases and returns a list of documents in which those keywords or phrases are found. Popular search engines include Google, MSN, Yahoo!, AOL, Alta Vista, Dogpile, and Ask.com. What follows is a list of search engines to which you should consider submitting your site:

- **Bing**—Visit www.Bing.com/webmaster/SubmitSitePage.aspx to submit your URL.

- **Google**—Visit www.Google.com/addurl/?continue=/addurl and follow the onscreen prompts.

- **Open Directory Project**—A bunch of search engines use Dmoz.org for their search material, and you can submit to Dmoz.org, too. Go to www. Dmoz.org/add.html and follow the onscreen instructions.

- **Yahoo!**—Visit http://SiteExplorer.Search.Yahoo.com/Submit and follow the onscreen instructions.

Once you do this, your virtual doors are open and ready for business!

Can I Make Money Selling My RPGs?

Tip

"You can only become truly accomplished at something you love. Don't make money your goal. Instead, pursue the things you love doing, and then do them so well that people can't take their eyes off you."

—Maya Angelou

There is a disclaimer from Enterbrain that says you can sell any game you make with RPG Maker—as long as you buy the proper licensed version of the software, you don't hide the fact that you made your game with RPG Maker, and you only use graphics and audio resources that shipped with the RTP or you custom-made yourself (which means, don't steal someone else's sprites and then use those sprites in a game you plan to sell!).

The subject of revealing to everyone that you made your game with RPG Maker is not that big of a deal. Almost all the top triple-A titles you see in game stores today say "Made with Unreal," "Made with the Source Engine," or some other game-creation application at the game's start-up screen and on the box. Showing that RPG Maker was used in the making of your RPG won't upset or restrict your developer role. Just be sure to publicize the software that has made your creation possible.

To give you some idea of what to charge for your game, an average price for an indie pay-on-download RPG is between $7 and $12. If you want to burn the game to disc and ship the CD/DVD to customers who order it online, you can do that, too.

Selling stuff online is a subject that surpasses the scope of this book, and is one with serious legal and financial specifics. You should speak to your parents and/ or investigate the best practices before embarking on a profitable game merchandising enterprise.

Gathering a Game Portfolio

Now that you've made two quick-and-dirty RPGs with RPG Maker, don't lose your momentum! If you truly want to become a game developer, or you've found that designing RPGs was a fun hobby, then by all means get back to work and make more. The more RPGs you develop, the more you will learn and better you'll get at it. All it takes is practice, persistence, and creativity.

As you start developing your RPGs, publish them to disc and put them together in a portfolio of sorts. Get a binder with clear plastic sheets and pockets for discs to slide into. Organize your games in this binder, with the labels clearly showing. Type up descriptions and print out screenshots of your games to entice someone to want to play the games. Keep adding to this portfolio, showcasing your best work.

Then, if you decide to go to a game school or attempt to get a job at a game company, you can pull out your portfolio and say, "Here. These are just some of the amazing games I've made!"

WHAT'S NEXT?

Hopefully this book has taught you a lot. You have gone through an arduous process. If you skimmed most of this book, now is probably a good time to go back and read the chapters that have interested you the most or read about specific areas where your skills might need improvement.

This book has shown you (a) how to make maps, (b) how to put items and characters on those maps, (c) how to develop stories and quests, and (d) how to put all those skills together into making RPGs other people can play.

Now it's up to you to carry what you have learned to the next level. Practice and improve your skills in art, animation, and game design. This can remain a hobby for you, or you can make it into your career goal.

Whatever you do with what I have taught you, I hope you have a fun time doing it!

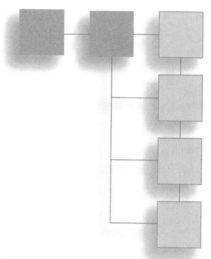

GLOSSARY

GLOSSARY TERMS

What you will find here are the definitions of the most important terms used within the text.

3D graphics: Virtual realistic scenes created from 3D polygon primitives rather than flat 2D vector or bitmap images; 3D graphics have become a big potential selling point for video games and are quickly dominating the console market.

action games: Games where the player's reflexes and hand-eye coordination make a difference in whether he wins or loses.

adventure games: Games that traditionally combine puzzle-solving with story-telling; what pulls the game together is an extended, often twisting narrative, calling for the player to visit different locations and encounter many different characters.

algorithm: A set of instructions, listed out step-by-step, for your computer, to make it do what you want it to do.

animated graphics: A type of animated sprite that is a prop or decoration but not a character.

animated sprite: A 2D rectangular image that will be animated, like a character walking across the screen or a waving flag on a pole.

anime: A Japanese style of animation; or an artwork done in the style of animation developed in Japan.

antagonist: Another word for the villain or dark force at work in a story.

archetype: An original model of a person, ideal example, or a prototype after which others are copied, patterned, or emulated.

audio compression: A process that restricts the range of sound by attenuating signals exceeding a threshold.

avatar: The onscreen representation of the player's character, or the protagonist of the game narrative.

back story: The events that take place before the game narrative actually starts.

bit: The smallest measure of digital data that comes from the phrase "binary digit," and is either a 1 or a 0.

bitmaps: Images that are fixed-resolution images, generally scanned paintings or drawings, composed of tiny squares of color information called pixels.

blood lock: A type of lock mechanism where the player is trapped within a single area until he beats all oncoming enemies.

boss encounter: A more difficult enemy battle that represents a major shift in the game narrative.

byte: The next smallest measure of digital data, composed of eight bits.

camera: An often invisible, arbitrary object in the game scene that defines the way the user sees the action on screen.

cascading style sheets (CSS): A computer language used to describe the presentation of structured documents that declare how a document written in a markup language such as HTML (Hypertext Markup Language) or XHTML (Extensible Markup Language) should look.

casual gamer: A person who plays for the sheer satisfaction of the experience and is less intense about the games he plays (as opposed to a core gamer).

class: A player character's occupation in a role-playing game world.

coin-op game: A coin-operated game, often enclosed in a box and set in an arcade.

collision detection: A method in game programming used to make sure that when objects come in contact with one another they behave with causal response as they would in the real world.

computer graphics: Anything of a visual nature that artists create using the computer as a tool.

control statement: A programming statement that involves looping or branching in the program code, offering random arbitration or depth possibilities.

core gamer: A person who routinely plays lots of games and plays for the thrill of beating games (as opposed to a casual gamer).

core/game mechanics: The particular rules of which a player plays a specific video game.

crunch time: The more intense period of game production as developers get closer to deadline time, resulting in overtime and working obscene hours to get a project finished on time.

currency: The use of script notes or coins to pay for things you cannot or will not barter for.

cut-scene: A brief cinematic that progresses the narrative of a video game while removing the player from game play temporarily.

Database: The management tool within RPG Maker that controls the characters, inventory items, common events, and naming conventions.

dialogue tree: A set of text dialogue common to RPGs, the dialogue tree has branching outcomes based on the player's choices.

door event: A scripted object similar to the transfer event that transports the player's character from one map to another (like an interior building map) when an animated door is opened.

draw order: A process used mainly to determine what objects are in front of others, which are behind others, and when one object collides with another.

Dungeon Master (DM): The person playing the *Dungeons & Dragons* tabletop role-playing game who is in charge of creating and sustaining the imaginary game world, enemies, and quests.

Easter egg: An industry name for a secret reward in a game, something few people but core gamers will find.

efficiency: A measure of how strong or weak a character is against a particular state or element.

emotioneering: A cluster of techniques seeking to evoke in gamers a breadth and depth of rich emotions to keep them engaged in playing a game.

events: Any scripted object placed in an RPG Maker map.

face graphic: A rectangular image of a character's face that can be shown in battle sequences and text boxes.

face set: A collection of eight face graphics.

feng shui: The theory that people's moods and reactions can be orchestrated by the placement of objects in a room or (in the case of level design) on the computer screen.

fetch quest: A common type of quest where the player must find and return with a particular item in their possession.

File Transfer Protocol (FTP): A set of instructions that allows you to upload and download files to and from a web server.

flowchart: A schematic representation of an algorithm or other step-by-step process, showing each step as a box or symbol and connecting them with arrows to show their progression.

fog of war: A darkened screen feature of many strategy games, which is opened up as the player travels the terrain—therefore offering uncertainty as to the placement of enemy units and resources on that terrain before they are approached.

Foley sounds: Sounds that are not natural but are recorded custom to emphasize sounds that should be heard in context.

function: The most common statement within an object-oriented programming language and a part of sequential logic.

game: Any activity conducted in a pretend reality that has a core component of play.

game design document: A written document that tells the team all the details of the game, including which levels and characters will be in the game and how the player controls will work.

game developer: A person who, frequently with the help of others, designs video games using specialized computer software.

game loop: A cycle of repetitive steps the player takes to win at any given game challenge.

game pace (or flow): The speed at which a player makes interactive actions and is guided through the game.

game play: The way a game is played, especially in the way player interaction, meaningful direction, and an engaging narrative come together to entertain the player.

game proposal: A written document intended to knock the socks off potential publishers and investors, that puts a game in its very best light.

game prototype: A raw unfinished game demo often used for business pitches.

game school: A place of higher education that offers degree or certificate programs in game development and/or design.

game testing: Often done iteratively to ensure there are no glaring mistakes; this means that testing is done every step along the way and after a mistake is fixed the game is tested again to make sure the fix didn't break something else.

game world: A complete background setting for a game.

gimmick: A clear and representational image of an idea; in level design, gimmicks are archetypal level types that are immediately memorable for players because of their familiar themes.

gold master: The final edition of a game with all the bugs removed.

graphical user interface (GUI): The look of the shell extension of a game, including the windows, interactive menus, and heads-up display.

green light: When you hear this, it means that a game development group has completed the preproduction phase, the required tools and finances to begin proper game creation have been acquired, and that the team is now geared up to start development in earnest.

high-concept statement: A two-to-three sentence description of a game, akin to film/TV blurbs.

Hit Points (HP): A measure of a character's health, or how much damage he can take.

Huizinga's Magic Circle: A concept stating that artificial effects appear to have importance and are bound by a set of made-up rules while inside their circle of use.

human-machine interfacing (HMI): The way in which a person, or user, interacts with a machine or special device, such as a computer.

if-else statement: A programming statement that checks against a variable before executing a code.

immersion: A key element of a game's popularity that creates addictive game play by submerging players in the entertainment form; with immersion, you get so engrossed in a game that you forget it's a game.

in-game artifact: An object found in-game, such as a journal or tape recording, that can be used to impart backstory.

inn event: A scripted object that allows the player the choice to rest and recuperate in exchange for currency.

interactive decoration: In RPG Maker, any object in a map that is part of the game world's landscape but that the player can interact with.

Internet: A global network of networks.

levels: Basic units, like chapters in a book, used for subdividing and organizing progress through a game.

lock mechanism: A structure that prevents the player's access to some area or reward in a game until the moment when the player beats the challenge and unlocks the next area or recovers the reward.

loop statement: A programming statement that makes all the code within the loop execute repeatedly, seemingly into perpetuity, until an exit condition is met.

ludology: The academic study of games for the features that are distinctly related to play, including rules and simulation.

Mana Points (MP): A measure of how elementally powerful a character is; MP is consumed whenever a character uses a Skill.

manga: The printed cousin to anime.

massively multiplayer online role-playing game (MMORPG): A role-playing game played over a network or the Internet that is played by many gamers simultaneously.

milestone: A realistic step of production that can be accomplished on a game production timeline.

monomyth: Also known as the "hero's journey," this is a pattern of legendary steps that follow one another in a chain of events common among most myths, fairy tales, and stories.

motion cycle: A looping animation of a character or other object going frame-by-frame through its motions.

moveset: A list of animations documenting a character's movements for a game, often found described in the character section of a game design document.

Multi-User Dungeon (MUD): One of the first types of online multiplayer role-playing games, MUDs are often text-based games.

non-player characters (NPCs): Characters not controlled by the player but by an artificial intelligence programmed into the game itself.

object: In creating a game with RPG Maker, this can be any item you place in your game world.

online communities: Websites designed to foster communication and social networking; they've been compared to bulletin boards, social clubs, and schoolyards.

pantheon: A group of gods and goddesses recognized and worshipped in a certain area.

parallax scrolling: A method in 2D sidescrolling games whereby dissimilar planes of graphics scroll by at unlike rates of speed depending on their perceived relation to the viewer, to create the illusion of depth.

pick-your-path game book: A book where the narrative is not linear but branching and the reader must make decisions that carry the story forward to multiple possible endings.

pixel: A tiny square of color, one of many that make up a bitmap, that has a dot of red, green, and blue information in it that sets the color tone for that square.

play: Any grouping of recreational human activities, often centered around having fun.

player interaction: A complex human-computer interface where the player gives her input or feedback to the game engine and the engine responds proportionally; this interaction can reside on mouse and keyboard or on a hand-held game controller, but it comes in the form of key or button combinations and directs the course of action in-game.

plot: The sequence of events that take place over time, from beginning to end.

portfolio: A list, often visual in nature, of what a designer has accomplished in their career thus far.

postproduction phase (of game development): During this development phase, testing, quality assurance, and bug-fixing are initiated, followed by a public relations campaign to get a game noticed by its target audience.

preproduction phase (of game development): The phase that takes place before designers ever get their tools out and get started.

production phase (of game development): During this phase of development, the artists design the assets, characters, and environments on their computers, the writers set out dialogue and scripted events, the programmers code the controls and character behaviors, and the leaders make sure no one walks off the job.

protagonist: Another word for the central character or hero of a story.

quality assurance (QA): Apart from game testing and beta testing, testing must be done to look at the game as a whole and check it against the initial concept for consistency.

quests: A special set of challenges that take place in both stories and games, thus linking narrative and play.

ramping: A game gets increasingly harder the longer someone plays it.

randomization: A method by which a computerized system can change the way in which a game is played.

rapid iterative prototyping: A production method where designers test ideas daily, see what's working and what's not, and abandon hurdles that are too difficult to get over.

reactive environments: The game world responds to the player in logical and meaningful ways that help immerse the player in that game world.

replayability: The "sweet spot" for game designers, where the player doesn't play the game only once through but wants to play the game repeatedly, either motivated by the need to excel or by the sheer excitement that comes from experiencing a compelling narrative.

Resource Manager: The management tool within RPG Maker that is used to import, export, and edit graphic and audio resources.

roguelike game: Any game where the world is not persistent but changes every time the game is played.

role: The part a player plays in a game, especially a role-playing game, often reflected as an avatar.

role-playing games (RPGs): Games where the main goal is for the player to gain enough experience or treasure for completing missions and beating monsters to make her near-infinitely customizable character stronger.

Scrum: A relatively new project management process that helps keep game teams organized and progressing toward product completion in a timely manner.

search engine: A program that searches the web for specific keywords and returns a list of documents in which those keywords are found.

shooters: Games in which the characters are equipped with firearms and focus on fast-paced movement, shooting targets, and blowing up nearly everything in sight.

shop event: An event whereby the player can purchase items, armor, and/or weapons, in exchange for currency.

sidescrolling: A visual technique in games where the player's character starts on the left-hand side of the screen (usually) and the player navigates the character to the right-hand side of the screen; the invisible camera that the game is viewed from is locked onto the player character, following its movements.

Skill: A magical or perfected ability that a character or enemy has that can be used in battle.

sound effects (SFX): Short, recorded sounds that are interjected relative to visual effects to enhance the whole experience and give aural clues to what's going on onscreen.

spawning: Making an object appear in-game at a specific or random location, often referring to the dynamic generation of enemies or pick-up items.

sprint: A short iteration in project development using Scrum.

sprite: A 2D rectangular bitmap image that makes up most of the visual elements in a 2D game.

state: A condition that affects a character (being a party member or enemy). States temporarily change the amount of damage a character does, drains his life, paralyzes him, or some other effect. Some states only occur during battle, while others can still take effect when the character explores the game world.

static sprite: A single sprite image that consists of a non-animating character, object, or element.

steampunk: The anachronistic merging of fantastical but archaic technology in a retro historic time period.

strategy games: Mental-challenge-based games, where the players build an empire, fortress, realm, world, or other construct, manage the resources therein, and prepare against inevitable problems like decay, hardship, economic depravity, revolution, or foreign invaders.

switch statement: A programming statement that checks against a variable and then executes a code based upon context cases.

symbiosis: A concept where two or more entities form a habitual relationship where they each gain something from each other.

tabletop role-playing game: Any role-playing game that is played with pencils, paper, and dice and/or around a table with multiple players at once.

target market: A specific group of people to sell to.

tile-based map: Any regularly spaced grid that reuses the same set of tiles.

tile passage settings: The definitions of whether or not a player character can or will walk on top of or behind a map tile.

tiles: Flat 2D images, which can be static or animated, that are repeated over and over in the background to make up the terrain or surface area of the game world.

transfer event: A scripted object that acts like a portal, transporting the player's character from one spot on a map to another or to a different map entirely.

treasure chest event: A scripted object that looks like a treasure chest and can be used to give the player items, weapons, and/or armor.

triple-A (AAA) title: A game that sells big; in other words, has a high cost to make and a higher return-on-investment; refers to an individual title's success or anticipated success if it is still in development.

troop: An enemy or organized collection of enemies that attack the player simultaneously within a single battle encounter.

variable: Any observable attribute in a programming language that changes its values when ordered to.

voice-overs (VOs): Sounds done by artists recorded reading dialogue and narration scripts in a recording studio for purposes of providing spoken dialogue and narration in games.

web browser: A software program that is used to locate and display web pages.

web pages: Specially formatted documents created using languages such as Hypertext Markup Language (HTML) and Extensible Hypertext Markup Language (XHTML).

web server: A computer that is hooked up to the Internet 24/7 that might have one or more websites stored on it at any given time.

work breakdown: A project management plan that breaks down the overall project into tasks and sub-tasks, assigns team members to those tasks, and estimates the time it will take to get those tasks done.

World Wide Web (WWW or the web): A subset of the Internet that supports web pages.

INDEX